'TILL I WAS TWI

INTRODUCTION

The following is an autobiography of the first 20 years of my life.

My reason for my writing it is that it may be of interest to my descendants one day - I'm sure that it will be of little interest to anyone else. I know for my part, that I have always been very curious about my forebears, but actually know hardly anything about them at all, little more than their names in fact. My parents rarely talked about their parents, and only my maternal grandmother was still living when I was born. I only recall ever seeing her once, when I was about eight, my father taking me for a visit, and all I can remember is that she was very small, still pretty, with dark curly hair, and she smelt of violets. I have never even seen a photograph of any of my grandparents.

My grandchildren all know me very well of course, and all those following will know what I look and sound like from my recordings, but my childhood and youth in the East End of London might be of some interest to them, the old pre-war London, the war, evacuation, the blitz, life for a teenager during the post war austerity, the Army and so on.

It might give them some idea of a very different time and place.

First published in Great Britian (1997) by Arlon House Publishing.
Printed and bound by Arlon Printers Limited
ISBN 0-946273 27 8
Cover design by Lee Collinson

CONTENTS

Chapter 1

LONDON BEFORE THE WAR

The Angel, Islington, is mentioned in the Pickwick Papers. Charles Dickens tells us that Mr Pickwick and his friends once set out from there on a coach journey and, on telling Sam Weller to get a move on with the loading up, was told, with some indignation: 'Coaches is like guns - they 'as to be loaded werry carefully afore they goes orf'. Nearby is Camden passage and Camden Walk, in Georgian times, a very select area inhabited by wealthy people, and so it is again today, but for a long period, from mid-Victorian till after the second world war, it was to deteriorate into a slum area. Also nearby is Chapel Street market, which has been there for a very long time, and just next to it is Parkfield Street.

That's where I was born, on August the 29th, 1932, the youngest of five children.

I remember nothing of this place, as my family moved to Hoxton when I was just a few months old. There we lived in Crossbow House, on the third story of a block of flats, where Wilmer Gardens joined the end of Hoxton Market. That part of London is called Shoreditch, and although the flats were comparatively new they were built in the midst of the old Victorian slums.

There is a large street map of London in the British Museum, dating from the 1880's, and the areas are all colour coded - Mayfair is gold for instance meaning: 'Aristocratic and Upper Class'. The colours get correspondingly darker as the class levels descend, and the black areas are termed 'Criminal and Lower'.

Shoreditch was black.

I suppose I am lucky in a way that I will be among the last generation to have very clear memories of the old pre-war cockney London. Very vivid memories they are too. For instance, London had it's own sound. If you see any film, or hear any radio play set in that time and place, they invariably have the obligatory barrel organ tinkling away in the backround, to set the mood. Well, they would be 100 per cent correct. We had one in Hoxton Market, and it never stopped. I doubt very much if anyone ever minded, as it is one of the most cheerful sounds on earth, although for the life of me, I can't remember ever seeing a monkey.

It is said that the most emotive of the senses, the one that most readily triggers off our early memories, is our sense of smell, and that's certainly true in my case. The all pervading whiff of the East End in those days was horse-dung. It is not an offensive smell, as I'm sure that anyone who's been in a stables will agree, and there was always a thick, dried up trail of it along every street, because the baker, milkman, coalman, brewery drays etc., all used horse drawn vehicles. There were also a stables in Wilmer Gardens, and dozens of others in the area. We all loved those horses, especially the colossal matched Percherons and Shire horses that pulled the drays stacked with beer barrels, and the waggons loaded with coal. Gentle giants with huge hairy hooves. I remember the steam coming off them and their heads toss-ing making the harness jingle. To this day, if I happen to pass near a stables, I can close my eyes, and I am back to my childhood.

The other familiar smells of those days were hot tar, fruit and veg, (espe-cially celery), beer, Lifebouy soap and Jeyes fluid. And smoke of course, as everybody had coal fires. The clean air act was still a long way in the future.

The sights - well, curiously enough, the Americans can show you. Any of their films showing the Lower East Side and Brooklyn neighbourhoods in old New York will show you just what the old East End of London was like. Teeming, bustling, noisy, street cries, quarrelling, laughing - just the same, just different accents. I've never seen it captured properly in a British film. They always seem to overdo it with the obligatory fog and slummy damp allyways, and slatternly old women saying - 'Gor Blimey guvnor'.

There was one difference in that although some areas were, like the American poor quarters, made up of old dilapidated, large houses, inhabit-ed by four or five families, and tenement blocks, London's working class neighbourhoods such as Hoxton, consisted mainly of small, two up - two down terraced houses, with the front door opening straight onto the pavement.

Before I go any further, let me tell you about my family.

My mother, Margaret, was born in 1898 in Finsbury - my father Arthur, in 1900 - I believe in Clerkenwell. When I was born, my sister Ivy was 11, my brother Francis 9, my brother Arthur 6, and my sister June was 3.

My mother started as a charlady in a Threadneedle Street bank in the city before I was born, and worked her way up, eventually becoming the boss of

My Mother, age 32

all the other charladies, retiring with a very good pension. My dad spent nearly all of his working life as a porter in Smithfield Market. He never really got anywhere career-wise, although he was a very intelligent man. He devoted all his talents to the Transport and General Workers union, reaching quite a high position. Although he was only ever a foreman porter, he had the respect of everybody in the market, and was very well liked.

My mother was a very strong, fierce and domineering lady, the type that did not suffer fools gladly. She had a very hard childhood and youth, my grand-father, a regular soldier, not being much of a father or husband. My poor old grandmother had an awful time of it, and she died when my mother was about sixteen. My mother watched her die, and never got over it, her eyes always filling up when she talked about her. She really loved her mother, and so consequently hated her father, and would never tell us any-thing about him, except that he had been in the Sudan, India and the Boer war. My elder sister told me that she saw him once when he visited one of our aunts I believe. He spent a couple or hours talking to my dad, made a fuss of the kids and then left. Mother would have nothing to do with him. That was the only time my sister ever saw him, and Lord alone knows what happened to him after that. My brother Frank tells me that he lived alone in a flat in another part of London. After my grandmother's death, he put the younger kids into an orphanage, the elder ones moving in with friends. Those were very hard times I suppose, and it must have had an effect on my mother's character. She was really formidable and very strict. She ruled the old man with a rod of iron, Frank telling me that they used to have stand up fist fights, although my dad was not a violent man at all, but she was never subdued. I suppose he gave up in the end. Anything for a quiet life.

In those days, the women used to fight almost as much as the men, and she was the guvnor in our block of flats. I'll tell you of one occasion that I can remember vividly, and which will give you an idea of how handy our mother was.

The Smiths were a scruffy, nasty lot, who lived at the other end of our landing. One of the Smith kids had pushed me off of my trike, and I had run in crying as usual. I was a very timid little kid, and was always running in crying, invariably getting a clout round the ear and being told to 'Garn 'it 'im back'. That is what happened on this occasion, even though the Smith kid was older and very much bigger than me. So my brother Arthur, who was just about the best street fighter for his age in the whole neighbourhood, decided to weigh in on my behalf, called the Smith kid out and punched him in the mouth, knocking him flat. Mrs Smith has come out screaming blue murder at my brother who told her to eff off, then toddled off to play football with his mates. Mrs Smith has gone back in, and emerged spitting bile with a bottle in her hand, ran along the landing to our door yelling "Come out 'ere you snotty cow!", and various other nasty things. I was still out on the landing watching all this.

Now everybody was scared of Mrs Smith, a dreadful harriden who had a reputation as a very nasty piece of work indeed. I can see it as if it were yesterday, my mother coming out the door chewing, with an egg sandwich in her hand. Up till that time, they had never actually quarrelled, each being aware of the other's reputation. They began a slanging match, my mother shouting with her mouth full of egg sandwich - Mrs Smith brandishing the bottle. There was a sound just like a wet flannel slapped hard upon a table, and Mrs Smith was flat on her back with her nose bleeding, and my mother yelling something to the effect that if she ever came round with a bottle again, she would stick it up her you know what. I distinctly remember - funny how things stick in your mind - a little round piece of egg from her sandwich spinning round and round on the floor. That was it, all over. We never had a peep from the Smiths after that.

Curiously enough, they became very friendly in later years, and I remember going in to see Mr Smith, who was bedridden, and had been a sniper in the first world war, been gassed and wounded and turned into an invalid, poor bloke. I recall he could only talk in a whisper, but nevertheless was always cheerful.

I must say that my mother was very hard on us kids, and rarely showed us much affection or understanding, but I've no doubt that she loved us in her own way. She just didn't show it very often. In those days, before child psychology was invented, it was the norm for children to 'be seen and not heard'. Mum's usual remedy for any transgression was a belt round the ear, right or wrong. But on the other hand we were always kept clean, well clothed and well fed. She held the purse strings, was an excellent manager, and always made sure that we had the odd outing and weekend trips to the seaside. She was also extremely attentive if any of us were ill or injured. I can remember being ill with measles, off school, sitting up in bed eating red jelly and blancmange, which was my favourite, while she read to me from a book of children's stories.

*June, Ivy, Francis and Arthur in 1931 –
the year before I was born.*

One other occasion when I saw her soft side was when I decided that I didn't want to go to school. I was only five or six years old at the time, terrified of the teachers, the other kids, and Orsman Road school in general. I used to go home to dinner, my mother being home from work by then (she used to walk to work at 5 o'clock every morning). So this particular time I opened the door, she being in the other room, and instead of going out, I shut the door, and went and hid under the sink, behind a little curtain. I sat there for a couple of minutes, feeling very clever, then thought to myself that perhaps she had not heard the door shut, so I waited till I heard her go into a bedroom, then crept out, opened the front door, and shut it again, to make sure, then crept under the sink again. Bad move! I heard her come into the kitchen, me crouching there frightened out of my life. "Who's there?" she said, went and had a look in the parlour, and then returned to the kitchen. Suddenly, the curtain was whipped back, and there she was glaring down at me. I really thought that I was going to be killed. She dragged me out and stood there with her hands on her hips, fixing me with that steely glare she had. 'This is it', I thought, and screwed my eyes up, waiting for the inevitable hiding. But instead, she started to laugh, and laughed till the tears ran down her face, picked me up and gave me a cuddle. She took me into next door, still laughing, saying to Mrs Carey "You'll never guess what this little bugger's done!". She still used to tell people about it years later.

You could never tell with my mother.

My father was completely different. He was very good natured most of the time, although it was best to keep out of his way when he was rowing with mum, which was quite often. But he was quite kindly in his own way, always joking around and singing, and, unlike my mother, did show us some warmth and affection. I think that perhaps I took after him, in that he was always reading - was very interested in every thing - always talking. He did have a quick temper mind - could dish out the odd clout, but really, it couldn't have been much fun bringing up a family in the East End in those days, and hard times make hard people. There was a time when he drank very heavily, before I was born - they all did in Smithfield Market - the boozers there being open early in the morning. Years later, he told me that one day, he came home dead drunk, crawled across the floor on his hands and knees and threw up on the carpet. He told me that mum glared down at him in disgust, and said very quietly, "If you ever come home like that again - just once more, I'll leave you", and went out for a walk. He told me - "Derek, I knew she meant it". He never drank again, except for the occasional half, and that very rarely.

I never saw them show any affection towards each other, but again, in those days it wasn't the done thing. What I do know is that many years later, when my dad was eighty, and fading away in hospital, my mother, eighty two years old, visited him twice a day, two bus rides and a walk away, despite having a broken leg in plaster, and hobbling along on two crutches. She never missed a visit. I took her a few times in the car, as did my sisters, and she used to sit by his bed, holding his hand, still telling him off, and giving him little sums to do, to keep his mind active.

I remember dad was always singing. He had a lovely voice, was a great fan of Richard Tauber, who he used to impersonate really well. My parents had quite a large circle of friends and relations, and there always seemed to be parties and get togethers at the weekends, always a piano-accordion playing, and -'Come on Arfur - give us a song!' We used to listen from the bedroom to 'Girls were made to love and kiss' and 'Oh Maiden my Maiden', as well as the old cockney favourites 'When farver painted the parlour', and 'The 'ouses in between'. We used to love those parties, because sooner or later, the piano accordion would be brought into the bedroom, and we'd be given our own recital, together with a bit of cake and some lemonade.

I recall an old fellow - I believe he was a great-uncle - old uncle Edward we called him. His party piece, when he'd had a few, would be to roll up his trouser leg and show us this big blue scar on his leg. "Them bleedin' Fuzzy-Wuzzies done that!" , he'd say proudly. He'd been in the Navy, serving on a gunboat up the Nile in the Sudan wars. Years later, I read that a party of sailors had been sent ashore, and they were ambushed by Afridi tribesman, two of them being wounded, and rescued by their comrades and carried back to the ship. Uncle Eddy had been one of them - speared through the leg.

Among other things that I remember about my dad when I was small was my very first day at school. Mum was at work, and he made me a cheese and tomato sandwich for my lunch, wrapping it up very neatly in newspaper, and saying to my brother Arthur - "Now you look after 'im, d'you 'ear?". That stuck in my memory, clear as crystal. Sitting next to the wireless, when the news was on yelling - 'Shurrup!' at us, and always giving me his bacon rind after breakfast. I used to love chewing that, all tasting of pepper and vinegar. 'Ere y'are winkle', he'd say, holding it out on his fork.

I mentioned earlier how smells bring back memories, and I always remember my dad smelling of smoked bacon when he came home from his work at the market. He took me there a few times, and I never forgot the hustle and bustle of the place, all the other porters patting my head and giving me a tanner - the old name for a silver sixpence.

My dad was only average height, and slim built, but he and the other porters could trot with a 200 pound side of beef on their backs. When he was in his sixties, he still had a lovely physique, like a twenty year old. He also had brown eyes, and an almost Latin clear light brown skin. On his side of the family, there was a lot of French blood, from the Huguenot influx into London. My grandmother's maiden name was Pinches, and her father had been a Sash weaver, which was one of the Huguenot trades, so I expect his looks came from that direction. Mind you, he had lost his hair and wore glasses by the time I came along, but I once saw a photo of him when he was 20, and he was really handsome. My mum often used to go on about how he looked when she first met him. 'Ard to believe now ennit', she'd sniff.

I suppose that my dad was very lucky in that he had been too young for the first world war, and too old for the second. He was the youngest of a very large family, the only other two that I can remember being my uncle Bill, who also worked in the market, and aunty Ginny, who lived in Wood Green.

My favourite person, throughout my childhood, was my eldest sister, Ivy. She was like a sort of fairy Godmother to me, the one I always ran to for protection and comfort. She was marvellous - my big sister. She used to read me stories and fairy tales, pointing to the words as she spoke them, and she had actually taught me to read quite well by the time I went to school. She was always kind and patient, and I used to really worship her. God knows what it would have been like if she hadn't been there. She was sort of tough and confident, like our mother, but kind and gentle as well, and extremely intelligent. I recall that she even got on quite well with my mother, and always knew how to handle her.

Of my other sister, June, who was three years older than me, funnily enough, I can remember very little at that time, almost as if she wasn't there. In our teens, June and I hated the sight of each other, but happily were eventually to become very close.

My elder brother Francis, or Frank as we all called him, was a real one off. He, like Ivy, was very bright indeed, and he had this air about him. We were

Mum, June, Ivy and Frank 1938

brought up in a rough, ultra cockney environment, with no other outside influences, and down-to-earth, no nonsense working class parents, but he blithely ignored all of this and went his own way. I never, ever heard him speak in a cockney accent for instance. He realised very early on, the value of correct speech, and from his early teens, spoke like a BBC announcer, in a perfect Oxford accent. He tells me that when he was a kid, an old Yiddisher fellow who he ran errands for had told him -"Listen, ya never gonna get anywhere if you don't speak properly. Ya wanna be someone, then ya gotta talk nice". It must have sunk in. The other kids used to call him 'Posh Franky'. Ordinarily, this would mean death in a neighbourhood like ours, but despite also being tall and slim, and gentle looking, he was actually as tough as old boots, with a lot of my mothers steel in him, so he was left very much alone.

To give you an idea of what Frank was like: when he was about fourteen, he saved up some money, (he always had the gift of making a few bob, doing errands, buying and selling etc.), and one Saturday morning walked to Portobello Road market, bought a broken gramophone, and carried it all the way home to Shoreditch, which was quite a long way. He then tinkered about with it and got it working properly. The following Saturday mornings he would spend walking all the way to Portobello, and there scour the second-hand stalls for classical records - Beethoven, Mozart, Chopin, and similar. My sister Ivy, I expect with his influence, was also very well spoken, and shared his tastes, and they used to play these records for hours. I grew up listening to the best music ever to be written and still love classical music - I can, to this day, listen to Dame Myra Hess playing Beethoven's 4th piano concerto, knowing every single note that's coming. I know where my tastes originate, obviously, but where Frank acquired his is to me a complete mystery.

Frank's taste in books was also very good. He simply set about educating himself, not to be better than everybody else, but because he had class. I bet he was the only fourteen year old kid in the East End who attended the Proms!

He was very good to me too. Like the time he wanted to go and see the epic silent movie 'Intolerance', and my mum made him take me. I remember it vividly, because these slaves in the picture started turfing Shadrach, Meeshak and Abednego down into the fiery pit, and I howled the place down in terror, and he had to take me out of the cinema. He must have been really unhappy about that, but I recall that he didn't show it, and was very kind, explaining on the way home that films were only people pretending.

Mind you, he wasn't always that nice, he and Arthur working out a nice little earner when we used to walk to the Tower of London. Mother would make them lug me along everywhere, to get me out from under her feet I suppose. What they'd do was wait till a likely looking tourist came towards us, then give me a crafty clump, making me cry, then ask for help, as they'd lost their fare home, and their little brother was tired and hungry. They tell me they used to rake in a fortune! Of course, little as I was, I soon caught onto this, and used to start hollering before I got the clump. I didn't ever get a share of the profits though, just a red ear'ole.

We were, all five of us, very bright - all passed the scholarship, but before the war, working class kids used to leave school as soon as possible after their fourteenth birthday, to help bring in the pennies. Frank, for instance went straight from school into Smithfield Market. I was the only one to go to Grammar school, but that was when I was the last one left, and things were easier. It was a real tragedy that Ivy and Frank, with their intellect, did not have the advantage of a really good education. Both of them would have gone a very long way I'm sure, although they both did a good job of educating themselves in later years, and Frank carved himself out a very good career.

Arthur has also got a very keen mind, and who knows how he would have got on had he been given the opportunity.

Still, that was the way of the world in those times.

My brother Arthur was very different to the others. He was small for his age, slightly built, curly haired with a face like a little angel. He was also completely fearless and absolutely devastating with his fists. He would fight anybody, any size, just for fun, and always won. He was cock of the school when there was a whole year above him, and the leader of the local gang. I saw him scrap many times, and the other kid was always bigger than him. I think that what used to un-nerve his opponents was that he would never argue, or even say a word, which was the usual thing. None of this squaring up, and saying 'come on then' or any of the usual preliminaries - none of that. When he knew it was on he'd just walk forward and start punching like a little buzz-saw. It was usually all over before they got their hands up. He was never a bully though - he just liked fighting. He was good at all sports, football, cricket, you name it, unlike Frank, who as far as I recall, wasn't interested in any sport. He was also very clever, and after passing the scholarship, went to the local Central school.

As for me, well all I can say was that when I was small, I was a total wimp, scared of my own shadow. I had unfortunately been born with a bad squint, one eye right in the corner, and wore glasses from a very early age. I was also called Derek, which believe me was not a very clever name to have in those days, and the combination of that cissy name and specs meant merciless micky taking from the other kids, and a certain target for bullying. The big kids would leave me alone of course, because of Arthur, but my own age group and even smaller kids were always having a go at me, because they knew I wouldn't fight back. I was also useless at football and cricket, because only seeing out of one eye meant that I had no co-ordination. This also meant that I was very clumsy - always bumping into things and having lots of accidents. I was scalded very badly, twice, when I was a toddler, and nearly died once, pulling a saucepan of boiling water over me. I was really accident prone, and spent an awful lot of time in the out-patients. The only thing I could do was run, Lord knows I had plenty of practise. Mind you, all this was when I was a little kid. The eyes learn to compensate as you get older, and I stopped wearing glasses when I was eleven, my eyes having straightened out, although I could only ever see out of one of them, and from then on my life was very different, and I learned to hold my own with the best of them, but more of that later.

I often think though, that if my eyes had been straight, and I had been called Bill or 'Arry, and our mother had been more like Mary Poppins, my whole life might have been completely different.

Who knows? As it happens, it hasn't turned out too bad.

. . . .

Let me tell you about the London that I remember before the war. It was never to be the same again.

One of my earliest memories can be very easily dated. I remember very clearly, the Blackshirts marching in column along Wilmer Gardens, Sam Brownes, swastikas, jackboots, banners, and led by a row of rattling kettle-drums. I have since learned that the government banned uniforms for all political parties in 1937, so I must have been five years old or less. The other pre-war memory that I can put a specific date to is of the coronation of George the 6th, as we had a massive street party for the children. I recall that it poured down with rain, but it was a great happy occasion with long trestle tables set out under canvas awnings, and we were all given a coronation mug, and a tin of chocolate with the new King and Queens' picture on it. It was 1936.

My other pre-war memories are still very clear, although they may not be in chronological order.

Our flat was at the end of the landing, on the third floor, and consisted of a living room, two bedrooms and a kitchen. Compared to the rest of the neighbourhood, we were very fortunate indeed, the flats being fairly new and well designed, with electricity, and a bath in the kitchen with a let-down top which served as a table. We didn't have the problems with rats and bugs that the old terraced streets had either. Hard to imagine now, but no matter how house- proud those cockney women were, there wasn't much they could do about it, the houses being so old. I remember that we had bed-bugs once - probably from one of us going into a mate's house and picking up some eggs on our clothes. Mum burnt the mattresses and got new ones, and I still remember the stink of that bug spray. We got rid of them, but in the houses, they lived in the walls, and it was one long fight to keep them, and other livestock, at bay. Another thing our dad used to do was to put each leg of the beds into a tin with an inch of paraffin in the bottom to stop them climbing up.

When we first moved from Islington, all five of us kids slept in the same bedroom, our parents having the other one, but later we had this big fold up bed, which looked like a wardrobe when not in use, and my sisters slept in that, myself and my brothers all sharing the same bed in the other bedroom. I was always in the middle in the summer, when it was hot, and on the outside in the winter when it was cold. It was no hardship though - I used to like bedtimes, laying there all warm with Frank and Arthur making up stories and 'telling pictures' and seeing who could blow off the loudest. Dad would yell out for us to be quiet - 'Don't make me come in there to yer!' he'd shout, and we'd get the giggles and bury our heads in the pillow. You'd get it under control and then one of us - usually Arthur - would drop another one and push my head under the blankets, and it would all start again and the old man would yell - 'I'm warning yer!'.

We used to have a paraffin stove in the bedroom during the cold weather - one of those upright cylindrical ones with holes in the top which used to make a pattern of lights on the ceiling, and although a bit smelly, would make the room really warm and cosy. No radiators in those days.

I used to love the evenings indoors. Dad would usually be reading or sitting next to the wireless listening with his ear cupped in his hand occasionally shushing us if there was something particularly interesting on. Mum would be constantly knitting, click click click, fingers moving like lightening, or getting us to hold out a skein of wool while she wound it into a ball. She was also an expert at crotcheting, making little hats. Sometimes, she would work with Ivy, who was a trainee dressmaker, always cutting and chalking from paper patterns, and sticking pins in a tailor's dummy, or bent over the sewing machine working the pedal with her foot. They used to make all their own, and June's clothes, as well as turning over a few bob making dresses for other women.

I remember that my pride and joy was a toy fort together with lots of tin soldiers and Indians, and a little field gun that used to shoot match sticks. I used to put the soldiers on the ramparts and try to knock them off with it. I'd play quite happily like that for hours. Arthur had a large Meccano set, always making models of cranes and windmills and things, really big complex affairs sometimes, that used to work off of a little battery motor. We also played a lot of Ludo and Snakes and Ladders and other board games. Dad used to join in sometimes and always beat us at draughts. Cards were very popular as well - the favourite game being Cribbage, which I learned to play at a very early age. That was the old cockney equivalent of Bridge - 'fifteen two, fifteen four, a pairs six and a pairs eight'. Mum used to play crib with us and she and Dad used to sometimes have friends round to play, although on those occasions the game would nearly always be Solo Whist. There was always something to do - we were never bored. I hear youngsters these days saying 'there's nuffink to do' - either that, or they're slouched in front of the tele watching endless cartoons, but in those days, we'd be worrying about what we were going to do next.

The radio, or wireless as we called it in those days, was always on, and we listened to all the serials and plays, the one I remember the best being 'The Count of Monte Christo'. The signature tune has stayed in my head all these years. My favourite song, to this day, and it always will be, is 'Just the way you look to-night' sung by Fred Astaire. If ever I hear that, I shut my eyes, and I'm back in Crossbow House, sitting by the big old wireless, with it's fretwork patterned face and the Bakelite knobs. The other song from those days which has always stayed with me is 'Little man you've had a busy Day'. I, and nearly every kid in those days, always listened to 'Children's Hour' with Uncle Mac, at 5 o'clock. Never missed it, the high spot of the day.

That was the pattern of life indoors, and I remember them being mostly happy times - with that feeling of comfort and safety - just doing the normal family things. If our mother had the hump, which was quite often, we had that children's knack of becoming invisible, keeping quiet, and if it got to the noisy stage, with the old man yelling back and the air turning blue, we could always disappear into the bedroom.

For all that, like most kids, we spent as little time as possible indoors. After 'Children's Hour', I would scoot out, down to the court, which was an area below the flats, with a high wall at the back, steps leading up to Wilmer Gardens at one end, and an opening leading to another block, 'Longbow House', at the other. The court was my little world at that time - all the children would be playing there - girls skipping - 'Salt-hop-Mustard-hop-Vinegar-hop-Pepper-hop', or playing 'dressing up', and clip-clopping about in their mothers shoes or playing hop-scotch, while the boys would pick sides for football, played with a tennis ball, or cricket, with the stumps chalked on the wall, also played with a tennis ball. Those were the bigger boys of course, I suppose they would have been about eight to ten year olds, known to us infants as the 'big kids'.

I had two great little mates at that time, and their names were Elly and Benjy and they were my best friends. We were together from babies until we were seven, when I was evacuated. Elly was a blond-haired blue-eyed chunky little boy, who had enormous energy, always whizzing around everywhere, always laughing. His name was Eldritch. I can't remember his first name, but he was always called Elly anyway. Benjy was a lovely little kid, and a bit quieter than Elly. His name was Benjamin Stone and I can still see his face, to this day. He was always smiling, and wore glasses like me, and they were always wonky. If ever I see a little kid with glasses, I always think of him. There was one other boy, called Alfy Wilkins who used to play with us sometimes. He lived in the flat directly above ours, and was a little older that us, but was very small for his age I remember, with a little pale, thin face.

We all had these little trikes - the ones with the pedals on the front wheel, and we used to race across the court, through the big kids football games - with them yelling 'Git aht of it!', dodging the clouts and giving them V signs - knowing we were fairly safe because of Arthur. We'd also play marbles and gobs - (fivestones), and flickums, which were games played with cigarette cards. We never ventured outside the court by ourselves, on strict instructions from our mothers.

At the end of the court, under the steps, was this big wooden door, which was always shut, with a big padlock on it. It was always a mystery to me and my mates what was behind that door. We used to imagine all sorts of things. It must have been some sort of tool shed for the caretaker I suppose, although we never ever saw anyone go in there. One of the big kids told us once that a bogie-man lived in there, and if we didn't watch it, he'd come out and eat us. I ran upstairs and told my mum, and she said he was right, but we'd be all right if we didn't tell fibs and be naughty, but when I told Ivy, she laughed and said she was just pulling my leg. We still gave it a wide berth for the next few days though.

. . . .

In those days of course, things like washing machines and fridges were still a long way in the future for the working classes. Monday was wash day, and we had a big wood burning copper in the kitchen, and the flat would be full of steam with mum pounding away with a big copperstick, or scrubbing away on the washboard, afterwards wringing the washing out through an enormous mangle, then humping it all down to the court to hang it out to dry, the same procedure being followed by all the other mums. No football or cricket that day, each family having their own two washing poles with the line stretched right across the court, which every Monday resembled the 'Cutty Sark' in full sail. Underclothes and socks and such, collectively known as 'smalls', were always hung up to dry in the kitchen, partly for modesty's sake as well as the fact that they were easier to nick! Mind you, in those days, folks were generally far more honest - burglaries in the neighbourhoods being just about non-existent. Everybody would have the front door key on a piece of string behind the letter box - a custom that existed right up until the 1970s - so that anyone could have just walked in, but nobody ever did that I remember.

Sunday was the best day of the week. All the front doors would be open, and there was a great deal of socialising, in and out of each others homes, gossiping and catching up with the news of the week, there being in those days much more of a sense of neighbourliness - mostly destroyed in later years with the coming of television. There was also a great smell of Sunday dinners cooking. The old expression -'dressed in our Sunday best' was very much in vogue in those days, everybody wearing their best clothes. Unlike the more rural areas, there wasn't much church-going in the East End, but it was the day for outings, and, weather permitting, we would be taken out to places like Clissold Park, Kenwood or Hampstead Heath. We used to watch the kite-flyers and model boats sailing on the ponds, in fact I had a little yacht myself at one time. Mum would sometimes make up a picnic, and we'd sit on the grass by the bandstands listening to military bands playing marches and waltzes, eating salmon and cucumber sandwiches, and little currant rock-cakes that mum used to make. Yes, we loved those Sundays - every-one seemed to be in a good mood.

Saturdays were quite eventful - going shopping with mother in Hoxton Market for the fruit and veg, which I used to enjoy, then going to Sainsburys, (I've forgotten where that was), for the rest of the weeks food, which I used to hate, as this was long before the supermarket - help yourself and pay at the till days, and you'd have to queue up first at the bacon and cheese counter, then the tinned goods counter, then the coffee and tea counter etc., etc., each time having it totted up with pencil and paper, and paid for separately. Seems hard to believe now.

The market was fun though, with the barrel-organ playing, and the stall-holders hollering away, - 'Ere y'ar missus - come and git yer luverly colly-wollys!' or whatever other particular item wasn't shifting too well that day. There was always a lot of wit flying about I remember, one Jewish fish-monger was always yelling out his favourite catchphrase - "Do me a favour lady - git ya baby's dirty bum orf me bleedin' counter!".

Sometimes on a Saturday, we would have our favourite treat which was a meal in the eel and pie shop. There were two of them, one called Cookes and the other called Manzes. Forty years later, I came upon a book about a blokes childhood in Hoxton, before the first world war, and I found that in those days, that shop was called Manzerelli's. My dad told me that when I was a toddler, I would always be begging for a 'pie and a pennerth', the pennerth being a scoop of mashed potatoes. There would be these marble topped tables with big metal salt and pepper pots, vinegar bottles, and

The Market Fish Stall

wicker baskets full of bits of bread, and sawdust on the floor.

No-one can describe the taste of that food. It was absolutely delicious. You could have hot stewed eels and mashed potatoes covered in what was known as 'liquor'- a white sauce with parsley in it, or pie and mash, again covered in liquor, the pies having a thin crust and filled with mincemeat, which melted in your mouth, or you could have pie, eels and mash, an unlikely combination, but one which somehow was absolutely perfect. The liquor and the pies were both made from secret recipes, handed down within the families. Ask any old cockney about the eel and pie shops and they'll tell you the same. We'd often see quite nobby, well-to-do people in there, prepared to mix with the lower orders for the sake of sampling something really special. Bit of an adventure for them I suppose. Dad said it was the same in the cafes in Smithfield market, where you could eat the best breakfasts in the world - better than the Savoy or Ritz, and a tenth of the price. There are still a few eel and pie shops about in London today, and they still do very well despite the competition from pizza parlours and kebab cafes. Perhaps it's because they were peculiar to London that they didn't survive as well as the fish and chip shops did.

Contrary to popular belief, although the depression was at its height, not many people starved in those days, or even went hungry. As the old man worked at Smithfield, we never really went short of anything, even during the war. If any family was really hard up, you could be certain that their neighbours would always make sure that they had food on the table.

Some of the meals of those days seem to have disappeared from todays tables - for instance, a great favourite with us was conger eel, served with mashed potatoes and white parsley sauce. We had that quite regularly, as well as breast of lamb, boiled hock of ham with pease pudding and carrots, rabbit stew with dumplings, steak and kidney pudding, boiled in a muslin cloth. Chicken was very rarely on the table, far too expensive, whereas today it's very common and quite cheap, and of course, we'd never heard of anything like pizza or hamburgers. We ate a lot more fish in those days - kippers, soused herrings, boiled haddock and bloaters. Spotted dick made with either currants or dates, and jam roly-poly pudding were also very popular.

Our mother was a super cook I must say.

. . . .

Something else that has disappeared is the 'Tuppenny Rush'. Saturday afternoons, all of us kids would be lining up at this church hall, just behind Hoxton market, surging in when the doors opened, scrambling for the best seats, then sitting there for a couple of hours watching Hopalong Cassidy, Tom Mix, Micky Mouse, Laurel and Hardy, Charley Chaplin and Buck Rogers. Lots of the films were really ancient silent shorts, but they were always very noisy occasions, with us all cheering the heroes and booing the villains and laughing at the slapstick antics of Charley, Olly and Stan, the Keystone Cops, Ben Turpin and Harold Lloyd. We also used to go to the proper pictures once a week. I've very vivid memories of Snow White and the Seven Dwarves, sitting there between Frank and Arthur absolutely enchanted, but the wicked Queen frightened the snot out of me, and I had nightmares for weeks. The cinema was an absolute wonderland for us, and we'd be talking about the last film we'd seen for the rest of the week.

Strangely enough I can remember watching the television before the war. Of course, it had only just come into existence then, and only rich people would have owned their own set, but I can recall sitting in the back of this big pantechnicon van on a bench, with about a dozen other children, watching a 'Felix the Kat' cartoon on this tiny little screen. My brothers and sisters have no recollection of this, but I have. I expect that it was some sort of mobile demonstration.

. . . .

Life in those days could be a lot more dangerous. Things like TB, known in those days as consumption, was nearly always fatal. There were also lots of other nasty things, like diphtheria, which very nearly killed poor old Frank , leaving him with a husky croaky voice, which he has to this day. The largest part of every hospital was the septic ward, mostly for post operation patients, but also treating lots of people with serious infections from cuts and scratches, or from what today would be quite harmless ailments. These were all swept away almost overnight with the discovery of anti-biotics thank God, just after the war, but in those days it was just accepted as hard luck. Any cut or deep scratch was always doused in iodine, which really smarted, but was a very wise precaution. Just get a book, and read up all the things that are treated with anti-biotics, and cured very quickly these days, and you'll have some idea of what I'm trying to convey. For instance, boils. I can't remember the last time I saw a boil, but they were very common then. Arthur always seemed to have one on his neck, the usual remedy being the bread poultice. I can remember dad wrapping the bread in a piece of lint, dipping it into the boiling water, squeezing it out, then slapping it on Arthur's neck. He'd let out such a yelp, and the old man would say 'It's for yer own good mate!' as he bandaged it in place.

Boys all wore short trousers in those days, till they were about fourteen years old, when they changed into longuns, as we used to call them, this being a big landmark in a boys life. Every other boy would have a scab on one or both knees, usually covered with iodine, and if it got infected, we used to say that it had 'turned poison' and, "e'll 'ave to 'ave a poultice!'. Today, you just take a couple of capsules. Impetigo and Ringworm were also very common, although fairly harmless, and blue unguent was very much inevidence in the classrooms. It all may sound horrible these days, but all things are relative, and I often think that we were very lucky when you consider that in Victorian and Georgian times, it must have been infinitely worse. For instance, Arthur had to be rushed into hospital with acute appendicitis when he was about twelve years old, and was operated on just in time. His breath really stunk for days after he came home. I expect it was something to do with the anaesthetic, or the medicine he had to take, but the point is that just forty years before, he would have certainly died, whereas he was out playing football and fighting a couple of weeks later.

I don't remember all that much about school, except that the teachers were very strict. It was all 'Sit up straight', and 'Be quiet', and they were always whacking us with a ruler. As I've mentioned before, I could already read when I went to school, and I was quite clever, but I can still remember that panic when we were given sums which I couldn't understand, and writing down any old answer, being too frightened to think clearly, and getting a rap on the knuckles. I expect that there must have been some kindly teachers, but I don't remember any. The playground was an absolute nightmare for me, without the protection of my brothers, always being called 'goggles' or 'foureyes', but I soon learned to hang around near the teacher who would be supervising the playtimes, which saved me a lot of grief.

I used to tag along with Arthur and his mates sometimes, although he used to treat me as a bloody nuisance most of the time, quite naturally I suppose, but on strict instructions from our mother to look after me, so he had no choice. I used to really enjoy those times though, feeling really proud, because the leader of the gang was my big brother. He used to totally ignore me most of the time, but I didn't mind in the least. I was quite happy to stay in the backround and just watch and listen. We used to roam all over the place - down to the Tower of London to play on the little mud beach under Tower Bridge or climbing onto the cannons and cheeking the Beefeaters, or down to the docks to watch the ships being loaded, or climbing down to the Grand Union canal, which was right near our flats, and fishing for tiddlers with nets and taking them home in a jam jar. They'd often go to another market and nick apples or oranges from the stalls then scarper with the stall-holder yelling blue murder, and sometimes chasing us, which was great fun. They often used to knock down those tin advertising stands which stood outside tobacconists - they used to go down with a terrific clatter, and then leg it, shouting rude things over their shoulders at the irate owner standing outside waving his fist.

One incident that has always stayed with me was when the gang was having one of it's regular wars with the boys in Wilmer Gardens. They were a really rough, scruffy lot and this particular time, the two armies were pelting each other with bad fruit that they'd collected from Hoxton market after it had closed down for the day. There was always lots of over-ripe stuff that they used to leave for the dustman, so both sides had plenty of ammo.
    I don't think that it was a particularly vicious encounter, more like a mock battle. However, there was this kid that Arthur really disliked, a tall lanky boy who was their leader. He's standing in front of his mates, waving his arms and encouraging them to greater efforts, with his back to our lot. Arthur picked up a big rotten tomato, and slung it up in the air towards the enemy, who were about thirty yards away. The kid has turned round with his arm back about to let fly with a rotten apple, still shouting, with his mouth wide open, and the tomato went straight in it. The poor bugger was running around choking and spluttering and our gang were in hysterics laughing. I can see it as though it were yesterday.

For us though, the one day, apart from Christmas, that we most looked for-ward to was Guy Fawkes day. We used to make a Guy out of rags and straw and old clothes, and take it to the City road, begging from the passers by with 'Penny for the Guy mister', everything we made going towards buying fireworks. There was something magical about selecting bangers and rockets and Catherine Wheels from the shop, the collection getting bigger - taking them out every evening to count and admire them, with the bonfire pile in the court getting higher and higher, and scrounging far and wide for anything that would burn to add to it, and posting sentries round it to stop the Wilmer Road kids from creeping in and lighting it, and thinking up ways to set theirs off. Then the big day, waiting till it was dark, and then whoosh! up it would go, and the air would be full of banging and flashing, and the sky full of explosions and colours...... Marvellous. Curiously enough, the fireworks of today are almost the same as those when I was a boy, although now people are a lot more safety conscious. We used to actually throw bangers at each other, although I wouldn't recommend it now.

I recall the apochryphal story that always did the rounds at these times, concerning some kid who dressed up as a guy, with a mask on, sitting in a pushcart, with his mates begging for pennies. "Penny for the guy mister?", shouts one of them outside the butchers shop. The butcher came out grinning, and thinking it was a dummy, said cheerfully, "'Ere y'are, 'e can 'ave this", and stuck a knife right through the kids chest. I hope it wasn't true, but it was always told in tones of hushed awe.

'Poor bastard', everyone would mutter.

It may come as a surprise to you that most of the sweets we bought more than half a century ago, are still around today, although there are of course, a lot of new ones. Something you don't see today however is Indian Toffee. These Indian blokes used to come round the streets with a little cart calling 'INDEEAAAN TOFFEE' at the top of their voices. We used to walk along behind them mimicking in chorus, but they were good natured blokes who took it all in good part. Indian toffee was a sort of spun sugar on a stick, a bit like candyfloss. The ice cream vendors were called the Hokey Pokey men, usually Italian, and they also had their own call, also enthusiastically mimicked, 'HOKEY POKAHEYYY'. They had beautiful little carts, multicoloured, with a striped awning and lots of little brass knobs.

. . . .

Every year the whole family would have at least one weekend at the seaside, taking the train or a char-a-banc to Southend, Margate or Ramsgate. I seem to remember going for the week, though my brothers dispute this, but the old man must have had an annual holiday the same as everyone else. Before I was born it would be hop-picking in Kent, one of the traditional Cockney holidays, and I've always regretted that I missed out on that. Arthur would tell me and June about it, and it sounded like paradise, living a sort of gypsy life sleeping in huts and cooking over an open fire and all the grown ups getting pissed every night and singing round the fire. I would have loved all that.

The only trouble about holidays was getting it all together. Once we were there and ensconced in the boarding house, everything was lovely, but the day before, the departure and the journey were absolute murder. Mother would always have the hump, ironing and packing etc., and dad would always be in a temper because of her, and flap and worry about, and they would always have an almighty row and dad would yell - 'F... it, I ain't goin'!' and storm out. We used to keep out of the way as much as possible, but somehow, it all used to come together and we'd end up having a good time. I remember the thrill at the first sight of the sea as we topped the last rise and descended towards the coast, and I also recall the ships on the horizon, and the way the haze used to make it look as though they were floating in the sky. The beaches used to be packed, every inch covered with people in various stages of undress. I never ever saw my dad in a bathing costume. He was of the old trousers rolled up and a handkerchief on the head brigade, although he used to enjoy a paddle. Mother used to wear a costume and come in the sea with us though. Always a couple of deck chairs, June and I making sand castles, and dad wending his way back through the throng carrying a tray with a pot of tea and thick china cups, and mum getting the sandwiches out of a shopping bag. The evenings and wet days were spent in the funfairs, which were heaven for us kids.

The old man was a terrific darts player, and he used to clean up the prizes on the darts stalls. I remember once him winning a policeman and a Popeye, both made out of papiermache and full of toffees. I had them for years, right up to the time I went in the Army. He also won a couple of pistols made of glass, and full of little round boiled sweets, and we kept those for many years as well. I have seen identical examples of both those papiermache figures and glass pistols on antique stalls recently, and they are worth quite a bit of money now.

Cockles, whelks, shrimps and winkles, ice cream, boat trips, we weren't denied anything, and even in those days, it must have cost our parents a fortune.

So, that is most of what I remember about the old pre-war East End, which was never to be the same again. One more recollection and a very clear one is as follows:

I was riding my trike up and down the landing, and I recall that it was a nice sunny day, but I got the feeling that something was about to happen. There had been a lot of too-ing and fro-ing among the grown ups, and my dad and a couple more men from the flats were leaning on the landing wall, talking.

All the windows were open, with the wirelesses turned up loud.

Someone called through a window - "Ere y'are, I think this is it', and they all moved over to listen. Mum came out wiping her hands on a towel, and began to say something to dad, but he held up his hand to stop her, and she joined them at the window. I heard this posh muffled voice making some sort of speech, which included the words - 'No such undertaking......'.

When he finished, one of the men said 'Ah well, 'ere we go again'.

It was September the third, 1939, my mother's birthday, and we were at war with Germany.

. . . .

Arthur, Ivy, June, our parents and me at Ramsgate.
I was about six.

26

Chapter 2

EVACUATION

You've no doubt seen all those old black and white films of evacuees, usually walking along in pairs towards buses and trains - dressed all in their Sunday best - all carrying gas masks in square cardboard boxes slung over their shoulders, each one with a label pinned to their coat -most of them carrying a satchel or a carrier bag containing food and various essentials packed by anxious mothers. Thousands and thousands of children moving out from all the big cities to the safety of the countryside, away from the air raids which were expected at any moment.

Three of those children were myself, my brother Arthur, and my sister June.

I remember it very well. It was just after my seventh birthday, and there we were, waiting in line at the top of Orsman Road, with the queue of charabancs waiting round the corner on the Kingsland Road to take us to Kings Cross station. There were crowds of anxious parents and lots of tears - grown ups saying 'don't worry, you'll be home soon'- 'You'll have a lovely time' and so on. Personally I wasn't in the least unhappy, looking forward to seeing all the cows and sheep and green fields, and had the feeling that we were going on a sort of holiday. I think most of the kids felt like that, treating it as an adventure, which I suppose it was. Of course, it must have been heartbreaking for the parents, seeing their kids off, and then returning to empty houses and worrying about what sort of people they were going to be billeted with. I really don't know how I would have handled it.

When you think about it, that must have been an incredible time to live through for the adults, watching the war clouds gathering as Hitler's armies smashed through Czechoslovakia and Poland - seeing the Luftwaffe blitz Warsaw on the newsreels, and thinking 'Christ, that could be London,' then realising that it had become a certainty; fathers wondering when they would be called up, what would happen to their jobs and families and so on.

The gas masks for instance, remembering the horrors that had occurred just 21 years before in the trenches, and knowing full well that the Italians had used poison gas on the civilian population of Ethiopia very recently, and little doubting that Hitler would do the same. The fact that it didn't happen is neither here nor there, in 1939 it was a very real threat. I recall going into the school hall and seeing a huge pile of these rubber things, and each being given one and shown how to put it on, the teachers tightening the straps to make them fit. We thought it was great fun as they made farting noises when we breathed out, but I don't suppose our parents thought it very funny when we brought them home, with strict instructions to carry them everywhere we went. Our parents had also watched sandbag walls being erected everywhere, and had been ordered to arrange for blacking out all the windows after dark - had been warned not to hoard food, turn off gas and water at bed time - all sorts of alarming things. All this after more than 20 years of normal peaceful living.

What a time it must have been.

So there we were, off to the country. I remember nothing of the actual journey, just that we ended up in a huge shed, which I subsequently found to be the cattle market in Market Harborough. There were lines of trestle tables with tea and cakes and sandwiches, and there was an awful lot of bustle and noise - then there was this big man with a moustache smiling down at us and asking us our names, telling us that we were going to stay with him.

His name was Bert Wright and he lived in Theddingworth, just 4 miles from Market Harborough, and was the village carpenter. Arthur, myself, and a boy called George went to stay with him, and June was with a family in the same village.

We felt very strange on our arrival at the house, sitting bolt upright and on our best behaviour as we tucked into an enormous supper, with Mrs Wright clucking around us, also another little old lady, who I think was her mother, both being very kind and attentive. They had no children of their own, so it must have made quite a change for them having three small cockneys to look after, but for the next six months or so they did a very good job of it, and we were very happy there.

It was a nice, ivy covered house at the end of the village, and it had that lovely country smell of apples and log fires. We went to bed that night, all three of us in the same room, and nodded straight off after a very long and exciting day.

I will always remember that first day, waking up to the smell of bacon, and looking out of the window overlooking a beautiful country lane, then having a wash at a marble washstand with water from a big china jug. George was a little younger than Arthur and we all immediately became good mates, and remained so for all the time we were together, and I remember George as being a very nice bloke. It was all so very new to us as we'd never lived in a house before, and everything was so utterly different, but at the same time very pleasant. We sat down to breakfast with Mr and Mrs Wright, the old lady, and the lodger - a dark haired young man who worked on one of the local farms, who we came to like very much. I wondered why they talked so funny, and said as much to Arthur which made everybody laugh, and the old lady said that it was us that talked funny, and not them, which made them laugh even more.

After breakfast, Mr Wright took us out to show us round. They had a yard with outhouses made of stone, and a big carpenters workshop which smelt of varnish and pine. There on a couple of trestles was a nice new coffin that he'd just made, which we thought very odd, until he told us that he made all the coffins for all the local area. I thought, 'wait till I get home and tell them about this!'. Then he took us through to the garden, which was enormous, with rows of vegetables, as well as a lovely herbaceous border, lupines and hollyhocks and all manner of flowers - a blaze of colour, again very new to us, as we'd only ever seen flowers in parks. At the end of the garden were a couple of old stone pig sties, all filled with junk and nettles, and another old disused shed, and this was to become my favourite place where I used to play for hours. That first morning, he marked each of us out our own little patch of garden, and said he would show us how to dig and plant it. We then went to visit the house where June was staying and then Mr Wright took us all for a long walk, through the village, and out into the country lanes.

It was sheer magic for us kids from the city, especially as the harvesting was in progress. There is nothing like the English countryside in the autumn, just like walking around in a picture book, a sight that we'd only ever seen on calendars, with Mr Wright telling us the names of the different cattle and sheep, explaining all about reaping and threshing, with George and Arthur asking him lots of questions all about this and that. Shoreditch already seemed a million miles away, and we were far too excited to feel homesick.

It must have been quite a time for the villagers when you come to think of it, nothing much happening for years in those sleepy little villages, then suddenly being invaded by hoards of kids with different speech and habits. Mr Wright used to try to get us to say 'booter' instead of butter, and 'think and thought' instead of 'fink and fawt'!

We had to go to church as well, something we weren't accustomed to, but which we quite liked. We were used to singing hymns, as in those days all schools had a little service at the start of the day in assembly, and most of the hymns were quite familiar, but I remember Arthur and some of the older kids got into trouble for singing their own words sometimes, which were often very rude.

It was a very happy time for us - like suddenly going to live in a giant play ground, the village kids introducing us to such things as birdsnesting, scrumping and playing mock wars in the woods, black-berrying and mushrooming and so on.

There was a big farmhouse at the end of the village. The farmer's name was Clark. His youngest son was about thirteen, and became a great mate of ours, and we'd help him gather in the eggs, and do little jobs around the farm, which was enormous fun. My favourites were the pigs, especially the little ones, although I got chased by the mother once, an enormous sow, and just made it over the fence in time, with all the others creasing up with laughter. Helping to bring the cows in for milking was also something we liked very much, as well as having a go at milking. We'd only ever seen milk in bottles up till then.

I recall that at that particular time, there were no other boys of my own age around, so I'd tag along with the big kids and stay in the back-ground most of the time, which I was quite happy to do. When we played wars they always made me a hostage.

. . . .

My next clear memory was of the first day we went to school in Market Harborough. There was a village school which we went to for a time, but it was too small for all of us, so some of us were transferred, myself and Arthur among them, as they always tried to keep brothers together. Market Harborough was about four miles away, so we had to go in by bus. There were already some children aboard when we got on, from another village, and I sat next to June, with Arthur and George sitting behind us.

Now I've already told you how fierce Arthur could be, although he never looked for trouble, and had been quite dormant since we had been away. I was sitting by the window, looking out at the passing countryside, idly kicking the seat in front of me, when this big ugly boy's head suddenly appeared over the back of the seat, and told me in no uncertain terms to pack it up. Frightened the life out of me he did. A few minutes later I started my usual daydreaming, forgot myself, and started kicking the seat again. Up comes the head again, glaring down, and he leaned right over me and shouted - 'Turn it in, you boss-eyed little git'. The next second, a fist whistled over my shoulder right onto his nose - wallop - a real fourpenny one. I'll never forget the shocked look of surprise on that ugly face, and he's started yelling - ' He 'it me - He 'it me!' like a big girl. Up comes the conductor with - 'What's going on here then?', and tried to drag Arthur out of his seat, but he wasn't having any of that and knocked his arm away and told him to piss off. I don't suppose a country bus-conductor was used to that sort of thing and let it go, mumbling something about Arthur being in big trouble. When we got off the bus at the school, the ugly boy was still holding a handkerchief to his nose. He was twice the size of my brother, which he hadn't realised until they were both standing up, and it looked for a moment as though he going to get brave, but one look at Arthur glaring back at him with no fear at all made him think better of it.

That wasn't the end of it that day either.

The two lots of kids, evacuees and locals, soon integrated quite happily, but that first morning playtime found all the cockneys on one side of the playground, and all the locals on the other, warily weighing each other up, quite naturally I suppose. Arthur was with a little group of kids we knew from home, and a couple of mates from the village, and they got someone to point out the one who the best fighter in the school, and it turned out to be this big blond kid with thick legs, called Jack, who was kicking a ball about with some mates. I don't remember how it came about, but after dinner, out in the playground, there was a big commotion with everyone shouting 'Fight Fight!' and a teacher running to break it up. When the crowd was dispersed, there was Jack sitting down holding his eye and looking very unhappy, and Arthur calmly walking away with his pals as though nothing had happened. He was the new cock of the school, and that was that.

As far as I know, that was the last scrap Arthur had as a boy. As I've mentioned earlier, he was not a bully, and never picked on anyone. Soon after, he left school at the age of fourteen, to work on a farm just outside Theddingworth. He certainly went out in a blaze of glory though, because Jack was to become very famous. He was Jack Gardner, the future British and Empire Heavyweight champion. It's curious that I remember him as having blond hair, because when he was boxing, he was dark. But it was him all right.

Do you know, although I was to attend that school for the next eighteen months or so, I can remember hardly anything about it after that first day - the classrooms - the teachers, the other children - it's almost a complete blank. I suppose that it must have been just uneventful. The only really clear recollection I do have is of the whole school practising singing 'Jerusalem' for weeks and weeks, in preparation for a visit from the Duchess of Gloucester. I'm not in the least religious, but I still love that hymn to this day. It's so very English and patriotic, and it became a sort of national theme song during the war. 'And did those feet - in ancient times - walk upon England's mountains green'. We sang it at the top of our voices together with about five hundred other children in the big market hall to the Duchess and the Mayor and a whole stage full of civic dignitaries, and I recall her wiping tears from her eyes with a lace handkerchief.

Stirring stuff.

Life back in the village went on quite happily - us children didn't think very much about the war at that time, although it must have been a worrying time for the adults. At that time, all the news was bad, especially Dunkirque, with our army being routed, and kicked out of France.

. . . .

We'd been away just a few months when there occurred one of the most magic days of my childhood.

It started one morning when George woke me up, all excited, and said - "Quick - come and look at this!". We went to the window, and what a marvellous sight it was. During the night about a foot of snow had fallen.

Now snow in the country is very different to snow in the East End. Everything was blanketed in brilliant shining white, and there we were gazing out at a Christmas card! That's exactly what it was like - the best description I can think of, because Theddingworth was a very beautiful, typically English village. The sun was blazing down out of a clear blue sky, making everything even brighter. What a sight it was. Obviously, in those days there were no such things as weather forecasts, as that would have been very handy information for the Luftwaffe, so it was completely unexpected, which made it all the more delightful. We all three washed and dressed in record time and bolted our breakfasts, as Mrs Wright had told us that there was no school that day because the roads were blocked, and Mr Wright was out in his workshop making us a sledge. We were soon wrapped up warm with our wellies and scarves on, out in the yard clearing the snow away and skylarking about chucking snowballs. Then we were trudging down the lane with the sledge to a big sloping field that Mr Wright told us was OK to sledge in. It wasn't long before nearly all the village was there, and we had a great time whizzing down the hill, the run getting faster and faster as the sledges smoothed it out. At the bottom of the hill, beside a wood, was a big frozen pond, and we had great fun sliding on it, with lots of laughter as people went arse over tip. The ice was really thick as 1940 was one of the coldest winters of the century, and the snow was there for quite a few weeks, so we all got to be expert sledgers.

All very nice for us children, but I don't suppose the farmers were very happy about it. Poor old Johnny Jones, the lodger, was out all hours rescuing sheep, and used to come home blue with the cold. He often went out in the evening, in the pitch dark, and we found it amazing that he could find his way about all over the fields, with no torch either, as they were banned because of the blackout.

We liked Johnny very much. He had a black and white sheepdog that he never let come into the house, although he was very fond of it, but apparently, that was the custom for a working dog, and it used to live in one of the sheds. He'd never let us touch it or play with it unless he was present, telling us - "'E's a working dog 'e is, not a pet, so don't try an' stroke 'im or 'e'll 'ave yer 'and orf!", although we knew that it was quite docile really.

Another memory of that winter was when a party of us were taken into Market Harborough one evening by Miss Beale to see 'The Wizard of Oz'.

Miss Beale was one of the village school teachers, a fat, jolly lady who was very popular with all us kids, always organising and finding us things to do. I think that 'The Wizard of Oz' was the greatest children's film that was ever made, although I was terrified of the witch and had nightmares about her for months afterwards, the way she kept trying to kill Dorothy. I nearly wet myself at the bit near the beginning of the film where she was riding a bike through the whirlwind and then changed into a witch on a broomstick with that long maniacal shriek of laughter. My brother could imitate it perfectly and he was always putting the wind up me with it, the rotten bugger. I remember once sitting on the outside toilet in the dark when he tip-toed up to the door and did it as loud as he could. I didn't need a laxative then I can tell you.

When we came out of the cinema, we had unfortunately missed the last bus home, and had to walk all four miles back to Theddingworth. I recall that it was a bright moonlit night, and the fields and hedges were still covered in snow. It was bitterly cold, and the road was very slippery with ice. Miss Beale was a tower of strength though, saying things like - 'Come on children - step it out, we'll soon be home round a nice warm fire', and leading us in singsongs. I was thoroughly miserable though, as my wellies were chafing my legs, and I was very tired, and Arthur kept teasing me about the witch, saying things like - 'Look out, she's hiding behind that tree - she's going to get you', eventually getting a clout round the ear from Miss Beale, which for me was the only good bit of that journey. Served him right.

. . . .

Early in the spring of 1940, I was moved from the Wright's house to live with another family in the village, who up till that time had not had an evacuee. They were Mr and Mrs Haig and their fourteen year old daughter Margaret.

I can tell you that my time with the Haigs was the happiest time of my childhood.

Mr Haig was a Scot, with red hair, who's accent was so broad, that I thought he was talking in a foreign language, and I could only understand him when he spoke very slowly. These days of course, people have hardly any trouble understanding all the accents, even the really strong ones such as Glasgow and Geordie. They've all become familiar with them because of the television, but in those days, it was a bit of a problem even for the adults, let alone us kids. For instance, years later when I was in the Army doing my National Service, for the first few weeks, all the Jocks sounded the same to me, whether they came from Glasgow or Aberdeen, and they told us that they couldn't hear any difference between us cockneys and the scouses from Liverpool.

Mr Haig was the chauffeur for Sir Humphrey de Trafford, who had a large mansion and an estate just outside the village. If ever you fancy visiting Theddingworth, you leave the M1 at junction 20 and turn east towards Market Harborough, and the village is about five miles along that road. The Wright's house is a little way in, on a left hand bend, just before a lane on

Mrs Haig, Margaret and me in Theddingworth, 1940

your left. Carry on and turn right just before the church, and about quarter of a mile down that lane, you will come across two little black and white lodges, on either side of the entrance to the estate. Almost opposite, on the left, are two cottages. Haig's was the first one.

To this day, I remember Mrs Haig as being one of the nicest, kindest people that I have ever known. As I've mentioned earlier, my mother was not what you'd call an affectionate type - that's not a criticism - it's just the way she was, but Mrs Haig was the complete opposite, and treated me as though I were her own child. It was a very happy household, and I'll always remember them with love and gratitude. There was also the fact that I moved there just as the countryside was waking up - the whole thing - snow-drops, crocuses and bluebells, the birds singing, and sunshine, all this after a long cold and grey winter. Being only seven years old, the cottage to me was like something out of Hansel and Gretel. I had been happy enough at the Wrights mind, but this was heaven.

My sister Ivy tells me that I was a very imaginative, excitable and nervous little kid, although my brother Arthur puts it just a bit differently, saying that I was a miserable little git, (that's just his sense of humour), but I do remember being in a sort of permanent state of panic as a child. The Haigs bless 'em, did a lot to put that right.

I was always asking questions - what's this and what's that etc. - like all children do, but they'd patiently answer and explain things, which was a change from 'shuddup' and 'gid aht of it!'. They didn't spoil me mind, and I got my fair share of scoldings, especially when I'd come home from the Clark's farm, which was just behind the church at the end of the lane, covered in cow dung, or pig dung which was even worse. But I never, ever got clouted. Funnily enough, just seeing her angry had far more of an effect, and I was by and large quite well behaved. I must have been, because I can remember her talking to another lady in a shop once, and her telling her that I was 'good as gold', and grinning down at me and saying - "Yer moi little soldier, ain't yer".

That was a lovely spring, and even after all these years, it's stayed in my mind. Every experience was new to us, things which country people take for granted, such as watching the new leaves appear on the hawthorn trees, - being told that another name for it was the 'bread and cheese bush', and that you could eat the first little leaves that appeared, they being the first greenery to appear. I found out years later that that was what the country people used to do in medieval times, to cure the scurvy, brought on by the winter diet, as it is a rich source of vitamin C. We learned the names of all the wild flowers that appeared, and how to press them in a book. The ground in the woods would be a carpet of bluebells, wild primroses and celandines, and I remember once bringing bunches of them home, and Mrs Haig saying -

"Now you mustn't do that. You leave them where they are, they look much prettier there".

We had a nice garden out the back, and I helped dig and rake it, and watched Mr Haig plant spring onions, radishes and lettuces, and he let me make the holes for the peas and beans with the dibber. There was an apple tree at the bottom of the garden, covered in beautiful blossom, and we were surrounded by grazing meadows. It was great fun watching the baby lambs hopping about. The Clark's farm was at the top of the lane, behind the church, and they had a couple of lambs that had lost their mothers, and they used to let me help to feed them with a titty bottle. I also remember Johny Jones showing us how to feed this little calf by dipping our thumb into a pail of milk, and letting her suck it, and then slowly lowering our hand into the pail until she was drinking on her own. Great fun.

My riding career started and finished on the same day round about this time. This little girl had her own horse - I think she was the daughter of the local squire or something, and she was a right little madam. The Clark boy could ride very well of course, and one day, he saddled up the horse ready for the little girl's daily ride, as it was stabled at the farm. He trotted round the field on it, then let Arthur and George have a go - just leading the horse at a walk. Then came my turn, and they had just helped me up in the saddle, when the girl appeared, all dressed up in her jodhpurs and riding hat. She started having a go at us for daring to use the horse without her permission, and the Clark kid had a go back telling her not to be so grumpy. I was sitting up in the saddle with my legs dangling, (it seemed at the time to be as big as a house), when the little cow gave it such a whack with her riding crop, making it leap forward, and me somersault backwards over it's rump. I came an awful cropper I can tell you. It's a wonder I didn't break my neck, and nothing would get me up on a horse after that.

That spring and summer was a great time for me. I became best friends with a boy of my own age who lived in a house a little further out from the village. His name was Oliver. His parents must have been fairly well off, as they had a miniature railway which went right round a very large lawn. Marvellous it was, with a real steam engine that you could actually sit on and ride and toot the whistle, with all the little points and signals, and a model station. It was a piece of real good fortune meeting Oliver, as he had all the toys and stuff that a boy could want, being an only child. He showed me how to ride this little two-wheeler bike I remember, and I know that that doesn't seem very interesting, but I can still recall that thrill when I finally managed to get to the end of the garden without falling off. Not only that but when I went home that day, his dad went into the garage, and came out with an old one of Oliver's that he said I could keep. I was in my glory I can tell you, and we had some great times with those bikes, having races and pretending to be despatch riders. I was hardly ever off it for the rest of the summer.

Another very vivid memory of that time was when the corn was being cut. The first bit of the field would be hand cut with the big scythes, to make room for the tractor pulling the reaping machine, and that would go round the edge of the field, and work in ever decreasing circles towards the middle. All round the field, each with their own arc of fire, there were men with shotguns, bowling over the rabbits as they bolted for the hedgerows. Of course, the smaller the square of uncut corn became, the more rabbits came hurtling out with that funny jinking run, and BANG - BANG! - another one bit the dust. It was one of the most exciting things I've ever seen and heard. They shared out the poor old rabbits at the end, and I was given two to take home to Mrs Haig.

The threshing was also quite an experience. This huge clanking monster of a machine, worked by a big traction engine, the two being joined by a huge long moving leather belt, all parked next to a corn rick . The men would feed the sheaves of wheat into the top, a couple standing on the rick, hoisting them up with pitchforks to another man on a platform on top of the machine. Bales of straw would come out of one side, and the corn out of the other, with two blokes catching it in sacks. The noise was deafening, and us kids couldn't help wondering what would happen if some poor bugger should happen to fall in and were told dark gruesome tales of just such occurrences. I don't know whether they were true or not, but they frightened the life out of us. Just like the rabbits in the fields, as the rick got lower, the rats and mice would make a run for it, and all round the area, they'd put a wire fence, about two feet high to trap them, and these little terriers would leap in, quick as lightening, grab them and toss them up in the air, breaking their necks. Everybody had a stick, ready to whack the ones that evaded the dogs, and when the rick was down to the bottom you've never seen such a sight - dozens of them pouring out, dogs yelping and snapping, people shouting and whacking - all this with the racket coming from the threshing machine and the steam engine - absolute mayhem .

Unforgettable.

. . . .

Arthur left school that year, and went to live and work on a farm, which was just outside the village, on the right of the road going back towards Husbands Bosworth. The farmers name was Austin. He took to it like a duck to water, and really liked the life, and stayed there till he was eighteen, when he went into the army. June moved into Market Harborough, and really fell on her feet, because they were a lovely couple, who doted on her, and she also stayed there till the end of the war, and was to remain very close friends with them till the end of her life.

We had the occasional visits from our parents of course, which we looked forward to, but all that time I was never homesick that I remember. I was very happy where I was, and London seemed a million miles away. I often used to think of Benjy and Elly though, and wished they were out in the country with us.

The war sort of passed us kids by really, although we heard about the Battle of Britain - how our Spitfires had duffed the Germans up, and chased them out of the sky, and we used to say prayers in school every morning for all our brave soldiers, sailors and airmen.

There were two incidents during my evacuation, one small, and one quite big that reminded us that there was a war on.

The first happened one sunny morning when Oliver and I saw all these patterns being traced in the sky - vapour trails, very high up. All we could hear was a faint droning noise from the planes, and a sound like a very distant typewriter - ticka-ticka-tick - ticka-ticka-tick. We sat there on our bikes, looking up at these big circles criss-crossing lazily against a clear blue sky and suddenly realised that we were watching a dogfight!. Oliver's parents came out and watched with us for a little while, then made us go in,

Mr & Mrs Austin, Mum, Arthur and me - 1940.
Arthur worked on the Austin's farm after he
left school.

suddenly realising that it could actually be a bit dangerous. It was so peaceful and tranquil down where we were, just that hum of insects, and the birds singing, but up there, there were young men actually trying to kill each other, and come to think of it, all those bullets had to land somewhere.

The other incident was a bit more serious, at least for us. One night, I was in bed, fast asleep, when I was woken up by a violent shake. Margaret, who I shared the room with, also woke up, and we both sat up in bed, in the dark, wondering what was going on. Then we heard sounds like things dropping on the roof, and then the light came on, and there was Mr Haig looking very worried, and asking us if we were all right. There was a big bulge in the ceiling right over my bed, and bits of plaster and glass everywhere. We all went downstairs, and Mrs Haig made some cocoa while Mr Haig dressed and went out to see what had happened. The next door neighbours came in and they all talked excitedly, wondering if a plane had crashed, or the Germans had invaded, and whether to all go up to the village, or whatever, but outside it was all quiet and normal.

The next morning we found out. ... A very large bomb had dropped in the field behind the cottage, about two hundred yards away.

All the next day this huge crater was surrounded by curious villagers and air raid wardens. It must have been a very exciting event for everyone really, a little bit of the war coming to Theddingworth. The blitz was raging in London at the time, and Coventry had been smashed quite recently, not to mention Liverpool and Plymouth and all the other important strategic places getting terrible air raids, but to the rural people, it was something they only read about in the newspapers. It certainly must have been a very large bomb, and it's odd how we tend to think of craters and bomb damage in black and white, because these days we only see the old mono newsreels of those times, but I'll always remember that enormous brown hole in the middle of a bright green field, huge clods of earth strewn all around, and the smell of earth and explosive, something that I was to experience a few more times before the war was over. Mrs Haig's description of it, quite accurately, was: 'You could turn a horse and cart round in it!'. If I heard her say that once, I heard her say it fifty times, talking to people she knew in Market Harborough when we went shopping on a Saturday, or discussing it with neighbours, as it was the big talking point in the village for months afterwards. Everybody reckoned that it must have been dropped accidentally, as there was just the one, all by itself, miles from anywhere of interest to the

Luftwaffe, but many years later, (about fifty actually), I think I found the answer.

It really is a fascinating story.

Late one night, I was driving home, listening to the radio, when this voice said - "If I'd been good at playing cricket, Wolverhampton would have been flattened". Naturally, my ears pricked up. I wondered what he was talking about.

It was the start of a dramatised documentary - the story of a scientist who had made a huge contribution to the war effort. Apparently, as a young man, he had obtained a university scholarship to study physics, but the one he wanted to attend wouldn't take him, as they only had so many vacancies, giving priority to good cricketers, as they were very keen to build up a good team. Our man was no sportsman, and for that reason alone, he was turned down. Sounds daft, but it was a fact. So he ended up studying at another university, which was at that time, the only one that included in it's syllabus the research into the embryonic science of electronics. He chose this as his subject - eventually becoming one of its leading experts.

During the war, he was employed as one of the boffins at the Ministry of Defence. He wondered how the German bombers found their inland targets so easily at night. It was no great problem to find London - just a matter of flying up the Thames Estuary, likewise the coastal targets, which was just a case of recognising the appropriate coastline, but the Midlands meant flying over a hundred miles or so of blacked-out countryside. There was no way that they could do it by dead reckoning with any accuracy, so he rightly surmised that they were employing some sort of guidance system.

He constructed a monitor, and sure enough, he found these strong directional radio beams coming from across the channel. All they had to do was fly along the main beam, crossing other beams which gave them their position, and on reaching the last one, being over the target. It was a very exciting play, as it was a sort of race against time, because he had a difficult job convincing the authorities of the urgency of the situation. It's easy enough for us to criticise the War Office all these years later, in hindsight, but of course, at that time, there were an awful lot of things going on, and lots of other people clamouring for priority. He managed to force his way into the inner sanctum, and talk to Churchill himself, who, immediately recognising the importance of the matter, gave him all the help he needed. He designed and manufactured a number of jamming devices, which succeeded in bending the German beams, and putting the bombers off course. Because of the lack of time, these devices were comparatively crude, and weren't always effective, which was why Coventry sustained that dreadful raid in November of '40. They smashed it to pieces, one of the worst raids of the war. It was a very high priority target for the enemy as it was a very concentrated manufacturing centre, and also the main producer of scientific instruments, it being the centre of the watchmaking industry in peacetime. Our chap rightly surmised that the next target to receive the same sort of attention would be where we made nearly all of our ball-bearings, this being an extremely vital product, invaluable to the war effort. That meant Wolverhampton. He also knew that they would hit it about a month after Coventry, at the next full moon, when conditions were at their best for the Luftwaffe. Unfortunately, this coincided with the discovery of an even more powerful, sophisticated guidance system that the Germans were employing, making our present counter measures all but useless. Again, the struggle with red tape, and the fight for priority, but he did it, just in time to save Wolverhampton, and all the other large inland targets for that matter.

Just a couple of weeks later, there were these big QL wireless lorries attached to generators parked all over the Midlands, waiting for a call from our coastal radar stations that would tell them when a large force of bombers would be crossing the Channel. Sure enough, just as, and when, he had predicted, over they came, and our transmitters started blasting out beams on the same frequency as the Germans, in all directions.

That night, there were bombs dropping all over the place, most of them quite harmlessly in open countryside, and very few hit Wolverhampton. He'd done it, bless him, and done the nation an invaluable service, although he bloody near did for me and the Haigs as well. And all because he couldn't play cricket!

I do realise that the Theddingworth bomb might have been dropped for some other reason, who knows?, but I thought that the story was well worth relating, and the facts do fit the case.

I've no other out of the ordinary recollections of my stay in Theddingworth. I can only repeat that it was the happiest period of my boyhood, from September '39 till the beginning of '41, I can't remember exactly when. Unfortunately, it all came to an end when Mr Haig got the sack. Why, I've no idea, but the cottage went with the job, which meant that we had to move to Market Harborough. It also meant that I had to be moved to a different billet, as there was no room for me in this little flat that they had rented. My sister June lived quite near, and the couple next door to her were willing to take me in, so that seeming the best solution all round, that's where I went.

I won't dwell too much about my time there, except to say that it was not very nice, and I was extremely unhappy. They were quite elderly, and very strict, and the house was gloomy and dark. I must say at this juncture, that I do realise that events seen through the eyes of a child do sometimes get exaggerated in ones mind in later years. I'm a lot older and wiser now, and I do realise that if I met that couple now, they would in all probability, turn out to have been quite nice normal people, and might have actually only been in their fifties, and not old and harsh as I remember them. There are two sides to everything and suddenly being saddled with a tearful eight year old, even though it was their choice, must have had it's problems. All I do know is that it was one long nightmare for me. Thinking about it all these years later, I reckon that they probably started out with the best intentions - otherwise, why volunteer to take in an evacuee in the first place? - then I think that once the novelty wore off, and I became more miserable, they started to lose their patience, and took it out on me.

Of *course* I was miserable. There was the fact that I was suddenly in the middle of a town, and not surrounded by fields, also that I had been so happy with the Haigs, and here I was with this stern old man and woman, in this horrible dark house. They used to shout at me at the top of their voices, and belt me at the slightest excuse.

There were two occasions that come to mind. One was when I was sent to Lipton's to get some eggs, which at that time were a bit of a luxury, and rationed of course. I somehow managed to drop them on the way home and handed her this soggy brown paper bag, every one of them being broken, and she beat the daylights out of me with a big copper stick, screaming at the top of her voice.

The other time was when I was sent to get a bag of chips. On the way home, I thought that they wouldn't miss one or two, so I ate them, and then thought to myself - 'well another one won't make much difference', and had another one, and so on, eventually arriving home with about a dozen chips. He half killed me with his leather belt, all the time both of them shouting at me. I know that I'm not the only kid to get a hiding for being naughty, but they went a bit too far, and too often.

I used to go round to see the Haigs, and I think that they must have had some relations in the town, because I remember going with Mrs Haig and

Margaret, to this big house where these two lovely old ladies lived, and eating cucumber sandwiches and cakes, and being made a fuss of. They used to play the gramophone all the time, one of those with a big brass horn. I remember that Mendelsohn's Cradle Song was one of their favourites. If I hear it now, I can shut my eyes and see that room, with all the knick-knacks and pictures and anti-macassars on the big old armchairs, and those two smiling old ladies. We used to go there most Sunday afternoons and it was something I always looked forward to.

Although my sister June lived next door, and I must have seen her every day, and at school, it's the same as before the war - I remember hardly anything about her. I've got a couple of photographs taken during the evacuation, with both of us in the group, and of course, I do recognise her as being my sister, but I've no recollection of us ever playing together, or going anywhere. Mind you, she was three years older, and had her own friends I suppose, so it's not surprising. Curiously enough, I do remember her guardians very well, perhaps because the man was in a wheelchair, although he wasn't very old - a very handsome man with curly hair, and they were a very happy couple. But I just can't get any picture of June from those days into my mind.

Very little of Market Harborough has stayed in my memory, only that I recall being told the facts of life by some older kids, and thinking it was hilariously funny, and not believing a word of it. I dimly remember a couple of boys I used to play with, and playing dares, one of which was hanging onto the backs of lorries, and dropping off before they got too much speed up. I hung onto one a bit to long once, till it was going too fast to let go, and clung on like a limpet, terrified, right to the other side of the town, when luckily enough, he slowed down to turn left, or I'd have probably ended up in Leicester. I still came a bit of a cropper though, and my gas mask, which was in a cylindrical metal case, something like a thermos flask, gave me an awful wallop on the head. I got another hiding when I got home because my shoes were all scuffed.

You remember earlier how I mentioned how smells bring back memories? Well, Market Harborough in those days, always had this lovely mouth-watering smell, because it was where they made Symington's Soups. They were sold as a solid block, about as big as a matchbox, which was dissolved in boiling water. There was a very big factory - well for all I know, it's still there, although you don't see it around much these days - pumping out a mixture of Oxtail, Lentil, Beef and Veg, and Tomato soup smells. No wonder we were always hungry.

Remember also how I wrote about how memory plays tricks?. Well although Arthur says that I didn't go back to London until '42, I think it was in the late summer of '41, as when I did go back, I recall the other kids asking how old I was, and I distinctly remember saying 'I'm eight'. Again, Frank tells me that he's pretty sure that I was taken back to London for a time, and then sent back to Market Harborough. If he's right, then it must have been in between the Haigs and the other place, although I have no recollection of it. I don't suppose it really matters.

Anyway, according to my mother, she got a letter from Mrs Haig one day, saying that I was very unhappy, and having a very hard time, and it really would be best for me to get out of there - either to another billet, or home.

God Bless you dear Mrs Haig.

I never saw her again unfortunately. The last I heard of them was from June, who told me that Margaret had married an American. My parents had moved to Tottenham soon after the start of the war, which was quite some way from the City and the docks, consequently a bit safer, and the main Blitz had petered out in the May of '41, so home I went.

Goodbye Market Harborough.

. . . .

Chapter 3

TOTTENHAM DURING THE WAR

Tottenham was very different to Hoxton. I remember that when I first heard that my parents had moved, being told that they'd moved to the 'outskirts' and wondering what an 'outskirt' was. I expect that when my parents were small, Tottenham would, to them, have been out in the country, but by 1942 it was just as cockney as Bethnal Green, but with a very different environment. The area that we lived in had been built after the first war, and a great deal of care and thought had gone into its planning. I don't know how my parents managed to get the move, but fair play to them. It was a far more desirable place to live than the old East End.

Waltheof Avenue, where we lived, and the whole surrounding area consisted of houses with gardens, front and back, and tree lined streets. At one end of the avenue was a tennis club, with three courts and a clubhouse. Opposite the other end, on the other side of Lordship Lane, was a big ornamental gate, the entrance to an enormous park, called the Lordship Recreation Ground. Because of the war, the tennis club was all dis-used and overgrown with weeds, and the 'Big Rec' as we called it, had been divided into little plots for growing vegetables, called allotments. One of the main slogans of the day was 'Dig for Victory!'. My dad had one, number 77, and most fine evenings and weekends, he'd toddle over there with his wheelbarrow and tools, happy as Larry. Sunday mornings, every single one of them would be occupied, blokes digging and raking and hoeing and talking about the best way to do things. I spent a lot of time there, helping the old man. We also had a very nice back garden, with an apple tree, raspberry, loganberry, and gooseberry bushes as well as the flowers.

Hell of a change from Hoxton.

The first thing I noticed, on my return, were the barrage balloons. The whole of London was protected by them, and they hung up there in the sky, at regular intervals, as far as the eye could see, like big silver whales, gently moving and turning with the breeze. There was something very matey and comforting about them, knowing that they were up there to protect us. Like a lot of kindly fat old uncles watching over us, and keeping us safe. They proved to be very effective in preventing low level attacks and dive bombing such as Warsaw and Rotterdam had suffered.

Life for people in the big cities was totally different from that of the country folk. We were far more aware that there was a war going on. Although the big blitz was over, there was still the occasional raid, and I very soon got used to the mournful wail of the sirens rising and falling. You'd hear one in the distance, then another would join in a bit closer, and so on, rising to a crescendo and then suddenly there would be an eerie silence.

Where we lived, people just carried on with what they were doing, except in the schools of course, where we'd all follow a well rehearsed drill and file down into the shelters. Sometimes nothing at all would happen and a half hour or so later, we'd hear the long single note of the all clear and all troop back into school. Most daylight raids were like that, as they were usually carried out by just a few fast fighter bombers, after a specific target, usually some distance from Tottenham. They used to call them 'hit and run' attacks.

The night raids were very different.

They weren't very frequent through '42 and '43, and nowhere near as severe as those in the big blitz, but at the beginning of 1944 there was to be what was known as the 'baby blitz'. Again, away from the city and the docks, it wasn't nearly so dangerous for us in the 'outskirts', but four miles was not much more than a minute away for a bomber, so we were often on the flight path, and after the sirens we would hear this horrid, distinctive throbbing drone overhead, very loud, and the roar and crack of the ack-ack batteries going off. We had a Morrison shelter in our living room, which looked like a large table, but had a frame of heavy angled steel and a top of thick sheet steel, the four sides enclosed in wire mesh. They doubled as a table and a bed, and a house could fall down on them and you'd still be fairly safe from anything except a direct hit. I slept in it for most of the war, and sometimes, when it was bad, my parents would get in there with me. They were named after one of the war ministers, Herbert Morrison, and I dare say they saved quite a few lives. The other kind of home shelter was of course, the Anderson, which was situated out in the garden, away from the house, but I wouldn't have fancied one of those in the winter. Some survive to this day.

It could be very frightening, laying there in the dark with gritted teeth and tight shut eyes, waiting for the bomber stream to pass, and the noise of the guns to gradually die away in the distance.

Some of the heavy ack-ack guns were mobile - mounted on very large trucks, and once a pair of them opened up right outside the house during a raid, with no warning. There was an ear-splitting crash followed by the sound of breaking glass, then another and another, on and on for about a minute. I was crying in terror and actually wet myself, clinging on to my mother. She held me very tight and said, quite calmly 'All right - I've got you'. We thought it was a stick of bombs you see, and we were waiting for the one that would hit the house. Dad was away firewatching that night, something most of the men used to volunteer for.

When the all clear sounded, we found that half of our front windows were broken. There was some very choice language when the old man came home.

Fortunately for us, our immediate area was spared from the worst of the bombing. There was one very bad raid on an area of old Tottenham called Scotland Green, which was almost totally destroyed, with lots of people killed and injured, but I think that was before I came home. They occasionally had a go at the industrial area around Tottenham Hale, and we'd hear the crump of the explosions, and feel the vibrations and hear the windows rattling. Sometimes we would go out in the back garden during a raid, when the gunfire was in the distance, it being quite safe, as we could easily scoot indoors if they came any closer.

I remember once standing out there with Arthur and Frank, who was home on leave, watching the searchlights as they swept too and fro across the sky. It was a lovely sight. If one of the beams picked a bomber up, there would instantly be an inverted cone of lights, with a little silver spark at the apex, (all this being a few miles away), and the cone would follow the plane for as long as it could, with the distant crackle of gunfire rising to a continuous roar, and we'd be cheering away yelling out "get the bastard!", but more often than not, they'd lose him, and the roar would quickly decrease to a desultory crackle, and the cone of beams would break up.

Frank had a narrow escape one night. He was standing with our dad on the front porch when a chunk of shrapnel as big us your fist smashed into the wall just a couple of feet from them. You can still see the scar in the brickwork. You've all heard about the wartime children picking up these bits of jagged steel on their way to school, and I can verify it. We all had biscuit tins full of the stuff, and I recall that the most prestigious find was a brass nose-cone. It's always been a mystery to me that there were so few casualties from shrapnel, as tons of it rained down on cities (nearly all of it from the guns of course), the other evidence being the number of broken roof tiles we used to see. If you look carefully today at wartime houses, you will notice many single tiles with different colouring to the others.

As far as the bombing went, there was only one serious incident on our estate. One night, a parachute mine fell in the Roundway, about 300 yards from our house. The Roundway is a long curved road, and the part where they dropped is very wide, with a green in front of the houses. Parachute mines were huge devastating things, and this one did a terrible amount of damage, and quite a few people were killed and injured. When we saw the scene the next day, our broken windows didn't seem very important any more.

One curious little thing that might be of interest concerning that incident: A small piece of shrapnel went right through the steel black and white post of a Belisha Beacon by the side of the road. Do you know that forty five years later, just out of curiosity, I went and had a look at that post and the two little holes were still there.

For all I know, they still are.

So those are most of my memories of the bombing. It stopped altogether in the spring of '44.   Later came the doodlebugs and the rockets, and I assure you, I'll be telling you quite a lot about those bloody diabolical objects, but for now, I'll return to the time when I first got back to London.

Just one more little thing that I'd completely forgotten about, until Arthur reminded me of it recently when he was over here visiting from Australia.

In one of the adjoining back gardens, somebody kept this duck. Whenever there was a burst, or a single shot from the ack-ack, there would be a couple of seconds silence, and then the duck would go quack. Just one single quack. We used to wait for it, and he never let us down. 'Boom baboom boom' - pause - 'gwaak'. We used to laugh till the tears ran down our faces. Even if the gun fire was very distant - always the same - ....'Rumblebumblebumble' - pause - 'gwaak'.

. . . .

There had been an addition to the family while I had been away. His name was Sammy. Sammy was a Dalmatian, what we used to call a 'plum pudding' dog. One of the characteristics of the Dalmatian is that they never grow up mentally I mean. They remain pups till they are old, and Sammy was typical, a complete idiot, and the most playful, boisterous and affectionate dog you could wish for. We'd never had a dog before, so you can imagine, for a small boy it was marvellous. I really loved old Sammy and we became great mates, and I'd take him everywhere, or rather, he'd take me, as he was quite a big dog, with enormous energy. I've never seen a dog whiz about so much as he used to, and he was absolutely tireless. Whenever I took him over the big Rec and slipped his lead, he'd shoot off like a rocket, disappearing into the distance, then come belting back full pelt about a minute later. I soon learnt to dodge out of the way, like a bullfighter, at the last second, or he'd knock me flat. Then he'd charge round in a big circle until I found a stick for him to fetch.

He always used to stick his head up in the air and howl when the sirens went off and would stand stiff legged and growl if it got noisy.

Lovely dog he was.

. . . .

When I got back from evacuation, there was just myself and my parents living at 20 Waltheof Avenue, and Sammy of course. It was a great pity for me that I was cut off from my brothers and sisters at that age. I used to see them occasionally though, but Ivy was in the Land Army, Frank in the RAF, Arthur still back in Theddingworth on the farm, where he stayed until 1944 when he was called up. He was in the Beds and Herts regiment, and served in Europe and India. June never came back from evacuation till after the war. But I soon palled up with the kids in our street. Johnny Gowan, Tony Seely and the Choules brothers, Lenny and Georgy became firm friends, and remained so until I left Tottenham when I joined the Army. Lenny was a year or so older than the rest of us, and he and his younger brother Georgy lived next door but one.

Lenny was a comical bugger, always laughing and joking, and the one thing I remember most about him was that he had this amazing sort of springy walk. It's very difficult to describe, but he used to bob up and down with each step, and take great long strides. He couldn't help it, and it really was peculiar. My mother nick-named him 'Springheeled Jack'.

There was another mate of ours who lived round the corner in Tower Gardens, and he deserves a special mention.

His name was Cyril Stewart, known to us as 'Skizza'. At that time, Cyril was about 12 or 13, and we were all about nine. He was a tall, boney sort of bloke with a long nose and a lantern jaw, and was a bit backward, in fact he had to attend a special school. He was very well liked in the neighbourhood, and no-one ever took the mickey out of him, but he was much happier playing with us than knocking about with the boys of his own age. He was just our mate. When we used to knock for him, his mum would fuss about doing up his coat and tying his scarf round his neck, and she'd whisper to us behind his back, "Now you look after 'im won't you". Actually it was the other way round. None of the big kids would ever take liberties with us or push us around while Skizza was with us. He had a reputation as a real nutter when his 'wild was up', although we never saw him ever have a go at anyone - far from it, he was a very gentle sort of bloke. But some years before, this big kid had started knocking him about and he'd just walked away, only to return a few minutes later with a toy cricket bat, and without saying a word had proceeded to half kill the poor sod, and would have finished the job if they hadn't pulled him away. Hence the reputation.

He was a head and shoulders bigger than the rest of us, which also helped. He couldn't read or write, and arithmetic was a complete mystery to him, but he was far from stupid. He had this very solemn, deliberate manner, and didn't lark about as much as us little 'uns, but he knew all the best places to find conkers and tadpoles and things, and he was by far the best at 'telling pictures'. He was very knowledgeable in his own way and we learnt quite a lot from him. His most common expression was 'issa fact'. For instance, after telling one of the cowboy films he'd seen, (and believe me it was almost as good as seeing it, he'd do it so well), he came out with:

"Do you know why they call 'em Indians?".

"'Cos they are, ain't they".

"Wotcha mean 'cos they are' you dollop?".

"Well, why do they then?".

"'Oo discovered America?" he asked.

"Christopher Columbus" we all chorused.

"S'right. Christopher Columbus did. Well, 'e was lookin' for India, wasn't 'e. Did ya know that?"

"Nah".

"Well 'e was, cos 'e knew that the world was round like, an' if 'e went west instead of east, 'e'd find it. Anyway, when 'e gets to America, the daft git fought 'e was in India, so that's why 'e called the people who lived there Indians".

"Yeah?"

"Yeah - issa fact".

"Why didn't 'e call 'em Americans then?".

"Cos America 'adn't been invented yet, 'ad it!" he replied.

You couldn't fault his logic.

'Telling pictures' was a favourite pastime of all children in those days. The high spot of the week for us was Saturday afternoons at the pictures. It was different from the old 'two-penny rush' in that it would be at one of the big cinemas, and would have a feature film as well as the shorts. We'd see great stuff such as 'Gungha Din', 'The Four Feathers', 'They Died with their Boots on' and 'The Sea Hawk'. We used to re-live them all, over and over again. After 'The Mark of Zorro' was shown, for weeks the whole of North London was covered in 'Z'eds slashed on walls with bits of chalk tied to the end of wooden swords. Even though we'd all seen a particular film, we'd never tire of recounting it to each other, taking turns with the scenes and acting them out. It used to lead to lots of friendly arguments.

"So this big bald 'eaded pirate gets out 'is pistol and shoots this French geezer straight between the eyes, an' 'e falls off the riggin' into the sea ...."

"No 'e never - it was 'im with the patch over 'e's eye an' a moustache who done that".

"Who's tellin' this - me or you?".

"Well - get it right you dope", and so on.

The only mention I've ever come across of this custom since those days is in Brendan Behan's book 'Borstal Boy'. It's a shame that it died out. I suppose you can blame it's passing on television, and the fact that kids these days see so many films and plays and cartoons, whereas we just had the one a week, and made sure that we got the most out of it.

I recall an occasion when we were all lining up in the rain waiting to get into the Bruce Grove cinema. I said what a great thing it would be if could have our own pictures in our houses. Something like a magic picture hanging on the wall that had buttons you could press, and knobs you could turn, and we could see as many pictures as we wanted. We had a long enthusiastic discussion about it I remember, all agreeing what a fabulous thing it would be, as good as having our own pirate ship, or being a Spitfire pilot. All harmless fantasy of course. We never for a moment thought about television, although when we played in the Big Rec, the Alexandra Palace and it's TV tower dominated the northern skyline. But that was only something for the rich people, and it was disused in the war anyway. No-one, not even the grown-ups, let alone us kids, ever dreamt that not many years later, it would come to the masses.

I'd been in Tottenham for a few months - I remember that I had started to go to Risley Avenue school - when I'm afraid to say that I received a terrible shock, something that I've never forgotten, and which affected me very badly, and even now, all these years later, I still have difficulty coming to terms with.

Two of my mother's friends came to visit us from Hoxton, and there was the usual - 'My - ain't 'e grown Maggy, all that livin' out in the country's done 'im good ennit' etc., and they both gave me a tanner. Nice jolly ladies they were. My mother told me to go out and play, which I did.

I came home some time later, round the side entrance, and through the kitchen, and started to do some drawing, my mother and the two ladies being in the front room having a chat. They'd been laughing very loudly when I came in, so they didn't know I was there. I could just hear them, although I wasn't paying any attention to what they were saying, when I heard one of them say 'Eldritch' and then my mother say something like "Oh no - never", which caught my attention, and I stopped drawing, went to the door, and started to listen.

I don't remember much about the next hour or so except for my mother shaking me and shouting in my face to stop it, and one of the ladies pushing her away and putting her arms around me. Apparently, according to my mother, they heard me shouting and crying and rushed into the room and I found me running at the wall, with my nose bleeding. Then I went for them, kicking and punching, completely hysterical.

Elly and Alfy Wilkins had both been killed.

I'd heard in detail about a direct hit on a shelter containing seven of the Eldritch family, and that only two of them had survived. I also heard that, according to some survivors, the Wilkins family had been on their way to a shelter, and had seen a parachute coming down, and had just stood there watching it, thinking that it must have been an airman, but it was in fact, a parachute mine. They'd found Alfy the next day, believe it or not, on the roof of St Leonards Hospital with half of his head missing. I'd been standing at the door listening to all this. My mother already knew about it, as both tragedies had occurred the year before, but her two friends were just giving her the details. I hadn't seen Elly or Alfy or Benjy for nearly two years, but whenever I had asked about them, my mother had told me that they were still away in the country. But I'd never forgotten them, and had still looked forward to seeing them again.

I don't know what became of Benjy, as I never saw him again, but please God he survived unharmed. I'm sure he must have, or I'd have heard. It's always stayed with me though, to this day, and whenever I see a little child with spectacles, I get a lump in my throat, and I can still see Elly whizzing around on his trike, Alfy's little pinched face, and little Benjy smiling through his wonky glasses.

We used to hear all the while about our brave boys in blue flying over and pounding the German cities, thinking - 'Go to it lads, give 'em some of their own medicine', and all the rest of it, and they were brave, they were heroes, and flew their missions with the complete conviction that they *were* doing the right thing, but how many other little Ellys and Alfys were smashed to pulp in Hamburg and Cologne?. I expect that Ludwig and Hans in their bloody Dorniers and Heinkels flew with just as much conviction. That's the tragedy of war. Just a brave, clear thinking young man peering through a bombsight and then squeezing his thumb down on a little button, whether he's looking down at Charlottenburg or Shoreditch, it's just the same.....They kill children. I'm not an Atheist, because I think that there must be some reason for us being here - I suppose I'm what you'd call an agnostic, but if ever I hear some clown of a cleric talking about God's will, I get very angry.

'Suffer little children to come unto me'.   What a load of bollocks.

. . . .

I can remember my first day at Risley Avenue Elementary school very clearly. As I have mentioned before, I was terrified of schools in general, so starting a new one with a lot of strange kids was even worse, although I knew Tony and Johnny, which took a little of the edge off of it. But what makes my recollection so clear was as follows:

I was standing by myself on the edge of the playground, during the morning break, when I heard someone yell - "Lookout!". I turned round and

Risley Avenue School – Tottenham 1942

My class, all age 9. Unfortunately, I'm not in the photograph for some reason.
Alby Dines, front row, 4th from left. Alec Jennings, front row, far right. Ronny Haynes, back row, 5th from left.
Roy Sutton, back row, 7th from left. The Headmaster Mr Powell and the nice lady teacher whose name I forget.

copped a tennis ball straight in the eye. I saw this little dot grow to a very big dot all in the space of a second, and wallop, I was seeing stars, then sitting down holding my face. It hit me in my left eye, a hell of a whack, and as I can't see out of the other one, I was in a bit of a state, sitting there doing my best not to start crying, when I heard this voice piping in my ear -

"You all right mate?". I took my hands away from my face, and there was this ginger-haired skinny kid with buck teeth, kneeling beside me, grinning quite happily. That was how I met Alby Dines. He'd just kicked the ball as hard as he could at the goal chalked on the brick wall, and miscued somewhat, and I'd been in the way. From that moment on we became best mates, and remained so for the next ten years, and are still in touch to this day. He helped me get up and I heard another kid say,

"It's that new kid ennit. His glasses are all bent - come on, we'll take him to the teacher". That other boy was Alec Jennings, and he was also to become a very close friend. That's why I remember that day so clearly. I got a black eye and two new mates.

Risley Avenue was typical of all urban pre-war elementary schools, and they can be easily described. Grim. I dare say the people who designed them did so with all the best intentions, but they were a far cry from the light and airy schools which my kids attended. In those days, they made sure that the windows were too high to see out of when we were sitting down, to save us from any outside distractions I suppose. Also, even small children were subjected to rigid discipline, no talking, sit up straight, and a whack with a ruler for even the most minor of transgressions. I dare say that this depended very much on what sort of teacher you had - a class just having the one teacher for all subjects.

Unfortunately for us, we had a real dragon.

Her name was Miss Boddie. I can honestly say that that bloody woman made my life a misery for the whole of my time at that school. She was a big horsy sort of woman, with glasses and a very loud voice, and we were all quite sure that she was mad. There were a couple of kids who she treated as pets, but she seemed to have this pathological hatred for the rest of us. Particularly me and Alby. Luckily, we were both very clever, so we were spared some of the grief, but even so, a single mistake in our sums for instance, might well mean being dragged bodily out from behind our desk and being literally thrown into the corner, with her shrieking at the top of her voice. Yet her favourite kid, a boy called Johnny Hough, who lived at the end of my street and had a face like a little angel, was as thick as two planks, and couldn't do anything right, but he'd get a pat on the head and a smile whatever he did. What a monster she was, a real lunatic.

A clear memory of Miss Boddie was of her pounding the piano accompanying us singing and screaming, "YOU'RE FLAT - YOU'RE FLAT!!". The trouble was that she never ever bothered to explain to us what flat meant, and we were all too terrified to ask. Let me repeat myself, and say that memory does play tricks, especially after so many years, but Alby Dines remembers her in much the same way. It might be the case that she wasn't as bad as we remember her, and I might well be doing her a disservice, but I do recall that whenever she was off sick, or otherwise engaged, another lady teacher used to take over the class, and she was really lovely and kind, and we worshipped her. I don't remember her name, but we'd do anything for her, and would always be on our best behaviour and it was such a change to get some encouragement and praise. We thought that she was going to be our teacher for our last year, but when we got back to the school after the long summer holidays we found to our horror, that we had Miss Boddie again, for the rest of our time there. Myself, Alby and Alec were among those that passed the scholarship to go to Grammar school, but I think we did it in spite of her, not because of her.

. . . .

As I have already mentioned, I was a complete duffer at any sport that was played with a ball. In the playground, we played endless games of football, using a tennis ball - a game that we called 'tooter' - (like it rhymed with 'footer'), and when they tossed up and the captains picked the teams, I was always the last one to be picked, because I was so useless. Alec, who was little and podgy, and not the slightest athletic looking, was absolutely brilliant, like a little Stanley Matthews, and could dribble round anybody, like the ball was stuck to his foot. It was also great to watch him do tricks and juggle the ball, using his feet, knees, shoulders and head. A common saying amongst us kids, shouted very often by Alec as he twinkled his way past one of the opposition was 'TrickiNESS!', the last syllable being shouted out in triumph. He was also just about the best cricketer in the school, again played with a tennis ball at a wicket chalked on the wall. I wasn't quite so bad at cricket, because Alec taught me to bowl, and sometimes I wouldn't be the last one to be picked, just the second from last. Try as I might, at that time, I could not catch the simplest of chances. I didn't realise then that it was because of my eyesight until one day, on the way home, Alec and Alby tried catching fast balls with one eye closed, and kept missing them altogether, which they found very funny, and made me feel a whole lot better. Alby was also brilliant at both sports, nearly as good as Alec, but, useless as I was, they never made me feel left out.

There was another boy of our age however, who used to make my life a misery whenever he could. His name was Ronny Haynes, and he was the playground bully. He got on quite well with my two mates, because they were good at sports, and playground heroes, but he was as nasty as they were good natured, and like all bullies, he picked on the wimps, and me in particular. He was a big sod, a head taller than all of us, and he was very fond of twisting my arm up my back and punching me in the shoulder as hard as he could, pushing me around and calling me 'four-eyes' and 'goggles'. I was terrified of him, and he knew it, which made him even worse. I had to put up with his constant bullying for about three years, because he also got to Tottenham Grammar school, and it only finished when I started to stand up for myself. I wouldn't mind betting that he's still an arsehole.

One thing I was good at though. Very good.

I still thank my lucky stars that although there was a war on, the Tottenham Lido was still open. It was a big open air pool, fifty yards by twenty five, shallow at each end and six feet deep in the middle, with a much wider bit where the diving boards were, where it was ten feet deep, with one, three and five metre diving boards. It also had quite a lot of room round it for the sun-bathers, and also some gymnastic equipment - rings, parallel bars and suchlike, a really first class pool. You could stay in there all day for threepence. It was when I was still only nine years old that Tony Seely, Johnny Gowan and myself went swimming for the first time.

It was the start of something magical for me, because to use a very apt cliché, I took to it like a duck to water. We had a terrific time, skylarking about in the shallow end, and couldn't wait to get back over there the next day. We all three became fanatical and practically lived there all that summer, rain or shine. I can still vividly remember that sense of achievement at every new thing we did, just jumping in off the side at first, then opening our eyes underwater and pulling faces at each other, then picking up stones from the bottom. Then the big step of taking your feet off the bottom and striking out for the side, grabbing the rail and yelling - "I dunnit - I dunnit, look I can swim!". Standing crouched on the side, screwing up the courage to go in head first for the first time, and that marvellous feeling when you come up spluttering and laughing. Every one of these steps was like a little victory, conquering the nerves. Then the pride we felt when we swam our first width, then the first length, then diving of the lowest board into the deep end. We did all these things together, geeing each other up. By the end of the summer we were completely at home in the water and were great mates with the life guards, who taught us to swim freestyle properly, (although in those days, it was called the front crawl). After being such a duffer at anything sport-wise, I'd found something that I was really good at. I was lucky to have this natural ability. Whenever we raced across the pool, I'd be finished while Johnny and Tony were still only half way. But the greatest fun we had was on the diving boards.

I remember the very first time we climbed up to the top board and peeped over the edge, and how our stomachs turned over, it looked such a long way down, and then the attendant yelling - "COME ON DAHN ORF A'THERE YOU!", and scuttling back down, and thinking - 'sod it - I don't fancy ever going off that'. But we did eventually. I can't describe that fantastic exhilaration the first time I jumped off it. This was towards the end of the summer of course, when we could swim well and thought nothing of diving to the bottom of the ten foot to pick up stones. We'd progressed by hopping off the one metre springboard, then the three metre and had climbed up to the top three or four times when the attendant wasn't looking, because little kids weren't allowed up there, but had chickened out and climbed down again. But came the day when I screwed up my courage, shut my eyes and stepped off, and I felt that thrill of falling - the heart jumping up into my mouth, then smacking into the water, then the bubbles streaming past and pushing up to the surface. Christ it was marvellous! - treading water and looking up at Johnny and Tony peering over the edge and shouting - "Come on - it's easy". Then the attendant saw them and yelled out but they both grabbed their noses and hopped off together - Splash - Splash, and there we all were laughing and whooping in triumph. I'll never forget it. We were as proud as punch, really pleased with ourselves, and it was well worth the telling off we got from the attendant.

Those were some of the happiest times in my life, and I can tell you that the Lido was my favourite place, right through my boyhood. I think that it was the start of finding my confidence and self reliance. We still went swimming at the Municipal indoor baths every weekend, right through the winter, and longed for the day that the Lido re-opened the next year. By the end of the next summer, I could swim like a fish, and was a really neat diver, doing somersaults off the spring boards, swallow dives and reverse and inward pikes off the top. OK- I was still hopeless at football and cricket - still a wimp in the playground, but I was King Dick over the pool.

. . . .

If a boy of today was to be transported back to those times he would think that they were on another planet. For a start, we were all dressed the same, more or less. Look at those drawings in the 'Just William' books, and they will give you a pretty accurate picture - cap, jacket, short grey trousers, baggy socks and black shoes. That was the universal uniform for all small boys, although the jacket was discarded in the hot weather, and we nearly all wore plimsolls when we played out. Short back and sides haircuts too. No television or video games of course, no coca-cola or hamburgers or hot dogs, no blue jeans, no multi-coloured T-shirts and bomber jackets. A real football or cricket bat would be a prized possession, making you the envy of all your mates, but the biggest status symbol of all was a bicycle. New ones were very rare, as they cost a fortune in those days, but we'd beg, borrow, scrounge and swap and until we had accumulated enough bits to make our own.

Sweets and ice cream were a rare luxury. Oranges, bananas and grapes were non-existent.

These would be the more obvious things he would immediately be aware of, together with things like the almost total absence of traffic and parked cars in all the side streets, also the fact that there were no black or brown faces to be seen anywhere. But there were other, more subtle things that would take a little more time to become apparent. For a start, even as kids, we were all very proud to be British - very patriotic, and being Londoners, we were very conscious of being at the centre of the greatest nation on earth. Yes, I know it may sound corny now, but that was exactly how we felt. None of us ever had the slightest doubt that we would win the war. It was sort of bred into us, and nurtured in the schools - the big world maps in the classrooms with huge splodges of red - Canada, Australia, most of Africa, India, and all the little splodges, from the Falklands to the West Indies. And there we were, living on this little island, and we were the guvnors of all of it. All gone now of course, but at that time, it was the greatest Empire that the world had ever known, and it was still intact. We didn't just think that we were the best - we knew we were the best, and had no doubt that one

Englishman was worth ten of any of that lot over the other side of the Channel, and twenty of anyone with a different coloured skin. Our only equals were the Jocks, Paddies and Taffs, together with the Aussies and Canadians, but that was only because they were Brits who happened to live somewhere else. I know that all this may sound dreadful in these days of political correctness, but I must point out that it was fifty years ago, at the time of writing, and the world was a very different place then.

Mind you, I must confess that I still feel the same.

Another fact of life at the time, was that we accepted the authority of all adults without question. For instance, if we were kicking a ball around in the street and a grownup would tell us to pack it in and go and play in the park, we would without any argument. We might call him a grumpy old sod when we were out of earshot, but nevertheless, we'd do it. Anyone trying that today would probably be told to eff off, even by the smallest children. The worst thing that could happen to us would be to 'have our name and address took' by a policeman. It actually didn't mean anything at all, but it made us little kids very apprehensive, giving us the feeling that we were half-way to the gallows, and we'd be on our best behaviour for the next few days.

Lying (except if it was very necessary), cheating, boasting, showing off, swearing in front of girls - all those sort of things, we looked down upon, and any kid found guilty wouldn't have many friends. That's not to say that we were all little saints - far from it, but I like to think that we had a lot more character in those days, and grew up all the better for it. Our heros were Rockfist Rogan, Stanley Matthews, Len Hutton, Guy Gibson and such, not effeminate overpaid pop stars. Just look at some of the well worn clichés dating from those times: 'Cheats never prosper' - 'truth will out' - 'never kick a man when he's down' - 'pick on someone your own size' - 'don't blow your own trumpet' - they're just a few that spring to mind. I'm not saying that we held to them all the while, but we did most of the time. It was part of the British character, and what made us such a strong nation.

I'd like if I may to tell of one occurrence that will maybe illustrate the difference between now and then:

My house in Hemel Hempstead backed onto an infant's school, which incidentally, my own kids attended. I lost count of the times that I had to hop over the fence and break up a fight between two red faced and angry little fellers, sorting out an argument after the days school had finished. I'd push through the crowd and pull them apart and make them shake hands and that would be that. But in later years, just before the school was demolished and replaced with houses, there were a few times when I'd have to rescue some poor little sod who was being kicked while he was on the ground by a number of other little heroes.

Say no more.

During the long summer holiday of 1942, I learned that I had passed the scholarship, with high enough marks for entrance to Tottenham Grammar School. Not only that, but Alec and Alby had also passed, so we were as pleased as punch. I wasn't too happy when I heard that Ronny Haynes was also going, but you can't have everything. Tony and Johnny unfortunately had not passed, and were doomed, (in our opinion), as they had to go to Roland Hill School where all the thickies (also in our opinion) went. Only about a dozen of us from Risley School made it, and we were all labelled 'clever dicks' by the others, but not with any malice.

I suppose that we all have little landmarks in our lives, events which we can hang the sequence of our memories on, and going to Tottenham Grammar was one of mine, but before I get to that, I'd like to relate one more event which took place during that last summer holiday.

The air raids at that time were very few and far between. Now and again, the sirens went off, but nobody took any notice, as the all clear always sounded about ten minutes later - sort of false alarms. This particular day I was in the Big Rec walking through the allotments with some mates, when we heard first, and then saw these two planes come over the houses at the end of the park, about a quarter of a mile away, just skimming the rooftops. They came straight towards us. We never even had time to duck. They passed us with an ear-splitting roar, no more than fifty feet from the ground, and about twenty-five yards from us, one just to the side of the other. We actually saw the pilots, as well as the black and white cross on the sides and the swastika on the tail. They came out of nowhere and had flashed past before we realised what they were. Then we heard a loud staccato banging when they opened up with their machine guns, and then they were gone. It was all over in a few seconds. There had been no air raid warning, nothing.

We all started to run back, our ears still ringing, as fast as we could, out of the park and across Lordship Lane, and down Waltheof Avenue where I lived. There were lots of people standing around wondering what had happened, and a man shouted - 'Go on, get on home you lot', but we were too excited, and wanted to see what damage had been done. We couldn't see anything actually, and stood around excitedly arguing whether they had been ME-109s or Fockewolfs, and telling all the others about it, and that they'd been so close that we could have hit them with a stone. What two German fighters were doing over north London on that bright sunny afternoon, and why they decided to strafe a perfectly innocent street I don't suppose anyone will ever know.

Sadly there was one casualty. We must have passed within a few feet of him without knowing it. He was an elderly bloke who had been walking along Tower Gardens road, just where it crosses Waltheof Avenue, and he had been hit in the elbow, the bullet going right through. He'd staggered into a front garden, and had died of traumatic shock, and wasn't found till the people came home from work. Poor old feller. The wrong place at the wrong time. The bullets had gone all along the back gardens and broken a window and a few slates at either end of the block, and one bullet had knocked a big chunk of bark from our apple tree.

. . . .

Chapter 4

TOTTENHAM DURING THE WAR Part 2.

Tottenham Grammar School was built between the wars and was situated in White Hart Lane. It was a very nice building, in the style known as 'red brick and white portal', quite modern in it's time, with a rugby field on one side, and a cricket pitch on the other, the whole stretching the length of Creighton Road. Curiously enough, White Hart Lane went round the other three sides of the school, then continued at the other end of Creighton Road, Lord knows why. The front of the school was really grand, fronted by a steep little rise, and a big iron ornamental gate and railings, which were level with the first floor windows, but all that imposing architecture was rather wasted, because that bit of White Hart Lane actually was just that - a lane. The big gates were never even opened. It was built sort of back to front with the back of the school and the playgrounds and fives courts facing the much busier Creighton Road. I realise that I may seem to be going into too much boring detail, but there is a good reason for this, for whoever decided to build Tottenham Grammar School the wrong way round, for whatever reason, was responsible for saving many lives, and probably averted the worst home disaster of the war.

More of that later.

I must say that I enjoyed the first year at the Grammar. I had been worried about whether I would be up to the standard of work that was required, but I soon found that it all came easy to me, and at the end of that first year, I was in the top half a dozen in all subjects (except woodwork), and overall third in the class. In those days, the brightest kids skipped the second form and went straight into the third, that class being called 3R. The idea was to matriculate a year earlier than the others, so consequently the work was more concentrated. I was among those selected.

Discipline was quite severe, but in that first year I worked hard because I enjoyed it, so I kept out of trouble. All the masters had degrees, obligatory for teaching at a Grammar school, and wore black gowns, and by and large weren't a bad bunch, and were, with a few exceptions, very good teachers. Our form master was called Mr Mitchell, an English teacher, and he was very popular and well respected, more so because he had earned a boxing Blue at Oxford.

We really did feel a cut above the other kids in the neighbourhood, going to school in a smart uniform and tie, carrying shiny new satchels, learning French and Algebra and what have you, and playing rugby instead of soccer. My father was always on about how lucky I was, and geeing me up to work hard, so that I wouldn't end up like him, humping sides of bacon about . But I didn't need any geeing up in that first year. It was nice to be taught properly, after two years with that dreadful Miss Boddie, and I used to actually enjoy my homework. I suppose that I was what you'd call a model pupil.

In that first year at least.

A big contribution to my happiness was that I had stopped wearing glasses a few weeks before I started Grammar school, and although I could only see properly out of my left eye, my squint had completely disappeared, so it was nice not being called 'foureyes' anymore, and not standing out as a playground wimp and getting picked on all the time. The only fly in the ointment was that bastard Ronny Haynes, who still continued to give me a hard time, but any playground bullying was always nipped in the bud by the elder prefects, so it was not nearly so bad as Risley.

Tottenham Grammar School had a great sporting tradition, particularly for rugby and swimming. Of course, none of us eleven year olds knew anything at all about rugby, so we all started off level you might say. It's a very different game from soccer, and I found to my surprise that I was much better than average. One thing I could do was run, which was very handy, and I found, also to my surprise, that I had no fear of getting stuck in, and I could tackle like a bullet right from the start. The games master was a little Welshman, who was an absolute fanatic. I can still hear him yelling "ON ON ON!!". He used to get really carried away, so much so that he used to join in sometimes, grabbing the ball and haring up the wing, scattering us little kids in all directions, and hurling himself over the line. He could never remember anyones name and for some reason he used to call me 'Brimmers' and sometimes even 'Brimmery'. He was a real character. "WELL DONE BRIMMERS" - "ON ON ON!" - "GOOD TACKLE BRIMMERY!". I really took to the game and played regularly for the school. All our teams seemed to win all the time. I remember once going to Westcliffe-on-sea with the under fourteen and a half team where we won 84 - nil. I suppose it must have been down to the mad Welshman's coaching. It was all such a change from always being picked last in the playground 'tooter' matches where I was still just as useless. Funnily enough, Alec, although still the same old twinkletoes at football was completely useless at rugby.

But it was in the swimming pool where I really came into my own.

The school had always had a great swimming tradition. I think that while I was there, as far as Middlesex Schools were concerned, which included all of London, we were second only to Isleworth Grammar School, and that was one of the best in the country. Again, it must have been down to the coaching, because our gym master had been an Olympic gymnast, and though middle-aged was a marvellous swimmer and diver. We really liked him, one reason being that he was the only master with a cockney accent, and although he was very strict, he had a great sense of humour. He was also a great boxing coach. His name was Mr Hawtin. There was also another young teacher, whose name I can't remember, an ex-naval officer, who had been a frogman during the war, a fabulous swimmer, also a very keen coach.

I couldn't wait for my first trial for the school at the Municipal indoor baths. It was just a one length freestyle race, and I crouched on the side with a line of other eleven year olds waiting for the whistle thinking - 'I'll show you buggers'. The whistle blew and off I went like the clappers but for the first half of the race, there was this blue pair of trunks next to my head, and I nearly killed myself trying to overhaul him, and just made it as our hands smacked against the rail. The kid's name was Curtis, and we grinned at each other, gasping for breath. We looked round, and there was another boy holding the rail looking at us. His name was Needham. The three of us had finished together, but the good thing was that we were about a third of a length ahead of all the others. I remember Mr Hawtin looking very pleased, and saying "Right you three - lets 'ave yer names".

We walked straight into the junior team, and together with a second former, a boy called Pierce, swam together in the relay team for the next three years, and were never ever beaten, even when we swam against Isleworth. We broke both junior and middle county schools records, and our school 200 metres record which we smashed in the third year was still standing after I had left the army. In the individual freestyle races, there was little to choose between us, but Curtis just about had the edge, and just pipped us in the school gala three years running, over a hundred yards, with either me or Needham a very close second, but I beat him once in the one length sprint.

I also won the diving every one of those three years, and was always well placed in the in the county matches, and my best sporting achievement was winning the Middlesex Schools junior diving title when I was thirteen. Mind you, in those days, diving was a lot less complicated than it is now, because it was before the advent of the trampoline, which completely transformed the sport, as you could do an hours practise in two minutes, and it became much easier to perfect somersaults and twists. I wish it had been around in my day.

So, as you will understand, my life took a few turns for the better in that first year at Tottenham Grammar. All kids like to be liked and respected by the others - it's quite a natural thing, and suddenly there was me, who'd always been useless at anything to do with sport, playing rugby and swimming for the school, and also no longer looking like Ben Turpin. It all gave a great boost to my self-confidence.

We all have turning points in our lives - little things that happen, which when you look back on, many years later, you realise altered the whole course of your future life. I suppose that they are actually very frequent. For instance, the night you met your future wife, she could have just as easily stayed in that night to wash her hair, and you'd have met someone else, but you would have never known the difference. I must say though, that I'm very glad that Jeanny wasn't washing her hair on the night we met. But some instances are very clear, and I'd like to tell you about the one event which I'm sure had the most effect on my own future life.

It happened as follows:

I hope I don't labour the point about being such a duffer at anything physical when I was a kid, but I also happened to be completely devoid of any courage when it came to fighting. As I've stated, I did get picked on quite a bit, but if anyone hit me, or even threatened me, I had two defences. For a start, I never tried to fight back. It never entered my head. I either legged it as fast as I could, or, if that was impossible, would immediately start to cry, which, due to the curious juvenile ethics of the time, meant that the other kid would immediately cease hostilities, and depart in triumph. Most kids somehow manage to get through without any sort of confrontation - for instance, I can't remember Alby or Alec ever being picked on, or having a go at anybody else for that matter, but I seemed to be a magnet for bullies.

To digress for a moment, I'll give you an example.

I was walking home from Risley School with Alec one time, along Risley

Avenue - I guess we were about ten years old, when a mob of big kids from Roland Hill came boiling out of the gates of the Little Rec and surrounded us. They were all about twelve or thirteen. The leader, a boy called Nobby Lacey, then punched me full force on the nose, for no reason at all, knocking me flat on my back, whereupon they all strolled away laughing, with not even a backward glance. I ran home crying, with my nose pouring with blood, but got no help or solace from my mother of course, even though the bleeding kept on for hours. I had a swollen face, and looked like a Panda for a couple of weeks, with two black eyes.

Years later, when I was in my thirties, I had to have my sinuses examined, and the specialist asked me when I had broken my nose. I replied that to the best of my knowledge, never, but he told me that I certainly had, and that the left side of my nose was completely blocked, and that I must have taken a hell of a whack. It could only have been that bastard Lacey, as that was the only time in my life that I had suffered a nosebleed.

But the point was - why did he hit me, and not Alec?! But, to continue....

In those days, as horrific as it may seem now in these more enlightened times, boxing at Tottenham Grammar School was compulsory for all first formers. You quite simply had to box. No way round it. I expect that some boys got notes from their parents for medical reasons, but a fat lot of good it would have done me asking mine! So, we were all weighed and matched, and the next day, there was the list of bouts up on the gymnasium notice board. I can well remember looking down the list, and seeing 'Brimson V Langridge', and the jolt of terror I suffered. No way round it. No legging it, or turning on the waterworks. The bouts were due to take place the next Monday after school. I don't suppose I was the only kid who was petrified, not for a moment. Alby wasn't bothered in the least, grinning quite happily and saying "I'm gonna murder the git", but Alec was as nervous as I was. "Sod that" he said, "I ain't going in no bloody boxing ring".

We therefore both decided that when school was finished on that particular day, we were off home - 'Die dog and shite the licence' as the saying goes which roughly translated means bugger the consequences. But unfortunately for us, the Wednesday before, when we were due to play rugby in the afternoon, it was pelting down with rain, so the Mad Welshman marched us all into the gym, where the ring had been assembled, and roared -

"Right boys - no rugby today, much too wet, so we're doing the boxing heats. Off and get changed now". Oh my God, there was no way out.

I didn't know the Langridge kid too well as he was in a different class, but he looked big and confident to me, and in the changing room looked quite at ease, laughing and joking with his mates. I'd also been getting some stick from Haynes for the last few days, to the effect that I was going to get done good and proper etc., so you can imagine what I was going through. I was shaking in my shoes. We all filed into the gym, and there was Gerry Hawtin sitting at a desk beside the ring.

"RIGHT LADS - PAY ATTENTION"- he shouted and then proceeded to call out our names - all those in the blue corner being told to go to one side of the gym, and all the red corner boys to the other.

"Right oh - now then. All the bouts will be two rounds - one and a half minutes each round. When I call your names, proceed to your corner and put the gloves on. You may each choose your own seconds". He called out the names of the first two protagonists, and when they were standing in their corners said -

"Pay attention all of yer. When I say 'BREAK', you step back and wait for me to say 'BOX ON' right?. When I say 'STOP BOXING' you stop and go back to your corner. This -", he held up this sort of tin can dangling from a piece of string - "is the bell". He gave it a whack with a metal rod - 'CLANG' it went.

"When you 'ear that, you start boxing - when you 'ear it again you stop and go back to yer corner. Any Questions?".

I sat there watching the other boys flailing away at each other midst absolute bedlam, with everyone cheering their mates on, dreading the moment when my name would be called out. When it was, I could hardly walk, my legs were shaking so much, and I remember how huge the gloves felt - they seemed to come right up to my elbows. I don't remember shaking hands or anything, although we must have done, but suddenly, there was Langridge looking very fierce, glaring at me from over the other side of the ring, banging his gloves together and then 'CLANG' - the tin rang. Now they say that panic and fear can give you extra strength. It may well be true, because I just flew across the ring, straight at him, and started belting away before he'd even left his corner. I just let go with everything I had. The next thing I heard above all the pandemonium was -

"STOP. STOP BOXING!", and there was Langridge crouching in the corner with hands over his head. When he straightened up, he looked very dazed and unhappy, with blood pouring from a split lip. The whole thing had lasted about twenty seconds. 'CLANG CLANG' went the tin and Mr Hawtin announced -

"BRRRRIMSON IS THE WINNAH! - Rightoh - next two - git the gloves on!".

Do you know, believe it or not, I was still as nervous as ever, despite all the pats on the back, and got changed and on my way home as quick as I could, in case Langridge came and hit me! Seems silly now, but I remember it very clearly. I walked home with Alec, (who had been beaten), thinking 'thank Christ that's over', and feeling like you do when you come out of the dentists, until Alec reminded me that now I was through to the next round, and would have to fight again next week.

The next day at school I was relieved to find that Langridge was quite friendly, even though he had a fat lip. But I had to go through it all again - the same jolt of fear as I looked at the list on the notice board and saw - 'GREEN V BRIMSON'. Now Jasper Green (yes, that was his name), was one of Ronny Haynes' cronies, and had won his fight quite handily. So I was even more terrified than before, and came in for a load of stick again, about how I was going to get massacred this time, and no mistake, some of it from Green himself. Again, there was no way out of it. My mates were quite encouraging though.

"What ya worried about? Just tear into 'im like you did last week - you'll be all right". Well, the dreaded moment arrived, and it was exactly the same as before, with Green over the other side of the ring looking very eager to get at me, and me standing there with those bloody great gloves on, nearly doing it in me trousers. 'CLANG', went the tin, and again, it was exactly the same, I just flew across the ring and let fly with both hands. I suppose it was just a release of tension, but about twenty seconds later, Green was sitting down in the corner with a bad nose-bleed, and one eye closing up.

"BRRRRIMSON IS THE WINNAH!". Same as before, I got out of there as fast as I could. Green didn't come near me the next day, but Haynes grabbed me by the tie and hissed "Think yourself lucky you ain't in my weight - I'd effin' kill ya".

"No you wouldn't mate" said Alec, which was a great help, because Haynes immediately challenged me to a fight, there and then, which I just as immediately declined. Mind you, the bastard was much bigger than me.

So there was I, still in it, through to the quarter-finals of my weight, just praying for the nightmare to end. It did no good at all being patted on the head by the bigger kids, and being told I was a little tearaway - I just wanted out of it.

The next day, I was in the corridor on my way to the next class, when this tough looking kid stopped me and asked - "You Brimson?". I said yes and he grinned at me and said "You're fighting me next. Good luck mate", patted me on the shoulder and disappeared. His name was Butcher, and he was a third-former, two years older than me, and had been champion of his weight the year before. Unluckily for me, he was very small for his age. I soon learned that he was very useful indeed, and boxed in the school team. Now funnily enough, I wasn't as scared as I thought I'd be. I knew that I'd get beaten, but it wouldn't come as a surprise to anyone, and anyway, I'd given a good account of myself, and soon I'd be finished with this bloody boxing for good. Also, the fact that he'd made himself known, and seemed a nice sort of bloke had taken a lot of the fear away. No disgrace to get beat by a champ I thought - and anyway, a first-former had never beaten a third-former. I just hoped that it wouldn't hurt too much.

I wasn't all that worried through the next few days, but as soon as I got to the dressing room, the same old nerves came back, and I was just as petrified standing in the corner looking across at Butcher. The gym was full, and a lot of the masters were there, and I noticed that Mr Mitchell was in Butcher's corner, him being one of the school's boxing coaches.

It wasn't at all like the other two bouts. 'CLANG' went the tin, and as before I ran at him like a lunatic, but this time - WHACK! and I was seeing stars. I ran into a perfect jab and it hurt! I thought my nose had been rammed through the back of my head, and he side-stepped and there we were in the centre of the ring. I went for him again, and WHACK! - I got another one. I must have got half a dozen of the same, but suddenly I had him in the corner and started flailing away. There was a deafening noise, everyone shouting for me, and I managed to get a big overhand right on the target, but just as suddenly, he wasn't there, and I actually had my back to him, and when I turned I got such a punch on the jaw and then another one on the nose, and there he was, in the centre of the ring out of harms way. I took quite a pasting, but still kept trying and had bundled him into a corner again, making him cover up, then 'CLANG' went the tin for the end of the round. I sat in the corner with this kid flapping away with a towel, and another one sponging my face to absolute bedlam. My ears were ringing, and my face felt all puffed up, and my right thumb was hurting badly, but I honestly wasn't scared anymore, and I just wanted the tin to ring so I could get at him again. I knew I was going to lose, but I didn't care. Believe it or not I was actually enjoying it! 'CLANG' and I sailed out, straight onto a stiff jab which made my eyes water. I took a couple more, and I think that it was at that moment that my life took that turn that I mentioned earlier. Because I lost my temper. I'd never done that in my life before. I just wanted to kill him. I didn't know how to box, so I just sort of grabbed him and pushed him onto the ropes where he couldn't dance away and pepper me with that sodding left hand of his, and punched away with all my strength. It's a lovely feeling when your bloods up - you don't feel the punches, you're too intent on getting at the other bloke. You can say that for the first time, I experienced the joy of battle! I hope all this doesn't seem all dramatic, because after all, it was only two little kids having a scrap, but it meant an awful lot to me. Then it was over, and everyone was yelling their heads off, and I went back to my corner feeling marvellous, on top of the world. 'CLANG CLANG CLANG' went the tin, and it all went quiet as Gerry Hawtin stood up to announce the verdict.

"Right. An excellent contest. Bout even. Another one minutes boxing to decide the winnah!".

There was such a cheer. This was always done if a bout was very close. 'CLANG'. Well, wouldn't it be nice to tell you that I won, but I didn't. We were both exhausted, but me more than him, and my arms felt like lead. He won the last minute easily, although I did my best, and I knew I'd lost, but I didn't give a sod. "BUTCHAH IS THE WINNAH!" and he crossed the ring, grinned and shook hands. Although I'd lost, and felt like I'd been through a mincer, that was one of the happiest moments in my life.

Perhaps here I should explain myself - why I'm sure that the afore mentioned events changed the course of my life. After the bouts were all finished, Gerry Hawtin took me to one side and said -

"Well done Brimson. Nah then, why don't you come to the boxing classes and learn to fight properly, instead of like a big tart?. You are allowed to duck now and again you know".

So I did. I never missed a class, and learned to punch properly with both hands, hooking and jabbing, how to bob and weave and block, proper footwork and balance. He was a great teacher, and made us really work hard. I suppose I was stronger than most kids in my arms and chest from all the swimming I'd been doing, which was probably why I was able to blow Langridge and Green away so easily, but that's no good to you if you're in the ring with someone who knows what they're doing, as I had found out with

Butcher. I was very keen, and soaked it all up. Remember, we were only little kids, but you're never too young to learn the basics, and it's like riding a bike - you never forget, and as I got older and stronger, the moves old Gerry Hawtin drummed into us became natural and automatic.

Now I wouldn't like you to think that I became a great fighter or anything - far from it, but I like to think that I did become a useful amateur, no more than that. I only lost once more at the school, in my second year to a boy called Luff, and in my third year, I became champion of my weight, none of the bouts going the distance. I joined a boxing club in Tottenham, and had a number of schoolboy and junior bouts, and I only lost one of those, in the Army Cadet Championships, when I got beaten by a certain L/Cpl White, who bloody near murdered me, the only time in my life I was ever stopped. I was about fifteen then, and had started to get fed up with boxing, and the grind of training, and had started to get interested in other things like girls and youth clubs and smoking, and having a good time with my mates. I had a couple more bouts, which I won, and then packed it in. I didn't fight again till I was in the army.

To get to the point, I honestly think that if I'd been beaten really easily by Butcher, I'd have never wanted to box again. But I'd given him a really hard time, and had actually enjoyed fighting in a temper, with all the fear gone, and dishing some out for a change, instead of just taking it. So I'm as sure as I can be that my life took a different turn that day, because I immediately became a different person, far more confidant and sure of myself. But the trouble was that I became a bit too sure of myself. What with the swimming and the rugby, and being suddenly one of the boys, I think that I let it go to my head. I suppose I had what was later to be called a 'personality change'. Up till then, I had been a swot, very interested and keen in the classroom, far happier in there than in the playground, but that was all to change I'm afraid. Not straight away - I didn't become a playground hard case or anything of that sort, but it was the start on a downward slope as far as the academic side of things was concerned.

But suppose I had got done by Butcher? Or equally, suppose I'd got beaten in the first fight? I'd have just carried on as usual, I'm sure. Alec and I used to do our homework together, working really hard to get it right, and I was actually much brighter than him. He didn't make it into 3R, yet he went on to get a degree in Modern Languages. In fact, more than half the boys in 3R went on to university. Just maybe, I'd have been one of them. Who knows?. But brains are no good without the application, and my new found cockiness was to have a very adverse effect in that department.

. . . .

They say that like seeks like, and that was certainly true of my circle of friends, in that we all had a good sense of humour and would do anything for a laugh. One of these, and I remember him with great affection, was Kenny Goldstein.

I would say that about a third of the boys at Tottenham Grammar were Jewish. and there was a curious sort of segregation in the playground. It wasn't of our making, but theirs. There was not the slightest animosity, in fact we got on quite well together, but they simply did not mix with us. They had their part of the playground, and we had ours. There was one exception, and that was Kenny. He sort of had his feet in both camps, but he and I hit it off from the start. He had this marvellous dry sense of humour, and knew all these great rude jokes, and used to have us in hysterics, and I don't think I ever saw him in a bad mood. Everything was funny to him, and he was a master at getting a rise out of the teachers, but he was so good natured, and also very clever in class, that he used to get away with it. He was a really good-looking kid, and very vain - always combing his hair and preening himself in a mirror, or whatever shop window we'd happen to be passing. We used to take the mickey out of him and ruffle his hair up, but he'd just smile - out would come the comb, and he'd say - "It's not my fault I'm lovely". I think he was the youngest sexual maniac I ever knew, always on about girls, even when we were only twelve years old!.

Kenny was an excellent swimmer and diver, in the school team with me. When we were about thirteen, and both competing in the annual school gala, he was representing his house in the diving, and he said to me, quite seriously -

"I'm going to beat you this year Brimo". There was a good chance that he would too, but I replied,

"My arse you will".

His very first dive - just an ordinary pike from the one metre springboard started out perfectly. The run up I mean. It was beautiful. He was so determined to do the whole thing in as perfect a style as was possible, and he walked along the board, leapt up as good as an international, down onto the board and up a good six feet into a perfect pike position. The trouble was, that he was so concerned with making a perfect dive, in front of the whole school, that he stayed in it too long, and dropped into the water in a ghastly bellyflop. It was so funny, we were all just helpless, but when he pulled himself out of the water he lay on the side of the pool sort of quivering, and it looked like he had hurt himself, and a couple of the teachers ran to him, but he wasn't hurt at all. He was laughing!, and the whole school, seeing that he was OK laughed with him and gave him a huge cheer as he favoured us all with a cavalier bow. He wasn't the slightest bit embarrassed. That was typical of Kenny.

Class, that was.

As I said, Goldstein used to get away with murder - had it down to a fine art, but there was one occasion when he came unstuck.

There was a part of one of the upstairs corridors that was directly above an opening onto the stairway. For some reason or other, we decided to bomb this kid called Crockford with a satchel. I borrowed Ken's satchel, because it was the heaviest, and always full of books, and a big ink bottle, and laid it on top of the wall, looking over down onto the opening. Alby Dines was in the corridor below, and it was his job to tell me when Crockford was coming, and Ken positioned himself half way up the stairs, to get a good view of the proceedings. Suddenly, here's Alby coming through the opening yelling up - "'E's coming!".

Now Crockford had blond curly hair. I look down and had a quick glimpse of white curls, and pushed the satchel off the wall. 'WALLOP'. Direct hit. I hear this shriek of mirth from Kenny and looked down to see Mr Bacchus, a young science teacher, who also had blond curly hair, down on his knees holding his nut in both hands, surrounded by a few startled passers by, (one of whom was Crockford). Oh my God. The other two took off like rabbits, but Mr Bacchus roared -

"DINES - GOLDSTEIN - GET BACK HERE IMMEDIATELY. BRIMSON - GET DOWN HERE!".

There was no way out of this one. He was in an mad fury, rubbing his head, and it did me no good telling him that I had accidentally knocked the satchel off with my elbow, as at the time I had my arm in plaster, with a sling, and couldn't catch it in time. Nor was Alby very convincing when being asked why he shouted out "'E's coming" said "I was trying to warn you sir". It was no good either of them saying they'd scarpered because they had gone to get help. Bang to rights, all three of us. So there we were, up before the headmaster the next morning. Alby and Kenny got six of the best on the bum, but I got out of that because of my broken arm, I've never understood why to this day, but I remember that I got an awful lot of detentions. I recall Goldstein ruefully rubbing his rear on the way back to class.

"Nazi bastard" - he said.

The Headmaster by the way, was one H.A.T. Simmonds, who we used to call 'The Hat' - for obvious reasons. Christ, he used to lay it on with that cane, as I was to find out on many occasions. I can still remember the terror, standing outside that door, and hearing that deep sonorous voice, saying, "COME IN - ENTAH", knowing I was going to get a whacking, wondering whether I was going to get it on the arse or the hand.

. . . .

I can't remember the exact year, but I know that I was well into my forties, when I did a concert at a school in Tottenham - a parent/teachers association gig, which went really well, a two encore job. I was talking to a group of people afterwards, and there was this chap standing behind them, looking at me with a grin on his face. He was the headmaster. He came forward, shook hands, and said -

"It's been a long time Derek". I replied -

"Refresh my memory. We know each other do we?".

"I should hope so - I wouldn't be here if it wasn't for you. I'm Roy Sutton". I couldn't believe it. We both started laughing - him because of the incredulous look on my face, and me because he was one of our best mates in the old days, coupled with the fact that he was a headmaster. Him of all people, who had been even more idle and disruptive than me when we were at school.

I did save his life too.

It was as the Tottenham Municipal baths during a school swimming period, and I was skylarking about at the deep end, under the diving boards, with some mates. I was standing on the edge, when I noticed this mop of hair floating on top of the water, near the edge. It was just sort of gently bobbing up and down, and at first I thought it was one of the kids mucking about. The baths were very crowded and noisy, and no-one else had noticed it, and I suddenly realised that who-ever it was was in trouble, so I dived in and came up underneath him, lifted his head clear, and shouted to the others to help me get him out. He was unconscious - actually drowning. We pulled him out and laid him on the side, and Gerry Hawtin, who'd just rushed up to see what the trouble was, started to give him artificial respiration, and yelled to an attendant to call an ambulance. Luckily, everything was all right, and he came too after Gerry pumped him out, and he was back at school the next day. Thank God I had noticed him, or he would have been a goner. And that was Roy Sutton.

Roy had been at Risley Avenue school with us, in the same class, but I didn't really know him very well then, and I remember him as a quiet little kid, but like me, he had come out of himself a little by now. He became one of our clique, easily fitting in, as he had the same sense of fun and irreverence as the rest of us. He was always in trouble, the same as me, for playing up, and getting into mischief, which on reflection, was probably my fault. I remember that like Kenny Goldstein he had a very advanced libido, even at that tender age. To tell you the truth, we were all horny little sods, not to put too fine a point on it. Roy lived quite near me, just off the Roundway, and I remember that he had a stepmother who was much younger than his dad - I suppose she must have been in her early twenties, and she was absolutely gorgeous, and we all lusted after her, (including Roy), and I can tell you that she was the centre of many a pubescent erotic fantasy. It's a wonder we didn't all go blind.

There's just one more school mate I'd like to mention, and that was Billy Budd. Billy was a great pal of mine, all through my schooldays, and after, up till we went in the army. He was a square-jawed chunky sort of kid, and as tough as nails, and hated all authority just as much as I did. He will always have my undying gratitude, because when we were in the third year, on his way to winning his weight in the boxing, he hammered the snot out of my old enemy Ronny Haynes.

I'd like to tell you at this point how I came to have my arm in a sling, that time we bombed Mr Bacchus. We used to have mock fights, like all boys do, sparring about with open hands, and wrestling - the object of this being to get the other kid down. One Saturday afternoon, I was over the Big Rec with some pals, and Lenny Choules and I were having a friendly grapple, trying to get a good grip on each other, when he hooked his leg behind me and gave me a shove. I fell straight back and stuck out my left arm to break my fall, and there was this dreadful cracking sound. I stood up, and Lenny was looking at my arm in horror. I looked at it, and the back of my hand was touching the back of my shoulder!. It had snapped at the elbow, and bent completely back as far as it would go. Then the pain hit me, and I won't even begin to describe it. I was screaming in agony and fright, and as I stood there, the bottom part of my arm fell down so that it was at right-angles, but still backwards, and I started running round in circles, till it fell down straight, but completely dislocated. I don't know how long it took, but someone had run to my house, which was only a couple of hundred yards away, and came running back with my brother Arthur, who was home waiting to go in the army. He took me to the Prince of Wales hospital on a bus, with my arm dangling, the elbow out of it's socket, and everyone looking making comforting noises, but I was in terrible pain.

We waited in the out-patients for two solid hours believe it or not, with Arthur getting more and more angry, and having a go at anyone in a white coat who happened to be walking by, and eventually collared a doctor, and said something like - "You f....ing well see to him, or I'm going to see to you". Eventually, I was taken into a room by two very young student doctors, and given some gas, and woke up with my arm in a sling. They told Arthur that I'd be OK in a couple of days - it was only a simple dislocation, and gave him some pain killers for me, and we rode home on the bus. But it wouldn't stop hurting, and I couldn't eat anything without bringing it straight up. That night, despite the painkillers, it got worse, and in the morning I was delirious, and bathed in sweat, so it was back to the hospital, again on a bloody bus with my father, and my elbow was X-rayed, which of course, it should have been the day before, before they put it back in it's socket. The ball joint was broken clean in half, and the whole thing had to be done again, under a general anaesthetic, and re-set properly, and immobilised in splints. They couldn't use plaster at first of course, because it was swollen like a football. I remember the old man went potty, and wanted the two young doctors reported for negligence, but I don't think anything ever came of it. It was no wonder I went through what I did that night. To this day, I still can't straighten my left arm properly, although I didn't lose any of the strength in it.

All through my time in Tottenham, as a boy, and as a youth, I spent as little time as possible indoors. My mother always seemed to have the permanent hump, and treated me as a nuisance most of the time, so as soon as I had finished a meal, I'd be out like a shot. If it was raining, I spent most of the time in Alec's flat, as his folks were really nice. We were never bored, and used to play chess and draughts for hours, or do experiments with our chemistry sets. We had this book called something like 'Chemistry for Boys', and worked our way right through it. If we didn't have the required chemicals, we used to go to this chemists in Stamford Hill that sold everything, all in little glass jars, as well as apparatus, and either buy them or nick them, which was great fun, if a bit naughty. The only time I saw his mum get angry, was when we manufactured sulphuretted hydrogen, and the whole flat was full of this sort of giant fart, and the old man was due home for his tea at any moment. Blimey, it did pen and ink! He came in and went straight out again.

We never spent much time round Alby's, as his mum was nearly as fierce as mine, as well as it being a bit crowded with six kids. Mrs Dines had black hair and brown eyes - very Latin looking, whereas Mr Dines had ginger hair and a very pale skin. It was really curious because the oldest, Billy, looked like a wop, whilst Alby, as I've already stated was red haired and pale, the image of his old man. There was only a year between them, but you would have sworn that they weren't even distantly related. The whole family was split, some dark, some copper-nobbed. Really strange.

We were all great readers, and started to graduate from the comics to books. The comics in those days were terrific, with great serials. There was the Rover, the Wizard the Hotspur and the Adventure, and we'd devour each issue as soon as it came out, to catch up with the doings of 'Wilson', this mysterious little bloke of indeterminate age, who would appear as if from nowhere, dressed in old fashioned Victorian togs, and smash every athletics world record, in both track and field, and all the swimming records too come to that, and then disappear back to where ever he came from. I remember once that he did an eighteen foot pole vault, which was absolutely ridiculous at the time, and we never imagined that this, together with his three minute fifty second mile, and many more improbable feats, would nearly all be actually surpassed in our lifetimes. This was in the days when it was said that a four minute mile wouldn't be run in this century. Good old Wilson. He was our hero, even above the 'Wolf of Kabul, and 'Rockfist Rogan'. The 'Wolf' would take on hoards of turbaned ruffians on the Northwest Frontier with nothing more than a cricket bat, which was called 'Clickyba', and lay all the buggers out. Brilliant stuff.

The school had a very good library, and in that first year, we all turned on to more substantial reading - Treasure Island, Rob Roy, Coral Island - and from then on I have never stopped reading. One of my great joys was reading in bed, especially in the summer when it didn't get dark till about ten o'clock, because during the war we had double summertime, and it became a habit which has stayed with me to this day. I always read for at least half an hour before I nod off.

We had some great times. There was always plenty to do, and plenty of places to go, and the bomb sites were all like adventure playgrounds to us. Every Saturday we'd be in the children's corner at White Hart Lane - there was always a top game, because during the war, Arsenal's ground was bombed, so they played their home games at Spurs, and we all supported both teams with the same amount of enthusiasm. Matthews, Finney, Raich Carter - we saw all of those, as even though all of the top footballers were all in the Services, they were still let out to play league football.

Also, at that time, people were in a far happier frame of mind because the war was going well, and everybody knew that it was only a matter of time before we'd win. All the news was good, after the awful early years, and the D Day landings, followed by the daily advances just about put the cap on it. We all, even at that tender age, got into the habit of devouring the newspapers, and it was like reading a daily exciting serial, except that it was actually happening. The friendly old barrage balloons still hung up in the sky, but the sirens had stopped wailing, and the unconscious nervousness which we all used to feel had all but disappeared.

But in June, 1944, the war returned to London.

. . . .

'Doodlebug'
1944

Chapter 5

THE 'V' WEAPONS

It was very early in the morning, and I was up and about for a change and out in the back garden, when I heard a siren wail in the distance, something we hadn't heard for some time. We did occasionally hear them, but nobody took much notice, as the all clear always sounded very soon after, and I expect that they were just exercises to keep the ARP on their toes. Then I heard a sort of motor bike noise in the distance, but getting closer and louder till it was a rattling roar. Then it stopped abruptly. A few seconds later there was a sort of flash, like someone taking a photograph, even though it was broad daylight, followed by an enormous deafening crack, then I felt a tremor through my feet. I ran outside into the street, and there was Tony Seely sitting on his bike, just on his way to knock for me.

"Quick, let's go and have a look" he shouted, and I ran back and grabbed my bike, and we shot up towards Lordship Lane to see what we could see. Sure enough, there was a big pall of black smoke rising over the roof tops in the general direction of the Lido. We started to hear fire engine bells as we sped towards Bruce Grove, past the Lido and then turning right up Mount Pleasant road in the direction of the smoke, then one of the engines went clanging past, making us jump our bikes up onto the pavement. Then we turned a corner.

I won't forget that sight. There was a sort of wall of thick red dust in front of us. The fire engine disappeared into it, and then this old lady staggered out of it, her face covered in blood, crying in pain. Then another lady, also dazed and bleeding, and then more of them in twos and threes, some staggering, some crawling. The old lady collapsed in the gutter and lay still, and a few people ran over to her. All the while there was this dust, like a giant curtain hanging, as high as the rooftops. Then it was suddenly very crowded, and an air raid warden yelled at us to get out of it and eff off home. "Git aht of it - gorn - fuck off 'ome!" he shouted and kicked my bike as he ran past. More of them were roping off the streets, and the air was ringing with ambulance and fire engine bells, and we could hear lots of shouting and screaming coming from the fog of red dust. That red dust was atomised brick, caused by high explosive.

That was the first doodlebug to fall on north London. We were to see many more.

I expect that you've all seen the newsreels of those flying bombs, and know how they rained down on London for the next few months. We saw many of them scudding across the sky, very low and fast, and watched a couple of them go down. You may have even seen films of them, and heard the recordings of that rattling roar suddenly cutting out, but it is very difficult to explain what it was like to be there.

The night was the worst time. As you know, most of them were shot down before they reached us, and there were guns all over southern England having a go at them, as well as our fighters shooting them down. But there were plenty left over, and some nights, we'd hear that distinctive drone every half hour or so, getting louder and nearer, gritting our teeth waiting for it to cut out. Sometimes, we'd hear it cut out while it was still a faint drone, and that was just as bad, because we soon learnt that there was no way of knowing what they'd do when the engine stopped. Sometimes they would plummet straight down. But they could just as easily glide on for three of four miles, and were even known to turn round and glide back the way they had come. They were hellish things, very hard on the nerves. It was that jet engine stopping so abruptly, Brrrrrup - and then that eerie silence which followed, everybody holding there breath, wondering if it was silently gliding towards you. Then there would either be a distant crump or a loud boom and then the rattling windows and clinking crockery.

The worst experience that I can recall was when one of them came right over, very low, with a shattering sound that made the windows rattle. One evening it was. It cut out very close indeed, but it must have gone on a lot further because we didn't even hear the explosion. Those thirty seconds or so until we knew we were safe were definitely the most terrifying in my life.

Lots of extra laundry in the neighbourhood next day.

Just the same as in the blitz, everybody went about their business as usual. I can't remember how we carried on at school, but we were on our summer holidays for most of the buzz-bomb campaign anyway, although they continued coming over well into 1945. It wasn't nearly so bad in the daytimes, but the nights, when my dad was firewatching, and there was just me and my mother laying in the Morrison shelter, were awful. They were far worse than the bombing psychologically, because they were just mindless machines aimed at random, just to kill people, like something out of a science fiction book. Also, there was the fact that they were the first jet engines we'd ever heard, or heard of for that matter. I think it was the Americans who gave them the name - 'doodlebug', but their other name was 'buzzbombs', and later, V1's.

I read some time after the war, that the first of these to cause any casualties landed in Bethnal Green on the 13th of June, and in the next 24 hours, 73 of them landed in London. By the end of the month they had killed 1600 people, and badly injured three times as many as that. Luckily for us, the Army had over-run all their launching sites by the beginning of September, but they still used to come over, although not nearly so frequently, and those were piggy-backed across the North Sea at night, by Heinkel bombers and launched near the coast. All that trouble and ingenuity just to kill innocent civilians. Mind you, our bombers were killing and awful lot of innocents as well, but that's war for you. Here, let me say that flying bombs and rockets killed people all over the Eastern Counties and Midlands, as well as Yorkshire and Lancashire. They got about half of them. We got the other half.

Actually, they were revenge weapons. Just that. The 'V' stood for 'Vergeltungswaffe', which means 'Revenge Weapon'. They ended up killing close to five thousand people in the London area.

I developed a habit many years ago, probably in the course of conversation to illustrate a point, of visualising figures. Just bare numbers often have little impact - in one ear and out the other, and 5000 doesn't sound much to some people, compared to 6000,000 Jews dying in the holocaust, and the 20,000,000 Russians who died in the war. Just numbers. They belittle the circumstances. Better to imagine a queue of people, little old ladies, house-wives, little children, teenagers and men, all standing patiently in a line. Imagine it starts at your house, and you go for a walk, and you say hello to every one of them. You'll still be saying 'hello' when you are three miles away. That's five thousand people.

I'll give you one more example before I continue, one that came to me when I was watching the Cup Final on the television. 90,000 people there, at least, and the TV cameras panned round Wembley as they were singing 'Abide with Me'. That vast great crowd...... . I suddenly found myself seeing them as all young men, all dressed in flying jackets and leather helmets and fur-lined boots, standing there in complete silence. All of them, and more than half as many again - British and American air crews, were killed in the war.

. . . .

Just as the main V1 campaign finished, at the beginning of September, the V2s started. No need to go into detail, you all know about them. A ton of high explosive hurtling straight down from the stratosphere. Over five hundred of them were to fall on the London area, the last in March of '45.

To tell you the truth, I can't remember my feelings about them at that time, or shall we say, not nearly as vividly as I remember the doodle-bugs. There was no warning with those bloody things - the sound of their approach came after they landed, as they were supersonic. There would be an intense blue flash of light, followed by a colossal explosion, and then two big booms. They were not nearly as scary as the V1s, and not nearly so frequent, and I suppose that everyone had become mentally hardened by then. As the old army saying goes - 'If your names on it, then it'll get you - if it ain't it won't'. It was the one with 'To whom it may concern' on it that bothered us. We'd hear them of course, mostly in the distance, most of them dropping on south London, and think - 'Poor sods. Glad it's not us', and carry on as usual, as there was nothing you could do about it.

I do recall going to school once, with Alec and Alby - our route taking us through the long path which cuts through the huge Tottenham cemetery, looking at the rows of tombstones and saying - "Just think - we could be digging up the daisies with them any day now", and we all laughed, and Alec said something to the effect that I was a cheerful sod and no mistake.

There were three that I remember very well. The first was a bit like that doodle-bug, as at the time we were again sitting on our bikes, just inside the Big Rec. There was this flash, even though it was daylight, as though someone had just taken a picture, then a terrific crack, just like the first doodle-bug, only louder, then a whoosh and two low booms. Something to do with them being supersonic I suppose. It was in the direction of Wood Green, so we took off, as fast as we could pedal, up Lordship Lane. I was really panicking as we got near, because my aunty Ginny, dad's eldest sister lived in that area, and I was very fond of her. But fortunately she was safe, her house being a couple of hundred yards away from the site. As before, we got there about the same time as the fire engines, but saw a huge area of devastation before we were shooed away by the coppers. Both sides of street were flattened, and again, the red dust. I have a very clear recollection of these events, but strangely enough, I can't recall seeing any injured people, as we had in Broadwater Road, although we heard later that there were a large number of casualties

There was something else that I'd forgotten to mention. Actually, it's only just come back to me. It was a sort of acrid smell, mixed with the smell of coal gas. I expect the former was high explosive, and the latter due to the fact that the gas mains had been fractured. It was a peculiar smell, and one which hung about on all bomb sites for weeks.
Funny I've only just remembered it.

The second V2 incident I can tell you about happened on 8th of March,'44. I wasn't there, but my father was. A rocket hit Smithfield market at the worst possible time, at midday, when the place was at it's busiest and most crowded. It went straight down a ventilation shaft of Farringdon Road tube station, and exploded upwards, with dreadful effect, and it was one of the worst home incidents of the whole war. Really dreadful.
My Dad didn't come home till the next day, staying to help in the rescue work and clearing up, without any sleep, right round the clock. He'd had a terrible time, and seen some terrible sights, and had lost many friends that he had known since he was a boy. He was completely exhausted, and looked a hundred years old, grey faced and sunken eyed. It took him weeks to get back to his old self. He'd been sitting on the toilet when it happened, believe it or not. We used to joke about that, much later of course, as to how it was about the best place to be in the circumstances, although I don't suppose that it was very funny at the time. He had to make his way out through a load of debris, and when he got into the street, he saw this lady sitting in the road, badly shocked. She had called him over, and said - "Please can you pull my skirt down mister". He'd said - "Of course love, I'll help you", but when he'd looked down, he saw that one of her legs was missing. She seemed quite calm, and didn't appear to be in any pain, so he put his arm round her shoulders and yelled for help, but she died while he was holding her.

It all came out over the next few weeks. How he saw a chap sitting quite calmly waiting to be seen to, who had a long piece of wood going through one cheek and out through the other. So many dead laying about, as a whole queue of housewives, waiting to buy sausages at Harris's had caught the full blast. Hour after hour, tearing at the rubble, with people saying that this bloke was gone, and that bloke was gone. Poor old dad. But the one incident of that day that affected him most, and did for many years to come was as follows:

There was an office block in Smithfield that employed a large number of pretty young office girls - clerks and typists and such. The porters knew most of them, and daily subjected them to a stream of good humoured cockney banter and flirting as they wended their way to work, and shared many cups of tea with them during their lunch breaks. All taken in good part, and anyway, they could give as good as they got, and nobody ever overstepped the mark. They knew most of them by their first names, and were very fond of them.

The explosion had destroyed the side of their building, which was about six floors high, and unfortunately, that was the side with the staircases. The rest of the building was intact, so there were all these girls on the top three floors with no way of getting down, the side of the building completely open to the elements, like a dolls house with the side taken off. They couldn't get any of the big fire engine ladders near enough to get them down because of all the rubble and debris, but there didn't seem to be too much danger, and the girls, who were all unhurt, were quite cheerful, and actually had a singsong as they enjoyed the sandwiches and flasks of tea that were passed up to them. By the middle of the night, the last of the debris was cleared, and a ladder started to crank up towards them, to cheers from the girls and the onlookers, and just then, the whole building collapsed. None of the girls survived.

That was the only time I ever saw my dad cry, when he told us about it. Heartbreaking. Even more so when you consider that everyone knew that the war was nearly over, at least in Europe. The Allies were smashing the enemy back, and were fighting in Germany itself. The Third Reich was in it's death throes, and we all knew it, and it was indeed all over just a couple of months later.

So now the third, and happily the final occurrence. It happened exactly one week after the Smithfield market tragedy, on the 15th of March, seven weeks before the end of the war with Germany.

A lady being rescued from the Smithfield Market V2.
March 8th 1945.
(My Dad was helping in the rescue work till well into the next day).

During the war, the great majority of the boys at Tottenham Grammar stayed to dinner. We didn't call it lunch in those days. Very good, wholesome dinners they were too I remember, despite the jokes we used to make about them. Those that couldn't be accommodated in the first sitting went into the hall when the first lot had finished. This was known as 'second dinners', and was much sought after, as there was always a bit extra of everything, and like all young kids, we were always hungry. I was one of the lucky ones this particular day, and I suppose that about a third of the tables were occupied. The rest of the boys were in the playgrounds, first and second formers in the east playground, and on the adjoining cricket pitch, the senior boys in the west playground. Luckily, very luckily, the adjoining west field, which was a rugby pitch, had been put out of bounds the previous week, exactly why, I can't remember. In all, there were about 450 boys on the premises. Here, let me quote from the official report, published a few days later, written by the headmaster. -

'I have to report that on Thursday March 15th, 1945 at 1.27 p.m. an enemy rocket bomb exploded on the waste ground about 20 yards north of the biology wing of the building. At the time the first sitting of lunch had just been completed and the boys were dispersing to their playgrounds while the second small sitting had just sat down. The staff were just concluding their lunch.'

I don't remember hearing the explosion. One moment we were all sitting down at the table, chattering away quite happily. The next thing I remember was hitting the floor, and laying there with this shrieking whistling and a sharp pain in my ears. I got to my knees and felt another sharp pain, as I was kneeling on broken glass, and it was as though I was looking at everything through a pair of dark green spectacles.

Those are my first clear recollections, and it all got a bit jumbled after that. I couldn't hear anything at all for the first few minutes, nothing except that whistling, and then my face started to hurt, and when I touched it, my hands were covered in blood. I had been among those that were facing the north side of the hall, and the upper half of it was all windows, and they had all blown down upon us. I remember that there was no panic and everybody was quite calm, and the masters were really terrific, moving around comforting everyone, making sure that we were all OK and then quickly shepherding us out, as the huge beams overhead were hanging down and looked as though the whole roof could come down at any moment. As my vision cleared, I looked up and noticed that the big church organ, which had it's own little balcony, was leaning over us at quite an angle - blown off of it's base. A lot of the boys, as well as myself, had cut faces, and there was a lot of blood about. Actually, to tell you the truth, we all felt marvellous, standing in the playground after the initial shock had worn off, and we realised that we were safe. I remember one of the masters examining my face and saying, "My, you are in a mess aren't you Brimson", then cleaning me up and applying iodine and sticking plaster, then smiling and saying - "You're all right boy, you'll live - off you go", then turning away to clean up the next one. None of the cuts needed stitches, and a couple of weeks later they'd all healed, although I still have a couple of very small scars. No-one who was in the hall was seriously injured. We all stood around on the east field, us walking wounded from the hall feeling very much one up on the others, with all our bits of sticking plaster and the odd bandage, exchanging experiences, although I remember that for some reason or other, I found it a bit difficult to talk.

You recall that I went into some detail in describing the layout of the school, and that at the front there was a steep little rise to the lane, which was level with the top half of the school. That was where the rocket exploded, just the other side of the lane, level with the west wing. It destroyed much of the top half of that wing, which included the biology lab, and the tremor broke lintels and doors even over the other side of the school, near the gymnasium, but the building was very solidly constructed, and stood up to it all very well. But the reason that I have told you that it was one of the luckiest escapes of the war, was that all the boys were well protected from the blast, the whole building being between the explosion and the playgrounds .

Sadly though, very sadly, there were two exceptions.

A small brick building in front of the school had recently been demolished, and some of the masonry was piled up beside the lane, and was in a direct line between the explosion and the west field. It blasted it like grapeshot across the rugby pitch, and even did a lot of damage to houses that were two or three hundred yards away. There wasn't a square yard of that field that didn't have chunks of brick and masonry on it. Normally, there would have been a couple of hundred boys playing there. Can you imagine the consequences?. Tragically, two boys, both fourteen years old, had for some reason or other, just climbed the little rise, and were standing by an air raid shelter on the corner of he field, just twenty-five yards or so from the explosion. They were both killed.

Their names were Peter Goodman and Harold Poulton.

There was only one other serious casualty. His name was Norman Burn, 13 years old. He had been standing very near the wall, with the whole west wing between him and the rocket, and should have been perfectly safe, except that, so we were told later, a piece of metal, part of the V2 apparently, came down, quite a few seconds after the explosion, when all the boys were picking themselves up, and hit his right arm, severing it above the elbow. He ran, screaming, the length of the playground, and Mr Mitchell, our form master, knocked him cold, and applied a tourniquet. He saved his life. He recovered quite well, and the next year, he was our monitor at the dinner table, and used to clump us with his artificial arm. When we were teenagers, I remember seeing him in Tottenham Royal dance hall, a tall good-looking bloke standing there eyeing up the girls, with his left handing holding his right, which always had a black glove on.

That is how I remember it, but memory plays tricks, and I did hear recently, that somebody says that he was on the field when he was hit, but I can't see how he would have survived the blast. We didn't know about Goodman and Poulton and Burnsy until the next day, when we all had to go to the school for a service. One of the masters was in hospital, as a roof had come down on him, but he made a good recovery. Another boy had lost an eye I believe. I remember that day, looking at the bricks on the rugger field, and the long trail of blood covered in sawdust where Norman Burn had run, and examining the vast crater, but we were kept away from the spot where Goodman and Poulton were killed.

It could have been so much worse. If the school had been built the other way round for instance, as it would have been but for the whim of some councillor, both playgrounds would have been exposed. If the rocket had been just a fraction of a degree off and landed on the school. If the west field hadn't been put out of bounds.

If, if ,if.   We were very lucky.

One curious little postscript: There was a big white billy-goat tethered to a stake, just the other side of the road from the school. We used to feed him sometimes - bits of fruit and bread, and on a few occasions, blotting paper.

He'd eat anything. The rocket must have landed right on him, as the crater was almost exactly the area that his tether allowed. I don't know whether there's any truth in it, but we heard that one of his horns was found a quarter of a mile away, in someone's back garden.

So that completes my memories of the Second World War. I can't say that I recall anything of VE day, or VJ day, although I'm sure I must have enjoyed them, and England was a very happy place at the time. I was left with a stammer, along with quite a few other boys, but that cleared up in about six months. I felt fine, not nervous or anything, I just had difficulty in starting sentences, but that was very common, due to delayed shock so we were told, and I ended up none the worse for it.

There were sixty thousand civilians killed in Britain, all of them appearing on the Commission's Roll of Honour. I'd like to quote two of the entries. Peter Goodman's is not quite accurate, as he died where it happened, but no matter.

GOODMAN Peter Gerald age 14 of 98 Sylvan Avenue, Wood Green. Son of Edward and Winifred Goodman. Injured 15 Mar 1945, at Grammar School grounds; died same day at Prince of Wales General Hospital.

POULTON Harold David age 14. Son of Thomas George and Lilian Beatrice Poulton, of 37 Buller Road. Injured 15 March 1945 at the Grammar School; died same day at Prince of Wales General Hospital.

Thank you very much, Werner von Braun.

. . . .

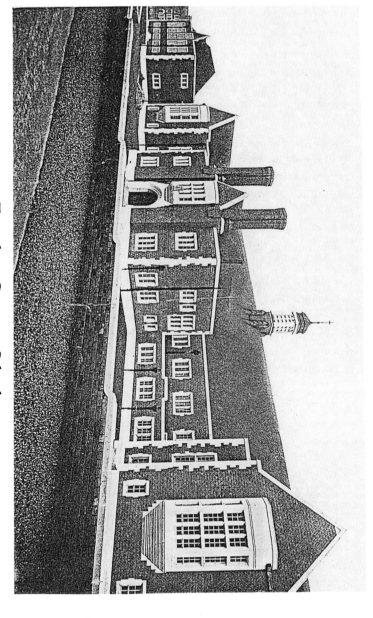

Tottenham Grammar School

The V2 landed almost exactly on the spot from where the photograph was taken. Much of the right wing was destroyed.

Chapter 6

AFTER THE WAR

So, the war was over at last. On came the lights and down came the barrage balloons. Actually, the blackout had finished quite some time before the end, but it was still just as though the country had emerged from a long black tunnel. One thing that I have omitted to mention was that all the windows in the shops and houses and office blocks had all been criss-crossed with sticky brown paper, to cut down the danger from flying glass, and it was good to see it all disappear overnight.

I remember very well the time after VE day, when, despite the euphoria, there was still a big question - 'What about them bloody Japs? Them crazy bastards are going to fight to the last man. Long way to go yet'. But then there were the photographs of the big mushroom clouds in all the papers. Hiroshima and Nagasaki. Suddenly, it really was all over.

Then the photographs of the prisoners of the Japanese. Those poor skeletons tottering along, and the news of those thousands beaten and starved to death. Any sympathy we had felt for the Land of the Rising Sun disappeared there and then.

Same with the Germans. All the pictures of the smashed and burnt cities were cancelled out in our minds with the gradual emergence of the dreadful scale of the Holocaust. Belsen had been big news just a few months before, because it was the first one to be found, like a nest of spiders when you move a stone. But then came Buchenwald, with it's gas chambers and ovens, then Treblinka, Ravensbruck, more and more of them, until finally, Auschwitz. God Almighty - how could a nation be capable of that.

The right side had won all right.

So, back to my memoirs, trivial as they may seem after all those big doings.

As mentioned earlier, I had enjoyed my first year at the Grammar. I suppose it was about half way through my second year that it started to go wrong, round about the time of he V2 incident, but I don't really think that that had anything to do with it. Up to that time I had always been very attentive and hard working because I enjoyed it, but my new found confidence seemed to shorten my attention span. I had started to become a bit more exuberant and cocky, naturally I suppose, and a little lazy, which in my particular class was fatal, as we were supposed to get through two years work in one. You could fall behind very quickly. I just wanted to have fun, and be with my mates, as Lord knows, I never had much fun at home. The only time I was ever happy there was when my sister Ivy came home on leave from the Land Army, and later when she became a nurse. She was still the same lovely big sister, and was the only one who ever showed me any affection when I was a boy. Some weekends, during the war, the house would be full of her land army mates and Americans from a USAAF base near to their farm. Ivy was engaged to one of them, S\Sgt Paul Kinney, and he and some of his B17 crew would be invited over. Marvellous blokes they were, and very fun loving. One of them, a chunky little bloke called Pete Camaniti, had been a circus acrobat, and used to walk up and down the stairs on his hands. Ivy tells me that Pete wasn't aircrew but worked as a ground technician. We used to crack up at his Bronx accent and Kinney's North Carolina drawl as we'd only ever heard Yank accents at the cinema. Those were some of the few times that I tasted sweets during the war, so I looked forward to their visits.

Frank occasionally came home on leave from the RAF, all smart in his uniform, and it was always good to see him, but for the rest of the time, it was not very nice at all, getting yelled at and clouted for the least little thing. Round about that time poor old Sammy caught distemper and died, so, as you can imagine, it was not a very happy home. I didn't get on too badly with the old man, but it was my mother who ruled the roost, and she just got worse. I remember I used to hear something about 'The Change' - whatever that was. She was always on about it to dad and Mrs Toohig, who lived next door. I know what it means now of course, but I didn't have a clue when I was twelve. We all know how that affects some women, making them bad-tempered and touchy, but she already had been. Now she was even worse.

So, resentment started to turn into rebellion, at school as well as at home. It gradually hardened into a hatred of authority, or to be more exact, unjust authority, that I retain to this day.

It wasn't all bad though - far from it. I had a great set of mates, which at that age, is very important indeed, all with the same sense humour - always out for a laugh. We had some great times.

The school had it's own Army Cadet Corps, which you could join when you were 13. Alec didn't fancy it, but the rest of us joined, because we were told by the elder boys that you got free cakes and tea at the twice weekly drills, and went away to weekend camps, and did all sorts of interesting things like manoeuvres, learning to take Bren guns to pieces, and charging round assault courses. And you got a uniform. In those days, a large percentage of the youth of the country joined the Army, Navy or Air Force cadets, and we didn't feel in the least out of place walking around in uniform. We loved it, right from the start, and were very enthusiastic recruits. Our officers were three of the masters, and luckily they were all popular ones. One of these was Mr Cooper, a maths teacher, and the most popular master in the school, another was a Mr Diaz, but the name of the other one escapes me. What really put the icing on the cake was the fact that very soon after we joined, our battalion formed a drum and bugle band, and employed an ex-army bandmaster. Myself, Alby and Billy Budd became drummers, and Kenny Goldstein, (incidentally, the only Jewish kid in the cadets), Roy and Hughy Geddes, another of our mates, took up the bugle. I expect that we made an awful row at first - just imagine - six side drums, two tenors and a base drum, and about fourteen bugles, all learning at the same time. But learn we did. It became our main interest.

We were fanatical, us drummers practising the taps every spare moment we had, on any surface that came to hand when we didn't have our drums, and the buglers blowing the tunes on their mouth pieces, which they carried everywhere. Every Sunday morning, you'd hear bugle bands all over London, marching through the streets, and we couldn't wait for the day when we'd be ready to join them, which we eventually did, but only when we were really ready, months later, after many hours practise, two nights a week, and every Sunday morning in the school playgrounds.

We were as smart as paint too, and took and enormous pride in our dress. Bandsmen had white belts and gaiters and a special coloured lanyard, and we'd polish our brasses and boots till they shone like glass, and iron our uniforms till you could cut yourself on the creases - webbing, drum slings and leg shields were blancoed as white as snow, and the instruments were given particular attention. We also took a great pride in the drill, which is very important in a band, as it means extra marks in competition, and we enjoyed every bit of it. All this is known in the army, collectively, as 'bull', and was to stand us all in very good stead when we all eventually joined up for real.

The most marvellous times of all were the weekend and annual camps. The weekends were spent at Cuffley, in Hertfordshire, and it was just the band that went. We'd pile into two army lorries, after school on the Friday and come home on Sunday evenings. There were always other bands there, with us all often practising together for a massed cadet band which was to play at the Royal Tournament at Olympia.

It's a great feeling being in the front rank of drummers, especially in a massed band, and I still remember those marches - Georgia, Burma rifles and the rest.

We went to Cuffley many times and for all of us it was heaven. All of it, the army food, drill, band practise, football and cricket, and all kipping together in the same barrack room, and telling jokes when the lights were out, and seeing who could blow off the loudest. All best mates, all together, not a care in the world, removed from the strictures of home and school.

I think that the highlight of my time in the cadets was when we went to Mytchett, in Aldershot, for a ceremonial do, part of which was a full guard mounting. I was the drummer for the old guard, and we were inspected by Lord Montgomery himself. He was second only to Churchill in the eyes of the British populace, so you can imagine how nervous we all were. I'd practised the drill for weeks and at last, there we were, all lined up, with Monty and his entourage slowly walking along the ranks, looking us all up and down. When he got to me, he really seemed to take his time, then looked me straight in the eye, frowned and barked - "Splendid" - and then moved on to the next cadet. Mind you, he said that to nearly all of us, but it was a great moment. We all gathered round him after we were dismissed, a couple of hundred of us, and he gave us a talk, to the effect that although we were only cadets, we were part of the finest army in the world, and all the rest of it.

Whenever I saw him after that, on a newsreel, or his picture in the paper, I used to say to the others -

"Oh look, there's my mate Monty. He reckons I'm splendid!".

There was only ever one unhappy occasion, all the time I was in the cadets. Not just unhappy; it was tragic.

For our first annual two week camp we went to Sudbrook, not far from Lincoln. We'd been looking forward to it for months, and at last there we all were, on the train, with two whole weeks stretching in front of us, happy as sandboys. It was a very hot day, and we had to march from the station to the

camp, so were really melting when we finally arrived. It was an ex POW camp, and there were a few Germans still there, who'd stayed on to act as permanent staff. We were naturally very curious about them and talked to them at every opportunity, asking them how they had been captured, and what was it like in the German army and so forth. They were really nice blokes, and were in no hurry to be repatriated, which wasn't surprising, as they all came from the Russian occupied east of Germany. One of the boys asked them if they'd been in the German cadets, and they laughed and said,
"Oh yes, but we were called the Hitler Youth!".

The camp was in a sort of marshy bit of country, and during the war, the POWs had adapted one of these big ponds into a large swimming pool, with a sort of wooden walkway round three sides of it and a diving board. So, as soon as we'd sorted our beds out, and dumped our kit, one of the officers said - "Right lads' who's for a swim?". We didn't need asking twice, and there was a mad scramble to get into our cossies, and in no time at all, the pool was heaving like a trout farm. So we're swimming and splashing around, having a good time, when somebody blew a whistle, and yelled at us that someone had gone under and hadn't come up. We good swimmers immediately started going down to look for him, but the water was very silty, and you couldn't see a hand in front of your face, so we just stayed under as long as we could, searching blindly, but couldn't find anything. We gave up in the end, but weren't all that concerned, as it turned out that somebody had thought he'd seen a boy slide down the slippery clay side of the pool into the water and gone under. But as it was so crowded, he'd probably come up amongst all the others, and anyway, so many of us had been looking, that surely we'd have found him by now.

I was sitting on the wooden walkway with Kenny Goldstein about five minutes later, and the pool was nearly empty, having been cleared of all but those of us who had been searching, when we saw one of the elder boys, a chap called 'Tank' Harding because he was so big, come to the surface holding a still, white figure. We dived in and helped him to the side and one of the officers immediately began artificial respiration. But it was too late.
He had drowned.

His name was Sullivan. He was a quiet kid, 13 years old, and had only just joined the battalion. None of us knew him very well, as he hadn't been at the school very long. Apparently, he couldn't swim. It was a terrible, sickening thing to happen. We soon shut it out of our minds, as we were determined to have a good time, and we did have a good time too for all that. There was nothing that we could do about it, and anyway, as I've mentioned, none of us knew him - we didn't even know his first name. I think that perhaps even though we were just boys, we had become hardened mentally because of the war.

But there is a postscript.

A few days after we got home, there was a funeral parade. We had a service at the school, and then we slow marched to the cemetery, where he had already been buried while we were away. There was another short ceremony round the grave, and the bandmaster, whose name I forget, played the Last Post on the bugle. Strangely enough, we'd never heard him play the bugle before - the buglers had been taught by one of the senior boys, our solo bugler, who had been in the Boys Brigade. We soon realised why we'd never heard him. He was terrible, and made a dreadful, embarrassing job of it. Not only that, there was Sullivan's mother at the graveside, really grief stricken, and we found that she was a war widow, and that Sullivan was an only child. It was so sad, and we all felt so sorry for her. Sorry too that we had not known him better.

I suppose that the last few chapters have been quite a bit doomy, but I've written about Sullivan, because I feel I owe it to him in a strange sort of way. He probably joined us to make new friends, but the poor bugger never got the chance.

Many years later, when I was about fifty, I had spent a day walking round my old haunts. I had gone to see my mother in her flat in Edmonton, and just on a whim, parked in Risley Avenue, and walked to the school, just as I had done so many times before, and got to the end of the cemetery lane, then suddenly thought of Sullivan and on an impulse, turned back and went through the gate with the intention of visiting his grave. I couldn't find it. I remember very well where it should have been - up by the railings about fifty yards from the path. I remember it all so well, the grave and the flowers and that poor sad lady. And that awful Last Post. But despite almost an hour of searching, backwards and forwards, examining all the headstones, I just could not find it. For some reason, I was furious when I eventually gave up, and walked away swearing out loud. But when I got to the gate, I stopped and looked back, and I said out loud - "I'll remember you mate".

And I always will.

. . . .

It was during the third year that I started playing the hop. I was always in trouble for being late, as throughout my life, I have always had trouble getting out of bed in the mornings. Funny thing that. Some people are early risers - some ain't. I am in the latter category unfortunately. I was often still in bed when Alec knocked for me, and I'd tell him to go on without me, as there was no sense in two of us getting into strife. Most days, I was the only one in the house, both of my parents being at work, so there was no-one to turf me out of the pit. So I was always getting detentions, and if you got three in a row for lateness, you got the cane. I can still remember running all the way to school, with my satchel banging on my back, trying to make it into assembly, knowing that if I didn't it was outside that office, waiting for that dreaded deep voice saying "COME IN", then wallop, wallop, wallop.

One morning, the three of us, Alec, Alby and myself were belting up the cemetery path, when we suddenly realised that we weren't going to make it, so we resignedly slowed to a walk. Might as well he hung for a sheep as a lamb. It was all right for them, but for me it meant the old "COME IN", and pain, not just a detention, so I said - "Fuck it, I ain't going".

And I didn't. It was a lovely day, so I went home and got my cossy and a towel and went swimming, and had a lovely time. That evening, Alec forged me a note to say I'd had the trots, and I got away with it. Easy as pie. It really was the start of the slippery slope I'm afraid, and it got to be very regular indeed. I had some very willing accomplices, my main partner in crime being Billy Budd, who had very much the same rebellious nature as myself. We were often joined by Roy, Kenny Goldstein and Alby, and very occasionally, Alec. And Kenny Handley.

I'll just digress for a few sentences, and tell you about Handley. I first met him in the railway carriage on the way to that first camp in Sudbrook. He came from Bethnal Green, and had joined the school at the beginning of the third year. He was a slim good-looking kid, with blond curly hair, and quickly hit it off with the rest of us, and we talked him into joining the band. He only lived a couple of hundred yards away from me, just round the corner in Gospatrick Road. You'll be reading quite a bit more about him later, because he and Alby and I became more or less inseparable right through our youth. When we got talking in that railway carriage, who would have guessed that I would be best man at his wedding, or that fifty years later, he and Alby and I, and our wives, would all go out to dinner together. Mates are very important, and he became one of the best.

But to continue.....

Of course, we overdid it, and eventually got tumbled, which had very painful consequences, I can tell you, at home as well as at school. I got a belting off of both my parents, but I'm not complaining. I suppose I deserved it. After all, they'd expected a lot from me, being the only one to get to Grammar school, and I'd let them down. Billy got half killed by his old man I recall. But I'm afraid it didn't cure either myself or Billy, and we were soon at it again, as we both hated school by now, but by this time, we were a bit more cute, and didn't overdo it.

We had some great times on these occasions, roaming all over the place. For instance, we got to know the museums in Kensington very well indeed. I suppose in a way, we continued our education, because we spent an awful lot of time in the Science Museum, downstairs in the children's section, playing with all the working exhibits, learning a great deal more about Physics than we ever did at school, and having fun at the same time. The Natural History museum as well, looking at the cases filled with all the animals and birds in creation. It was all free of course, which was handy, and so was the zoo, or at least it was to us, because we found a place where we could bunk in.

Regents Park Zoo was a real wonderland to us. I recall a time when Handley, Goldstein, Alby and I were in there early one morning, when it was practically deserted. We'd always bunk in near where the birds of prey were kept, and there was this row of cages which all seemed to be empty. The last one however, held these four big owls, with pointed ears, all perched in a row with their backs to us. I rattled the wire at the front of their cage, and without their bodies moving, the four heads turned in unison right round 180 degrees, and solemnly blinked and stared at us with these huge eyes. I just can't begin to describe how funny it was. We were helpless with laughter - on the floor in hysterics. It is simply one of the funniest things I have ever seen..

Some time after I'd left the army, Jeanny and I were over the Lido with Kenny Goldstein and his wife, all laying there, soaking up the sun with our eyes shut, when right out of the blue, Kenny said - "Remember them owls

Del?". I said "Yeah". We started to giggle, and a few seconds later were laughing just like we did all those years ago.

. . . .

I don't suppose I was the worst boy in the school, but I was certainly one of them. I just couldn't take the discipline, and there was an awful lot of that at Tottenham Grammar I'm afraid. If you ever answered back, or played up, or cheeked any of the teachers, you were asking for trouble, and in those days, they didn't muck about. You'd get a box round the ear which would make your head ring. It got to the stage where I was averaging at least one clout a day, which I expect I deserved, but this obviously has the effect of fermenting resentment. Christ, I got enough of that at home. Some of the teachers I would never play up, because they were good at their jobs, and made the lessons interesting, and if a kid misbehaved, they'd give him a good sensible talking too, and nip it in the bud. Our form master, Mr Mitchell was one of these, and we all liked him, even though he was strict, so English, which he taught, was my best subject, and I never fell behind, and in the mock matriculation, I came close to getting a distinction. Mr Cooper was another teacher who we wouldn't dream of giving a hard time, so I maintained a decent standard at Maths. These were two of the better ones but some of the others weren't so nice.

For instance, there were two German masters at the school, a Mr Adler, and a Mr Schlartz. Now Mr Adler, who taught economics and German, looked like a typical Prussian officer, which indeed, he had been, in the first world war, one of the enemy. He was very big, ramrod straight, and the back of his head went straight down into his shoulders, and he actually had, believe it or not, a livid scar across the back of his neck, that he had got in a duel when he was a young cadet. He didn't talk, he barked, in a clipped Conrad Viedt accent. A very fierce and frightening character. He was an anti-nazi refugee, as was Mr Schlartz. Mr Schlartz was also a refugee, and Jewish, and he was a small, chubby man, with a very kind face, with little glasses, which he peered over benevolently, not unlike Pinoccio's father. He also taught German.

Looks deceive.

Mr Adler's nickname was Max. Come to think of it, it was his real name. He was one of the nicest blokes in the school, with a great sense of humour. He would sweep into the class, glare at us and shout -

"Now poys, here iss your beloffed Mex! Let us heff some quviet PLISS! Now den, let us open up our - 'DEUTCHES LEBEN' et page ein hundert sieben und zwanzig, and ve vill BEGIN!" He always had our undivided attention.

Beloved Max. He was too.

Mr Schlartz was quite simply, a sadistic bastard, and a complete martinet. He was always twisting ears and clouting and punching shoulders; a real tyrant. He didn't do all these as the result of any misbehaviour, he was one who we'd never dare play up - we were terrified of him, no, it was if you made any mistakes or didn't have a correct answer, or so much as made an ink blot on a page. I expect he'd learnt to teach like that in Germany.

The following episode was I think, just about the last straw for me:

I had this unfortunate habit of sometimes whistling through my teeth, very quietly, almost inaudibly, if I was engrossed or giving something my undivided attention. I didn't realise I was doing it half the time, and it was during one of Schlartz's lessons, which were always conducted in complete silence, I heard him say - "Who iss vistling?". I realised it was me, but didn't own up to it, and he just glared round and let it go. Ten minutes later, I was leaning over my desk, writing, completely absorbed, when I heard a faint rustle, and saw this pair of black shoes poking out from underneath a gown, right beside me. At the same instant, I realised to my horror that I was whistling through my teeth again. The next second I got a terrific whack on the back of my head, which banged my face down onto the desk. It was just the same as having a hard punch on the nose, and you know how that can hurt. I was dazed for just a couple of seconds, and then really lost my temper and stood up and swore and squared up to him! I was thirteen years old at the time, and nearly as big as him, and he jumped back looking very surprised and nervous, and then walked quickly back behind his desk, yelling over his shoulder for me to get out and go and wait outside the head-master's office. I had completely lost it by then and yelled back at him, calling him everything under the sun, then chucked my books at him and walked out the class, and then just kept going, out of the school. There was hell to pay the next day, and there I was in the headmaster's office, but my nose was all swollen, so I expect that was why I only got caned instead of being expelled.

But I was a hero in the class, and the bastard never touched me again. The trouble was, I didn't learn any more German either.

After that, I knew that I'd be leaving as soon as I possibly could. I knew that there was no way that I could matriculate. I'd have passed easily in English Language, and probably got through Maths, but in those days, you had to pass in at least eight subjects to matriculate if I remember rightly - you didn't get individual passes like they do today. I was miles behind in all the other subjects, because of playing the hop, and not working when I was at school, but I didn't give a sod, I just wanted out of there.

It was a pity really. For instance, I hated History, which was about the least popular subject for all of us for some reason. Most school children find it very dull and uninteresting. I don't really understand why, because it could be the most interesting if it's taught properly. But even at a grammar school, they just turn it into a memory test. I was near the bottom of the class in the third year, because I simply didn't pay attention, and the History teacher was a complete tosser as far as I was concerned, one that you could play up easily. But a few weeks before I left school, we had to write an essay on what we think would have happened if the South had won the American Civil War. Well, by coincidence I'd just read a book about John Paul Jones, which included a condensed account of the whole war, and also 'The Red Badge of Courage', as well as a book about slavery. As I mentioned earlier, I was always reading. So I enjoyed writing the essay, really worked on it, and handed it in with all the others. The next day the History teacher saw me in a corridor, and took me into an empty classroom.

"I've just read your essay Brimson" he said. He looked quite stern and continued - "Now did you really write it? I'm not a complete fool you know". I told him that yes, I had written it - so what?. So he asked me a few questions, which I answered, and when he was finally convinced that everything was above board, he said -

"You really are such a bloody fool Brimson. You're hopeless in the classroom, yet you turn out the type of essay that I would expect from a sixth former". He glared at me and poked me in the chest.

"You've thrown it all away haven't you eh?" - poke - "Eh?". He whirled round and stomped out, tut-tutting. He'd made his point though.

I used to get the same sort of thing from Mr Mitchell. Mind you, English was my best subject. We were asked to write a short poem - subject: An historical event. I had chosen the battle of Waterloo, as again, I'd just read a book about it, and how Napoleon's Old Guard had turned their backs on the enemy for the first time in their history. He knew I was leaving, and gave me the same sort of talking to that I had got from the History master. He waved the poem under my nose, and said -

"You'll be working in a factory soon I expect boy, and you can do THIS. You CLOWN!".

I might as well show it to you.

"When the Old Guard Broke" by master D.Brimson.

'And the waves of Blue and Silver crashed and battered
Against the walls of Red and Gold -
And broke and shattered -
Up from the ranks there came a sigh - a moan - a cry
That pierced the soul of France -
"La Garde recule!
"Allons mes enfants! Nous sommes trahis -
Nous sommes perdu!
A les Anglais le victoire!".

Not bad, although I do say so myself.

. . . .

But, too little to late. My thoughts at the time were 'bollocks to 'em. I'll do all right, I've got brains'. I just wanted to get out into the wide world and earn some money. Alby and Kenny were leaving too, Alby because he came from a big family, and I expect that they couldn't afford to keep him there. Also of course, we had friends who were already working, and they always had a few bob in their pockets and were to us men of the world, while we were still schoolboys. Billy Budd was on his way out too, his circumstances being similar to mine. Billy was totally fearless, and inclined towards truculence if threatened. He'd been hauled up to be punished for some dark deed or other, but had flatly refused to be caned, and had even threatened the headmaster, telling him that if he tried, he'd stick his cane up his arse, which didn't go down too well if I remember rightly, so I was in good company. In those days, the minimum school leaving age was fourteen.

So after the first term of my fourth year, at the beginning of the Christmas holiday, Tottenham Grammar School and I parted company.

I wasn't sorry.... At the time.

. . . .

Me, aged fourteen, with June, Mum and Dad
– Torquay.

Me,
same year,
same place.

Chapter 7

TEENAGER Part 1.

The period between leaving school at the end of '46 till the day I went in the Army in January '51 were extremely eventful or me. I have a sort of kaleidoscope of memories from that time, and so many things happened that I think I could probably write a separate book about it, but I won't attempt to go into too much detail. I'll tell you some of it, but I'll go mainly for trying to give you some idea of life in the Forties - what it like to live in those times.

The one big word which all historians employ to describe those times is 'AUSTERITY'. I think that the word is over-used, as it is retrospective, by which I mean that at the time, we were not conscious of being particularly deprived or poor. No doubt, if you later generations were to be suddenly transported back to that time, you certainly would be in for a shock, and would very quickly wish to scuttle back in your time machine to your own far more comfortable present, but remember, we had never known any different, and all the time things were slowly improving. What you've never had, you don't miss. Rationing was still in force for both food and clothing, but no-one starved, and neither did people walk around in rags.

No, to tell you the truth, it wasn't too bad at all.

The one big plus for the nation in the Forties was that there was full employment. You could get a job anywhere - factories, offices, building sites - you name it, they were all crying out for people. All this was just as well as far as yours truly was concerned, because I must confess that I lost count of the jobs I had as a teenager. My dislike of authority had a lot to do with that, coupled with the fact that I was bone idle, with a very low boredom threshold. But I can say, with my hand on my heart, that looking back, I don't regret it in the slightest, and that's the truth. At the time I was a free spirit, with only myself to worry about, and I don't feel that the time was wasted - far from it. You've only got one life, and I believe in filling it up with as many experiences as possible, at least while you're young and single. So I look back upon it all as an education, and an invaluable one. This is with hindsight naturally, as I didn't deliberately flit from job to job with those ends in mind, but never-the-less I got to know so many diverse kinds of people and what makes them tick, from those that my father used to call the 'bread and dripping aristocrats' in offices to the Poles and the Paddies on the building sites; from the Yiddish street traders in the markets to the blokes on the factory floor; from the marvellous cockney women in the brewery to the bargees on the Grand Union Canal. And I had a lot of fun, and learned an awful lot. I wouldn't have had all that if I'd have stayed in the same job for four years. This is a very personal point of view of course, and there's just as much to be said for getting a good job that one enjoys, sticking at it and embarking on a career, but I just didn't go through that gate.

No regrets though. None at all.

. . . .

Mr Mitchell was right, because my first job was in a factory. I went there for no other reason than that a couple of mates of mine talked me into it, and it was one of the best paid jobs for a fourteen year old. It was at Gestetners, by Tottenham Hale, and they made duplicating machines. It was lovely to have a few bob in my pocket for the first time, but Christ it was boring! I lasted about three months before getting the sack for swearing at the fore-man. A bit unjust really, because he'd just sworn at me, but I didn't mind in the slightest, as a good pal of ours, one Freddy Buddin, had said that I could get a job with him, and be apprenticed as an upholsterer. His father was the foreman at the firm, so it was no trouble getting taken on, and it worked out very nicely, as the fact that it was a good trade went a long way to allaying the wrath of my parents for getting the tin-tack.

I must say, I enjoyed my time there. The upholsterers, or 'tackers' as they were known were a great bunch of blokes, and were always singing and cracking jokes. It wasn't a formal apprenticeship, like engineering or print-ing, with a certificate at the end of it, more a case of learning as you went along, as well as fetching and carrying and sweeping up.

One of our jobs was to strip the armchairs and settees that had come in to be re-built. Right down to the bare frame. We used to love this, because when you ripped the back fly of the seats off, everything that had found it's way down there, over many years in some cases, used to cascade down onto the floor. That was one of our perks. Sometimes, there'd be nothing at all, where some tight-fisted sod had already searched down there, but other times it would be like Christmas! Combs, lighters, hair clips and even the odd watch believe it or not. And money - tanners, pennies, florins, half crowns, and once, a silver cigarette case.

The first time I ever got drunk was at the firm's Christmas booze-up. It wasn't a formal do by any means, just a matter of knocking off early the day before the Christmas break, and then getting stuck into the beer and spirits and sandwiches and cakes that had been provided by the governors, right there in the workshop. I don't remember too much about it, except that we all had a marvellous time, and there was an awful lot of singing and skylarking about, but us youngsters not being used to drink, and with the enthusiastic connivance of the tackers, all got monumentally and totally pissed very quickly. Mind you, so did most of them, but what I do remember is waking up in pitch darkness and a strange eerie silence. I was laying in the flock box - a very large wooden thing, something like an over-sized coffin. I didn't realise where I was for the first few moments - and then complete panic, thinking I'd gone blind and deaf. I sat up and banged my head on the lid then threw it open and clambered out. My head was splitting, and I brought everything up, right back to yesterdays breakfast. God I felt terrible! The reason it was so quiet and dark was that I was alone - the only one in the building. I must have passed out very early on and fell in the box out of sight, and been forgotten and they'd all buggered off and left me there.

I climbed out of a window and had to walk all the way home from Hackney, as it was one o'clock in the morning and the buses had stopped running. What with the freezing cold fog, and my poor aching head, I swore there and then - 'Never again' - and I also knew I'd be in big trouble when I got home. That was a very long miserable walk I can tell you, but luckily for me, Frank and his wife Pip were there, visiting for Christmas, and were waiting up with my parents, and they all thought it was hilarious, so I escaped retribution.

Part of the reason that they thought it was so funny was that I looked Al Johlson! My face was as black as Newgate's Knocker, not surprising after two hours stumbling through the smog.

Thank the Lord they're a thing of the past. London has more than it's fair share of fogs in the winter, but in those days, it sometimes combined with all the smoke pouring out of the houses and factories, and became so thick that you couldn't see more than a couple of yards. The smoke actually combined with the water droplets, and it was really dreadful filthy stuff, hence smog, fog and smoke mixed up. You never hear of it now, because of the clean air act, but it actually killed thousands of old people every year, and at that time it was particularly bad, as the factories were all working full blast, some of them round the clock. 'KILLER SMOG INVADES THE CAPITAL" was a typical headline in those days. They had to have chaps walking in front of the buses with these yellow flares, as the drivers couldn't see anything at all - this during the rush hours as people had to get too and from work. Apart from the bikes, they'd be the only thing moving on the roads, and even they'd pack it in once the rush hour was over. That was why I had to walk home that night, and I only found my way by walking along the kerb, all along the Kingsland Road and on and on, not knowing where the bloody hell I was, but luckily knowing that it was the same straight road all the way, through Hackney, Stoke Newington, then Stamford Hill, then High Cross, to Bruce Grove railway station in Tottenham. What a nightmare. Just me and the smog and the kerb, frozen stiff and with a headache, like walking through a long endless tunnel.

So I walk in with these two red eyes, black face and white mouth where I'd tied my hanky, and blurted out - "I got drunk and fell asleep in the flock box!".

No wonder they cracked up.

The upholstery lasted almost a year, by far the longest time I was ever to spend at any one job, and one of those that I enjoyed the most. The one big drawback however, from my point of view, was that it was unhealthy. I was at the time, going through that phase very common to teenagers - terminal hypochondria. Sounds silly now, but most of us go through it - every bellyache is appendicitis, every earache a mastoid, every pimple a catastrophe. This coupled with the fact that spending so much time over the Lido, and getting to know all the muscle-men, I'd got very interested in weightlifting and bodybuilding and had started to work on building myself a good physique. I'd lost all interest in boxing, and all this had become my new passion. Freddy Buddin too, in fact it was him who had turned me onto it, and we'd both joined Reub Martin's gym.

One afternoon, the sun was shining through the windows of the work shop, and I realised that I could not see through the beam of light because of all the dust from the fibre and flock that was hanging in the air. I pointed this out to Freddy, and as we were discussing it, we heard one of the old tackers hawking and gobbing as he was busily tapping away. Freddy said -

"Christ, you're right Del, come to think of it, they're always doing that. My old man uses two hankies a day". We there and then decided that we didn't fancy breathing in all that shit for the rest of our lives, and we both asked for our cards. Freddy's dad was none too pleased, and tried to talk him out of it, without success.

So ended my career in the furniture business.

Freddy and I both got jobs together the next day in a shoe factory, and Freddy stayed there till he went in the Army, but I didn't last too long. I found it seriously tedious.

. . . .

I won't bore you with a catalogue of all the jobs that I went through in the next three years - that is if I could remember them all anyway - suffice to say that they were many and varied. Some lasted a couple of months, some a few hours. I only had one responsibility, and that was to give my mother thirty bob every Friday for my keep. God help me if I didn't. It may not sound much, but a good wage for a boy of my age at the time was three pounds ten shillings a week, and a man would only be earning about six or seven. So it was actually quite a chunk of change, and didn't leave too much over.

It is a fact that a high percentage of blokes who spent their formative teenage years in the immediate post-war Britain drink very little. It's because we simply couldn't afford it in those times, so we never got a taste for it. We all used to get drunk very quickly at parties of course, but never bought any drink, and were too young to go into boozers anyway, so our alcohol tolerance was very low. Add to that the fact that we all went into the Services when we were eighteen, and we definitely could not afford it on twenty-eight shillings a week. By the time we came out two years later, most of us had formed the habit of not drinking.

We did however, all smoke. Non-smokers were quite a rarity, in fact as far as I remember, Alec was the only one of my mates who didn't. I had my first fag when I was twelve, when Lenny Choules gave me a DeReske Minor over the Big Rec.

"Go on' he said 'take it down like this", and inhaled a big gob full of smoke, then slowly blew it out through his nose. So I did, much to his amusement at my coughing and spluttering. But I was a regular smoker from the age of fourteen, the same as nearly everyone else at that time. Still am. But at least, I never got to be a drinker, thank God.

I consider myself very lucky in the fact that when I am left to my own devices, I am never bored, and have also been blessed with an enquiring mind; an insatiable curiosity. It really is a blessing especially when I consider people that I know who never even read a newspaper, let alone a book, and have no hobbies and few interests. It takes all sorts I suppose, but I'm glad that I'm the way I am, as I consider that it makes for a much fuller life. Different strokes for different folks. There will always be youngsters who are forever saying 'God I'm bored' and 'There's nothing to do in this dump', but I was never one of them, and fortunately, nor were any of my friends. You can take it from me that we were a very lively bunch, and made the most out of what there was going for us. And that was quite a lot.

Although we had left school, Alby, Kenny, Billy and myself were still allowed to stay in the cadets, so the band practices and weekend camps continued. We were all just as keen, and the band was by now very good indeed, one of the best in north London, and we looked forward eagerly to the street marches on Sunday mornings, as well as the various competitions and functions we appeared in.

We did our second annual camp at Dover, and Glory be we were camped with the pipes and drums of the Ist Battalion of the Scots Guards. What a bit of luck. We simply could not believe that drumming could be that good, and quickly realised that we were complete beginners compared to them. To watch one of the best pipe bands in the world marching with an awesome precision, playing such superb, stirring music was a marvellous experience for us boys. They paraded just after reveille every morning, it being a regimental custom, counter marching on the parade ground, and we'd all be there for it, washed and dressed, before breakfast, loving every minute of it. Lovely tunes - 'Farewell to the Creeks', 'Bonny Dundee', 'Johnny Cope', 'Blue Bonnets' - then forming a circle to play the beautiful strathspeys and reels. We couldn't get enough of it, and for me it was the start of a lifelong passion for pipe band music.

Do you want a tip? Go and buy a recording of any of the massed pipe band performances from the Edinburgh Festivals. If you're feeling a bit low and fed up, put it on your sound system and wind the volume right up, and let the music fill the house. You'll feel very much better in no time.

Bugger the neighbours.

We got to know the drummers of course, and they were great blokes and didn't mind in the least giving us a bit of coaching. Scots drumming is far more elaborate than any other kind of military drumming, but a little of what they taught us rubbed off, and our own taps to the simple bugle marches became a lot more complex, and improved the band no end.

Another bonus which came with reaching the grand old age of fourteen was that you could join the youth clubs. It only cost us two bob a week, which was a bargain, as it was somewhere to go if it was cold or raining. We all joined the one at Risley Avenue school, and had a lot of fun there. We had all suddenly started to take a great interest in girls, quite naturally, and youth clubs were perfect places to start our apprenticeships in the pursuit of l'amour. There comes a time in a boys life when girls are no longer regarded as a bloody nuisance, and suddenly become something very different. This can occur quite a bit earlier than fourteen years of age, but none of us would dare own up to it for fear of being dubbed a cissy, but comes the day when it's the done thing, and off we go. It's the start of the Great Game, and we all embarked on the journey with enthusiasm. All very innocent at that time, and at that age, but none-the-less, very very nice.

Table tennis was about the most popular activity in the youth clubs, and we all very quickly became addicted. There were eight tables at Risley and they were all occupied throughout the evening and you had to get your name down very early if you wanted a game. I was mad keen - well, we all were, but I was never any good. They could all beat me nine times out of ten, but I didn't mind, and enjoyed it just as much. There was however, one big drawback as far as I was concerned, and a very curious one.

It takes a few weeks to learn to play table tennis with any degree of competence, and not just patting the ball over the net to each other. It was about the time that I'd reached this stage and had just had three good games on the trot, and had actually won one of them against Alby, when the others started looking at me with amused interest. Kenny said -

"What are you doing that for?". I replied - "What?". Then Billy said -

"Are you doing it on purpose?". I had no idea what they were talking about, and said,

"Doing what on purpose ?". They all started to crack up laughing, and I made it worse by getting all humpty, when Kenny said -

"Go and look in the mirror". I went to the bog grumbling, followed by my so called mates, and on looking at my reflection, saw that my right eye had gone right into the corner. Ben Turpin all over again! It really did look funny, but I was horrified and panic-stricken. When they saw the look on my face, they laughed even louder, and thought it highly amusing. Well, to cut a long story short, the eye returned to normal again after about ten minutes, to my intense relief, but it always wandered inwards when I played for any length of time, God knows why. I guess that it was something to do with following the ball with my one good eye so intently. It didn't stop me playing, but I had to be very careful on the occasions when I had amorous intentions towards any particular girl, and had to time my games accordingly.

Difficult to do any chatting up looking like that.

So what with the cadets, youth clubs, Spurs, cinema, and all sorts of other things we got up to, we didn't have a bad time of it at all. We all hated staying in, and for my part, home was just a place to eat and sleep and play the piano.

I haven't mentioned the piano yet. We had a really nice one, which my parents had bought when they first moved to Tottenham. I never did find out why they bought it, as neither of them played, but in those days, many households had one - a sort of status symbol suppose, and it was always in the front room.

That's another custom that has long gone. The front room. That was where the best furniture - the three piece suite, the best carpet, the china cabinet - the pictures on the wall and the family photographs standing on the mantle piece in their silver frames - the aspidistra and the ornaments were all kept. And the piano. It was a curious custom, in that the front room was rarely used. Most families lived and ate in the kitchen and the back room, and the front room, which was always kept spotless and neat was treated like a sort of shrine, only used on special occasions.

I loved our front room, as we had a bay window, and it always seemed to be much lighter and less gloomy than the back of the house. It was beautifully furnished, as my mother had very good taste, and always bought the very best that we could afford. We had a very expensive damask covered three piece suite, a lovely French black and gold ormolu cabinet full of pretty china ornaments, which my mother collected, and the very latest, top of the range radiogram. We still had all Frank and Ivy's classical records, as well as dad's Richard Taubers. When I first came back from evacuation I was rarely allowed in there, but I soon learned the trick of asking if I could go in and play some music on the gramophone - the old fashioned wind-up job that preceded the radiogram. It always used to work.

"Go on then, but don't make a mess, and don't touch anything".

There were a few jazz and piano records in the collection, and among these was one called 'Pine-top Blues', by Pinetop Smith. Obviously, at a very early age I used to tinkle about on the piano, and pick out tunes with one finger, and they were among the only occasions that I can remember my mother showing any interest or approval. She'd come in and say -

"That's it - now try and join in with the other 'and". Ivy taught me to play 'Wonderland', a very simple little waltz, and I used to play it over and over again. Must have driven them mad. I was about thirteen when I first discovered 'Pinetop', and kept on and persevered till I could play it. It's a nice little twelve bar boogie piece, very simple actually, but it gave me the taste to learn more. Somehow or other, I acquired other boogie-woogie records and worked out the different eight to the bar recurring base lines played with the left hand, peculiar to that style of blues. Billy Penrose, Albert Ammons, Meade-lux Lewis and Jimmy Yancey, which all seemed to be on the old blue and white Parlophone label. I gradually worked all of them out, with a lot of help from a pal of ours called Johnny Gibbs, who was having piano lessons, and shared my love of boogie. By the time I was fifteen, although I say so myself, I was bloody good, but only however in that style. Just twelve bar, and nearly all played in the key of C. One exception was 'Honky Tonk Train Blues', which was always my party piece. I did it all by ear, like the old black fellers who invented it. I never learned to read music, and never got any further with the piano, although I did learn some Fats Waller tunes later on, but it took ages, and was very hard work. But like they say, if you don't buy a ticket you won't win the raffle, and it was all very good grist to the mill, (excuse the clichés, but I'm not entering this biography for a Pullitzer Prize), and was to stand me in very good stead in later life.

Jumping ahead a good few years; when I first acquired a guitar I remembered that frustration as a boy, laboriously working everything out by ear. I wanted to play classical guitar, so I had lessons, and learnt to read guitar music and it was the start of a very good career for me. I also had two of my own tutors published, as well as writing tablature for instruction records.

One of the by-products of our sudden interest in girls was that we started to be much more conscious of our appearance. I had always been a scruffy kid, second only in scruffiness to Billy Budd. The only time we ever looked smart was when we were in uniform, but suddenly, we were putting Brylcream on our hair, polishing our shoes and putting a crease in our trousers. Later, clothes became almost an obsession with us, and we'd stand outside Davis's men's wear shop very much like the Bisto Kids, gazing longingly in the window at the drape jackets, gabardine slacks, pinstripe suits and spearpoint shirts. We'd save up for weeks to buy a poplin shirt, which in those days cost about two pounds ten shillings. A jacket would set you back about seven or eight quid, and the cheapest suits were thirteen or fourteen. Work it out for yourself, translating the present average weekly wage with the seven or eight pounds which was the weekly norm in those times. And that was for an adult. We earned half that much. So you see, unless you were lucky enough to have indulgent parents, it was very difficult to be well dressed. Also, clothes were not nearly as well made and hard wearing as they are today, and had to be really well looked after. Very few of us had more than one decent outfit - usually a drape jacket, spearpoint collar shirt, a pair of hopsack or gabardine trousers, and a pair of suede, crepe-soled shoes. I didn't own a suit till I was seventeen, and I got that on hire purchase.

Remember when you were little and hated getting clothes for birthday and Christmas? Well, that all changed when we were fifteen. Please Father Christmas, for God sake give me something to wear!.

I fell in love for the first time when I was fifteen. Her name was Theresa Klaxton, and I met her at a dance at the Lynch House Youth club in Bruce Grove. Of course, I didn't know how to handle it, and it's something we all have to go through - part of the learning process which none of us ever complete. I'd taken a few girls home and kissed them on the doorstep, but never really fallen for any of them, but suddenly here it was - the real thing.

Well, it was at the time.

Theresa was like a little film star, with a face like an angel and long curly blond hair. Needless to say, she was very popular with all the chaps, but I was the one who took her all the way home to Seven Sisters that night, and walked home treading on air, having arranged to take her to the pictures the next afternoon. Sunday afternoon pictures at the Bruce Grove Cinema was a regular part of our social lives - a sort of teenage club. My mates were green with envy.

"Lucky bastard" they said, "How did you manage that?". I really fell for her, and she did for me and we were together for about a month, which is quite a long time for the age we were. Theresa was a very affectionate little lady and a brilliant snogger, but I never dreamt of anything carnal of course - it just wasn't done if you really respected a girl in those days -'nothing below the waist' as we used to say. We swore undying love and devotion and all the rest of it, but it all ended quite suddenly as most very early romances do. I had never been shown much affection before, so of course I did it all wrong and showered her with it, which is a very sure way of putting a girl off. And it did. I got the elbow. I was heartbroken, completely mystified and was very miserable for quite a long time. We laugh at it all years later, but calf love is very real and extremely painful when it goes wrong. My mates were a fat lot of help.

"You should have give 'er one while you had the chance Del" said Alby. Always the gentleman.

. . . .

I'd like at this point to tell you about my life of crime. It won't take long because it was extremely brief, and quite funny when I look back upon it.

My immediate circle of pals were by and large, a law-abiding lot. We weren't hard cases, although we could all stand up for ourselves, but apart from the odd minor scuffle, we kept out of bother. We were all far to good natured to go looking for trouble anyway, and to tell you the truth, that applied to the very large majority of teenagers in those days. Mind you, those that did go looking for trouble always found it, but fights were far less frequent than they are among today's youth. They talk about the tough old back-streets of London, but that is a myth. Vandalism was practically unknown - it never crossed our minds, and as for thieving - well, that was a mugs game because all thieves ended up in the nick eventually, and we didn't fancy that in the slightest. Borstals were very nasty places indeed, and due to the fact that there were far fewer miscreants, the law was far more harshly applied in those times. No letting off with a caution or community service and cosy chats with a kindly social worker, - down the steps you go pal, and see you next year.

The whole business actually started with a fight, which may seem strange after reading the previous paragraph. I was still fifteen at the time and was on my way to the Lido carrying my towel and cossie under my arm, jogging along Tower Gardens road, minding my own business and at peace with the world in general. There was a little group of youths hanging out at the entrance of the Little Rec and as I went past one, of them, a bloke called Billy Ayres, stuck out a foot and tripped me, sending me flying, flat on my face. There was this big laugh from all of them, but I was furious, and picked myself up and went for Billy Ayres like a lunatic. It wasn't like me at all, and as far as I can remember, it was the first time I had had a serious go at anybody without a pair of boxing gloves on. If I'd have stopped to argue, I would probably have backed down, as Ayres had a bit of a reputation as a hard nut, and was the leader of that little team, and was older and bigger than me. I was still quite timid despite being useful in the ring, but it all went off so quickly that I didn't have time to get nervous. I just sailed straight in belting him all over the place, and didn't give him a chance to fight back. I bloody massacred him. It was over very quickly, and there he was, sitting down holding his hands over his head and yelling -

"All right all right you fuckin' lunatic - wassup with ya!". His mates were just standing there, looking very surprised, but my blood was still up, so me, bloody John Wayne, turned on them and shouted -

"How about any of you wankers then?!", but none of them wanted to know and put their hands in their pockets and started examining their shoes. I just glared at them, picked up my togs, and walked on, still in a temper. Billy Ayres called after me, not very convincingly -

"I'll 'ave you mate, don't worry". I walked back, put my togs on the hedge, raised my fists and said -

"Let's go then". He was only trying to save face in front of his mates, and mumbled something about not being ready, and next time he would be, but it would have to be tomorrow because he was still dizzy. So we arranged to meet in the Little Rec next afternoon and sort it out.

"I'll be ready for you then mate", he said.

"You'd better be", I replied and went my way.

Do you know, when my temper left me, I started to get really worried, and couldn't think of anything else for the rest of the day and was very nervous waiting there with Alby and Fred, with my stomach in a knot, although I was fairly confident. But he didn't show up, much to my relief and Freddy and Alby's disappointment.

I saw him a few days later at the shops in Lordship Lane. He came over with a sheepish grin and held out his hand and said - "Call it quits eh?", which was all right with me. I actually got to know him quite well after that, and soon found that he was one of those who looked and sounded tough, he was actually a bit of a wimp, and could scare the shit out of people with his mouth, so much so that he'd rarely had to do any actual fighting, and then only when he was sure of winning. But he wasn't a bad bloke for all of that, and we became quite friendly.

There was a little cafe opposite Bruce Grove station, known as 'The Little Caff' appropriately enough, and it was where all the local young villains and wrongdoers used to hang out. I was passing by one day, at a time when I was in between jobs, and this curly haired youth stuck his head out the door and called -

"Come 'ere a minute". I asked him what he wanted and he said -

"You're the one who done Billy Ayres ain't you".

"That's right mate, so what?" I answered.

"'Ave a cup of tea" he said with a grin.

That was how I met Georgy. I passed the next hour or so with him and two of his mates, and had a great time, because they were all comedians. They were also thieves. But they were all three so likeable - latter day Artful Dodgers, and kept me in stitches with stories of jobs they'd pulled and scrapes they had been in. I remember Georgy offering me a fag, which I took very gratefully, as I was skint as usual.

"Ain't you got none then?" he asked.

"'Fraid not" I said, whereupon he reached in his pocket and gave me a whole packet of Woodbines. He saw the surprise on my face and said;

"Don't worry cock, there's plenty more where they came from", and they all cracked up laughing. They simply never paid for anything if they could help it. If they were out of cigarettes they'd go into a tobacconists and nick them. I got to know all the local young villains, as I spent quite a bit of time in the 'Little Caff' after that, and was readily accepted into that society, although I wasn't a tea-leaf, which they didn't hold against me, but because I'd gained a bit of a reputation as a scrapper, which actually was far from the truth. Billy Ayres was a regular there, and they were all still under the impression that he was a hard case, which was also far from the truth, but I went along with it quite happily, because I really liked them, and fitted in quite well. Georgy and his two mates, who were both called Johnny, were brilliant company and we had some great laughs. I used to call them my day-time mates, because I never knocked about with them in the evenings or at weekends, as they weren't exactly into youth clubs and army cadets. They were more for pubs and clubs, and going 'up West', as the West End of London was called, and getting in with the big time, real villains. That was when they weren't robbing and stripping lead off church roofs and suchlike. Of course, I couldn't afford the former, and was definitely not up for the latter.

I learned a lot in their company. One thing was that habitual thieves, like Georgy and the two Johnnys, all have one thing in common, and that is a colossal nerve, and will happily take chances that the normal person would-n't dream of, and nine times out of ten, they will get away with it, and the times when they don't, they'll still wiggle out of trouble most of the time by sheer cheek and front. They also enjoyed their knavery, and got a kick out of the danger, and treated it all as fun. Naturally, I'm talking about the suc-cessful ones who are bright. The thick ones spend most of their life in the chokey.

As much as I liked them and enjoyed their company and friendship, I always resisted the numerous invitations to join then in their nefarious activities.

"We got summink on Del - it's easy, a real doddle. D'ya wanna come wiv us?. It'll mean a few bob in your pocket son", but I'd always laugh and decline the offer saying - "Nah, leave me out. With my luck I'd get you all banged up", and they'd smile and let it go, and never thought any the less of me for it. But a few times, I admit I as tempted. Let's say I was at an impressionable age. I must also own up to being shit scared at the prospect, but the more they asked me, the more I was tempted, and finally, just like the time I jumped off the top board for the first time, I found myself saying,

"Yeah, I'll have some of that". Georgy and the two Johnnys grinned in sur-prised approval. "Don't worry son - we'll look after ya".
So began my brief life of crime.

"Yeah - I'll have some of that". I'll tell you what 'that' was. There was a lit-tle tobacconist's kiosk next to the station in Seven Sisters road, and they'd hatched this plan to get onto the railway line further down the track, walk along till they came to the bridge, then let themselves down to this little roof and then get in through the skylight window, climb down and take everything that was not nailed down. All this in the middle of the night obviously. It sounded very simple - a doddle, to use their favourite expression.

Actually, they were right, it was a doddle, but unfortunately, there were to be what I can only describe as unforeseen circumstances.

So that night, I crept downstairs, avoiding the squeaky ones, at one o'clock in the morning and tiptoed out of the house feeling extremely nervous, and made my way through the deserted and dark streets to the rendezvous in an all night cafe in South Tottenham. There they were, with all the bus drivers and dossers and gave me a big cheer when I came through the door. 'Hurray - 'ere comes Public Enemy Number One - someone get 'im a cup of tea for Gawdsakes'. We stayed in there for an hour or so, chatting and joking, with me trying to appear all unconcerned, till finally Georgy said -

"To work gentlemen".

About half an hour later, we scrambled up this grass embankment in the pale moonlight. We got to the top, and there we were standing on the railway track. One of the Johnnys was carrying a length of knotted rope which they'd hidden near the hole in the fence the day before.

"That's clever", I said.

"Plannin' son - plannin", said Georgy. We walked for about a quarter of a mile along the track, with them chatting away without a care in the world, and me chain-smoking furiously, wishing I was somewhere else and trying to appear as unconcerned as they were till we were about a hundred yards from the bridge, then dropped halfway down the bank so that we couldn't be seen from the road. We clambered up onto this flat little roof, and Georgy began working on the skylight with a screwdriver, but found that it was already unlocked. He looked up and smiled.

"Easy", he whispered. Johnny secured the rope and dropped it down into the darkness.

"Ere we go then - me first", and Johnny lowered himself down. We waited a few seconds, peering down into the gloom, then heard him say -

"Come on then - all clear". Georgy stood up, and had a final look round.

"Right Del - you next". Christ I was terrified I can tell you, but down I went, only about ten feet, till I felt Johnny's hands round my waist. We were joined by the other two, and there we were, all four of us standing in pitch darkness. Georgy took a torch from his pocket, but it didn't work.

"Oh fuck it, someone light a match" he hissed.

We were standing in this little storeroom, and immediately saw a dreadful mess, with boxes open and strewn all over the place. It didn't dawn on us at first, but when we went through the door into the shop and lit another match, and saw even more of a shambles, with the till on the floor, fags and sweets and tobacco tins and more empty and torn boxes everywhere, plus the broken window in the front door, we instantly knew that the shop had just been done by someone else!!

We were up that bloody rope and out the skylight like four Polaris missiles, and we ran and ran back along that railway line till our lungs were bursting, finally collapsing in a heap on the embankment, and just lay there laughing uncontrollably. I suppose it was the release of tension as much as anything else, but it was also such a ludicrously funny situation. We laughed till our sides ached, and it was all well worth it as far as I was concerned because of that alone.

Needless to say, my career as a criminal finished right there and then. There was no way I was going to go through that again thank you very much. The story of the 'Seven Sisters Road' job went the rounds many times, and was responsible for a great deal of hilarity in the 'Little Caff', and I was quite pleased that I had been a part of it, but never again. At least I had proved to myself that I had the bottle, but I had also proved to myself that I was never cut out to be a villain. I've often wondered about what would have followed if the occasion had been successful, and whether I'd have got a taste for it. But I very much doubt it.

I still continued to frequent the 'Little Caff' and remained great mates with the boys, but made it plain that I was content to tread the straight and narrow, and they accepted it quite cheerfully.

I've often wondered what became of them.

. . . .

My sister June stayed on in Market Harborough for some time after the war ended, as she was very happy there, and I suppose my parents thought she should stay and finish school, so she would have been about sixteen when she came home - a young woman. She had for some reason become a dreadful snob - very prim and proper, and well spoken, and also very short tempered. I was a scruffy little cockney schoolboy, so inevitably, we very quickly developed a virulent mutual hatred. She really did fancy herself, and I suppose I used to fan the flames somewhat, because I was always calling her a 'toffee-nosed stuck up cow' and taking the micky in general. Unfortunately, I was at a bit of a disadvantage, because my mother doted on her, and let her get away with everything so life got even more uncomfortable for me at number 48. Just out of devilment, I used to play some awful tricks on her, and wind her up whenever I got the chance, but blimey, she used to ask for it! She'd never say a word to me unless she could help it and when she did it was as if she was talking to a cockroach.

My mother enrolled her into Pitman's College to learn shorthand typing, and she got even more up herself because 'going to college' sounded really classy - much better than working. June had learned drama and dancing while she was evacuated, and was very good at both, so she joined the Amateur Dramatic Society whose headquarters were at Lynch House in Bruce Grove. That lot were as toffee-nosed as she was, and naturally, they became her circle of friends, and the front room was often full of them at weekends - blokes with cravats and long hair, and pretty, well dressed women, all calling each other 'dahling'. I thought it was hilarious, but was always shooed out when they came in case I showed her up.

I remember making my dad laugh once, when I had to go into the front room, for some reason or other. It was full of Luvvies.

"Hello, who's this?" asked this middle-aged fat bloke with grey hair.

"My brother", answered June between clenched teeth.

"He's a very nice looking young chap isn't he" he said with a syrupy smile
"So you're the young rascal we've heard about. Derek isn't it?".

"Right", I said, and got out of there fast. My dad was sitting in the kitchen drinking a cup of tea, and I said --

"Dad - I reckon they're a load of irons". He cracked up and sprayed a mouthful of tea all over the kitchen and replied -

"Shh - yer mother will hear you - go on, bugger off". Iron is cockney rhyming slang for gays - 'iron hoof - poof'. He told June what I'd said, because he thought it was hilarious, but she was furious, and warned me to stay out of the way when her fellow thespians were about, or she'd kill me.

Some time in '47, Arthur came home from India, where he'd been since the end of the war, and I really looked forward to seeing him again. He was as brown as a berry, and looked terrific in his uniform, more so because his regiment, the Beds and Herts, had been issued with the Australian bush hats. He was demobbed very soon after coming home, but didn't stay with us too long, leaving home and going to work on a farm, which had always been his ambition. I recall that he did have a job somewhere in Tottenham for a time, and was always bringing home soldering irons and various other things that he'd nicked from work, but I'm not sure whether that was before or after he went in the army. He hated the city, and couldn't wait to get away. As far as I was concerned, it was a great pity, as it was nice to have a brother around again. He was just as touchy and sarcastic as he had always been, and didn't suffer fools gladly, but he had a great sense of humour, and actually did talk to me, which was more than anyone else did. We shared a bedroom for the short time he was there, and we'd sometimes talk far into the night, with him telling me all about the Army and his time in India, where his regiment were deployed to quell the riots when India was partitioned. He was dreadfully prejudiced.

"Fuckin' wogs' he'd say, 'they ain't worth a carrot". He was as hard as nails, physically and mentally, and still is for that matter, and has all my mother's characteristics, except that he became a marvellous husband and father, and dotes on his family. As far as I know, he only ever had one serious girl-friend, and that was Jesse, his wife, who he met when he was farming, and is one of the nicest people I've ever met. They married, had six kids, and eventually settled very happily in Australia.

. . . .

Kenny and Alby were always on to me about getting a regular job, and stick-ing to it, the main reason being that I was always skint, and cadging fags off them. They both worked at Hammonds, the spectacle manufacturers, and never had a day off work, and consequently always had a few bob in their pockets. I naturally wanted to go and work with them, but it was only a little place and it was quite some time before a vacancy came up, but eventually, I did join them.

I'd just got the sack from the Rex Cinema in Wood Green at the time, under what were rather amusing circumstances. I was learning to be a pro-jectionist, which doesn't require all that much skill, but the one thing you do need is the ability to concentrate. At the time I was rather lacking in that department, but after a couple of weeks, I could change the reels and switch over from one projector to the other perfectly. You have to watch the top

Arthur in the Beds and Herts in India - 1946
(He's the one on the right).

right hand corner of the screen just before the reel runs out and start the other projector running when you see this little dot appear. You've probably seen those little dots and wondered what they're for. Well, now you know. I expect it's all automatic now but in those days, you had to wait for the second dot, and then switch over manually. Easy. I did it quite a few times with the projectionist looking over my shoulder, and came the time for me to go solo, which I did quite successfully, alone in the room while he was off chatting up one of the usherettes. It was in the afternoon of course, when there were only a few people in, just in case. My other job was to rewind the reels and put them back in the rack in their correct order. A feature film used to consist of four, sometimes five reels, marked Part 1 & 2, Part 3 & 4, etc.

So a few afternoons later, matey's off on his relentless pursuit of the usherettes honour, and I was alone in the projection room again, watching for the dots with my hands ready on the switches. There's Errol Flynn flailing away at Basil Rathbone with his sword - 'Go on my son, sort the bugger out' I whisper. I knew he was going to win - I'd seen it twelve times already. Dot. Click. Dot. Click click. And there's Laurel and Hardy falling down the stairs. Oh my God I'd put the wrong bloody reel in! It was Part 2 & 3 all right, but I hadn't looked at the title.

There were a few very confused old age pensioners and a very angry manager, and me down the road with my cards.

A few days later, I started work at Hammonds Opticians. It was quite a nice clean little job, in pleasant surroundings, but the foreman was an absolute arsehole, and I fell out with him very quickly and was out on my ear after a couple of weeks. I just could not take being told off and shouted at, and in those days, all teenagers were told off and shouted at as a matter of course, and accepted it without question, but not me matey. I'm pretty sure that I would have stayed at Hammonds if it hadn't have been for that git, but it was just one of those unfortunate things, and in those days it just wasn't done to question a foreman's parentage to his face, or to threaten to shove a pair of spectacles up his nose.

Well, he shouldn't have been so rude.

. . . .

The only time my father ever gave me a real hiding was during this period.

I was flitting from job to job, staying till I got bored or sacked, because I never exactly put myself out at any of them, and tended to prefer the swimming pool when the sun was shining.

I got a start at this little engineering firm, but after being there for a couple of hours decided that it was not for me, and buggered off during the first tea break, and spent the rest of the day in the 'Little Caff'. I hadn't even told my parents that I was out of work, let alone starting a new job, which was the usual course of events, as it saved me a lot of grief, and anyway, their only concern was that I coughed up the old thirty bob come Friday night. So I walked in the house that evening, and my dad just got up, walked over and punched me straight in the mouth. I staggered back, and he came at me again and started belting the daylights out of me, shouting and swearing, and calling me all the thieving bastards under the sun. He then dragged me bodily up the stairs by the scruff of my neck and threw me into the bedroom. All the time I had been covering up and yelling, asking what the bloody hell was this for etc., but it fell on deaf ears and he really laid into me. It was such a shock, as he hadn't laid a finger on me since I was a little kid, and then it was just the odd clump.

But this was different, and I took a hell of a beating.

The reason was that two plain clothes policeman had come to the house that afternoon. They'd established that I lived there, then marched straight in, pushing my mother aside, and asking where my room was, and had then proceeded to search the house, despite my mothers protestations. Apparently half a dozen quite valuable micrometers had gone missing from the firm that I had started work in that morning. They'd phoned the law, and given them my address, assuming, not unnaturally, that I was the culprit. My old man was very old fashioned, and detested all crime in general, and we'd never had any trouble with the police, so what with having the house searched, and my mother being pushed around, and also the fact that I hadn't told them I was out of work, it was no wonder that he had the serious hump.

I went back to the place first thing the next morning in a blazing temper, and quite prepared to do some damage, but the foreman was as nice as pie and very apologetic, because they'd caught the thief smuggling the gear out the day before. I told him what had happened, but he made the point that it had looked suspicious to say the least - no-one had ever jacked the job in after just two hours before. He also couldn't understand why the police had not been back to my house to put it right. I asked him for a note explaining things, which he readily provided, and left there still fuming and indignant.

I presented the note to the old man in triumph when I got home that evening, but he just snatched it out of my hand, read it, slung it on the table and started reading his paper again without a word. I started to give him a mouthful, but he shut me up and growled something to the effect that I'd been asking for it for a long time, then told me to piss off before I got a bit more of the same. I couldn't believe it, and ran out of the house in tears. I had fully expected him to go tearing round the police station to create hell, and also to tell me how sorry he was. Boy, was I wrong.

I've never understood it from that day to this and it was never ever mentioned again. I suppose it's possible that he had already been round there that day to get to the bottom of it, and had already known the facts when I came home, and was too embarrassed to admit it. I don't know why he acted like he did, and I never will now. I expect it was a mixture of exasperation and disappointment, and I have to admit that I had let them down somewhat.

There was a very strained atmosphere in the house after that and it all came to a head a few weeks later.

I was just sixteen, and had actually started to toe the line a bit. I'd found a job in the office of a little welding firm called Pinders. The Pinders were two very nice old gentlemen - brothers, and the office staff consisted of them and me. I was treated very kindly, and consequently worked willingly and well. It was nice to go to work looking smart, and using my brains for a change. I was only an office boy, but it was a pleasant and interesting little job, which I enjoyed, and I also got on like a house on fire with all the welders. A very happy little outfit indeed and I'd made up my mind to stay there, and I would have done too, but it wasn't to be worse luck.

The reason I didn't stay at Pinders was that my parents had chucked me out. They'd been threatening to for ages, but when ever they did I'd say, "That's all right with me, any time you like", so it had been on the cards for quite some time. So one day, I came home from work, and there was a suitcase in the hall, and the old man saying - "Go on - fuck off. You're on your own", with my mother standing behind him, glaring at me with a face like thunder.

This had all been brought on by the events of the previous evening.

Me, age 16 (and Mum).
The only picture I can find of me as a youth,
unfortunately.

Chapter 8

MY EXILE

I can't remember exactly why, but that evening, just for a something to do, we decided to go and ask to join the Lynch House Amateur Theatrical Society. We had no intention of actually joining. It was just for a laugh, to see what would happen. I'd told my mates about June's arty-farty friends, and they wanted to have a look at them. It was also a very good way of annoying my sister, so it seemed a good idea at the time. It was just for the crack you understand, with no harm or malice intended.

Myself, Alby, Billy Budd, Freddy and a mate of ours called Georgy Lemon set off to Bruce Grove in the best of spirits, all singing 'Hi Diddly Dee - an actor's life for me,' twirling imaginary canes like the Fox in Pinocchio. We arrived a Lynch House, went up the steps, through the door and into the large hallway, and saw this girl pinning something up onto the notice-board.

"'Ello love, who do we see about joining?" says Georgy. She looked a bit startled, said -

"Wait here", and disappeared through the door which she shut behind her.

"I'd give her one," said Freddy conversationally, "is she one of June's mates Del?".

I'd just told him that I didn't know her, but I'd like to when the door opened and in came Curley. I can't remember his name, but that is what I used to call him, and he didn't like me and I didn't like him. He'd been to the house quite a few times, and was a real snotty type, and always looked down his nose at me. He was the dead spit of those old pictures of Oscar Wilde, with a built in sneer. He was one of the leading lights in the group, a big soft looking sod - about thirty, a typical Luvvie.

"Oh - it's you is it. What do you want?" he said, looking at my mates as though someone had just farted.

"We wanna join don't we", replies Alby cheerfully.

"Yeah" says Billy, we wanna be actors like", and Georgy and Freddy laughed and sang - "Hi diddly Dee".

"Out", said Curley - and walked towards as waving his hands towards the door - "Come on - OUT". Alby, still smiling good naturedly says -

"Now that's no way to get new members is it cock?". Curley stood by the open door pointing dramatically out into the street.

"OUT - I said" he yelled.

"Fuck you" said Billy. We'd all stopped smiling, and I felt myself getting really narked - I mean, who the Christ did he think he was?.

"Get out, or you'll be thrown out", hissed Curley.

"Not by you - poof", said Georgy quietly.

"Right, we'll see about that", and Curley hurriedly departed back into the building.

"Oh dear, I think we're in trouble lads" I said, by now feeling very annoyed indeed. We all were, even Alby, and it took a lot to annoy him. As I mentioned before, we never went looking for trouble, but we'd never duck it either, and we didn't like being threatened. The door opened, and Curley re-appeared with three companions, two young blokes in their twenties, and the grey haired bloke who had reckoned I was good looking.

"Now what's this lads?" he asked, and Alby again replied -

"We wanna join, don't we".

"Now come on - don't be silly. Off you go now".

"Bollocks" says Georgy.

One of the others, a bit handy looking, with a moustache and a cravat, took it up, stepped in front of grey hair and said between clenched teeth in his best Oxford accent -

"Right you - (he meant me), out - now - and take your yob friends with you".

"Who you calling a yob?" said Billy. It had suddenly got a bit ugly, and the other bloke had stepped forward looking all humpty and Curley had also got brave and confident and was trying to stare me down. Another couple of blokes had come into the hall. The moustache went up to Billy, poked him in the chest and said menacingly -

"I'm calling YOU a yob". He gave him another stiff poke and shouted in his face - "Now - OUT".

Billy hit him so hard his mother must have felt it, and he flew back and hit the wall. Then the balloon really went up. As I went for Curley I could hear grey hair yelling like a big tart - "Call the police - Call the police", and there was a hell of a bundle - punching, kicking and cursing. I just went straight for Curley, as I was in a rage by now, and the moustache, who was no mug, had got up and gone for Billy, but it would have been much better for him if he had stayed down. Billy murdered him, and Georgy, Freddy and Alby went for the others and very soon sorted them out. What a lively couple of minutes that was, and suddenly there was my sister, mad as hell, screeching and slapping, dragging me off of Curley and a crash as Georgy flung a chair through the window. That was the signal for us to get out of there, and as we ran down the steps Alby laughed and yelled back over his shoulder -

"We've changed our minds - we're not gonna join now!", and so we departed, victorious and in the best of spirits.

. . . .

"I think we're in trouble", says Freddy as we were walking back along Lordship Lane, after we'd got our breath back.

"No we're not" I said, "They started it. That bloke poked Billy with his finger. That's assault that is."

"Yeah, that's right - the bastard poked me. Self defence wasn't it." Georgy said something to the effect that I had really self-defenced Curley, and that they had also self-defenced the others, but Freddy, pretending he was a barrister in court, holding his lapels, said -

"They advanced upon these poor boys, who were after all, only enquiring as to the feasibility of joining the Society, in an aggressive and threatening manner, and it must be obvious to the jury m'lud, that they had no other recourse than to defend themselves".

"Yeah, that's right" growled Billy - "Fuck 'em".

"Yeah - fuck 'em" we all choroused.

But the next day, I was out on my ear.

In those days, it was very unusual for someone of my age to be homeless. I don't suppose I was the only rebellious teenager to be turfed out of the parental home, but the usual thing was that some alternative home would have been arranged, either with a relative or a friend. Not me though. There I was, standing outside 20 Waltheof Avenue with no money and nowhere to go. Just me and me suitcase. I was really furious, and at that moment hated my parents and that cow of a sister and felt very much like chucking a brick through the window, but thought better of it.

I can't quite remember how it came about, but about an hour later, I was talking to my brother Arthur and his girlfriend Jesse at the end of the street, and he seemed quite concerned I recall, and bunged me a couple of quid, and advised me to go to the Church Army Hostel in Wood Green. I spent one night there, and that was enough.

The couple who ran the place were like something out of a Dickens novel, very stern and forbidding, rapping out the do's and don'ts just as if it was my first day in the nick. I was shown into a big room containing a number of beds - very Spartan, with the blankets folded as if it was a barrack room. There was no-one else about. "You can make your bed up", said the man, "Supper is at nine o'clock, lights out at ten".

I liked the idea of supper, as I was starving hungry, but I didn't reckon to the rest of it very much. I asked him a few questions, but he just ignored me - I think he must have just had a row with his dragon of a missus. You can say that I wasn't exactly made to feel welcome.

I was sitting in the lounge reading a paper, feeling very lonely, waiting for nine o'clock, when the door opened, and two youths walked in - scruffy looking buggers with close cropped hair. They looked at me curiously, and one of them said - "'Ello, you new?". I replied in the affirmative, and told them that I had just been chucked out, and asked them what sort of a place it was etc., and in the ensuing conversation, found out that nearly all of the blokes staying there, including themselves, were ex-borstal boys and young offenders.

Sitting down to supper, I felt really out of it and uncomfortable. There were about twenty of them, nearly all of them with that cropped hair, which in those days was a dead give-away for someone fresh out of borstal. Half of them were eighteen or nineteen years old - hard, nasty looking customers. There were also two or three boys who were obviously simple.

I lay in bed that night, listening to them all talking about thieving and fighting and maiming, and who had done what, and what they were going to do feeling very uncomfortable indeed. I woke up the next morning with everyone crashing and stamping about, looked at my watch, which said six o'clock, and just turned over and nodded off again. I woke up about an hour later, washed and dressed and went down to the dining room, which smelt very invitingly of frying bacon. There was no-one about, so I poked my head into the kitchen, and there was Wackford Squeers and his old lady sitting there drinking tea.

"Can I have some breakfast please?" I enquired. They looked at me as though I was insane.

"Breakfast's finished lad. Too late. We've got rules here. If you ain't on time, you go without. All right?". It did no good telling them that no-one had told me.

"You was told last night mister. Now then, you've to be out of here at eight thirty and not allowed back in till five o'clock".

It wasn't even eight o'clock yet. I went back to the dormitory, just in time to see my two erstwhile companions about to rifle through my suitcase, which they'd got from under the bed, said - "Thanks very much" - and took it from them and went downstairs, passing Wackford in the hall.

"Where you going?" he says.

"Off" - says I. Didn't even say goodbye.

What a nightmare of a place that was. But at least, I was able to walk out of it, and it was only when I was a lot older, with more experience of life, that I realised how lucky I was to have had the choice. I thought at the time what a nasty bunch of no-good losers those blokes were, and what sort of life was ahead of them. Then I thought about the fact that nearly all of them had been institutionalised from birth - orphanages and children's homes, years of mental and physical bullying and abuse, plus the influence of the older kids. All these sort of things must have shaped their characters, and led them to approved schools and borstals, and inevitably the nick. When I look back now, I feel sorry for them, and all those like them. I'm in no doubt that some orphanages, even most of them, are very nice places, and do a very good job of bringing children up, and giving them a good start in life. But these chaps were the unlucky ones. It wasn't really their fault. They were just surviving.

I sat in a cafe that morning, cheering myself up with a very large breakfast, and decided that as soon as I could, I'd head north to Buckingham. That was where Pip, my sister-in-law lived, Frank being away in Singapore working for the Government at something or other. He had a very good position with the Civilian Inspectorate of REME as far as I remember, but I was never sure what he actually did.

That evening, I went with Ken and Alby to a school in Wood Green where the 4/6th Middlesex cadet band practised. They were all mates of ours, and a very good band indeed, nearly as good as us, and we were thinking of joining. I got talking to their solo drummer, a nice bloke called Emmy (short for Emlyn) Harris, and he said that if I liked, I could go home with him, as his mum took in lodgers, and he'd have no trouble in talking her into taking me in. Good old Emmy.

His mum was a very nice lady, and made me very welcome, and I was to spend the next couple of weeks with them in their house in South

Tottenham. I was able to pay my way well enough, as I had collected my wages and holiday money from Pinders. Both the brothers were very understanding, and said that I could go back there any time I wanted, and we parted on the best of terms.

I shared a room with Emmy, and laying in bed that first night he came out with an idea that for some reason, I hadn't thought of myself. Why not have a go at joining the Merchant Navy? "Now there's a thought" I said. It was too, and it would solve all my problems. Emmy had been thinking of it for some time, and had a couple of mates who had joined and trained as stewards, and were working on one of the big liners. The more we talked, and the more I heard about what a great time his mates were having, the keener I became.

A few days later, Emmy and I were on our way to Leadenhall Street to have our medical. We were happy and excited, thinking about Tangiers and Lisbon and Rio De Janiro, and shagging all the women tourists and suchlike, and couldn't see any reason why we wouldn't be accepted. We had an interview, then an intelligence test, and finally the medical. The very last thing to be tested were my eyes. First the left one. I didn't only read the bottom line, I read the makers name and address underneath it. Then the right eye.......Nothing....

"Can't you read the top line?" asked the doctor.

"I can't even see the card" I answered, and explained that I had been born with a squint etc.

"I'm sorry son, somebody should have told you. You need two good eyes to get in the Merchant Service".

"But I only want to be a steward" I said.

"Sorry son. It's a very strict rule. No exceptions".

That was a very miserable ride home from Leadenhall Street. I don't mind admitting that I was close to tears. Emmy had sailed through the medical and signed all the forms, and for him, it was just a question of waiting for the confirmation, but good fellow that he was, he was nearly as unhappy as me that I had dipped out. Whether he went in the Merchant Navy or not, I can't tell you, because shortly after, I headed north, and I never met Emmy again. Nice bloke though, and I hope it all went well with him.

BUCKINGHAM

I wasn't in Buckingham for very long - a couple of weeks or so, but it was a very happy visit. Pip, my sister-in-law was, and still is, one of my favourite people. Astonishingly pretty, with jet black hair and huge brown eyes and a beautiful figure. She was also as nice as she looked, and we had always got on well even though I was nothing like Frank in any way. She was a lady, and spoke like one, whereas I was a bit of a young cockney yob, but I was always able to make her laugh, and she had always had a lot of time for me. She lived in her mother's house in the centre of Buckingham, and a nice old house it was too, smelling of apples and floor polish. Her mother, Mrs Beck, was a nice old lady with a country accent, and was always saying "Joost saw", which was Yorkshire for "Just so". I liked old Mrs Beck. Then there were my two little nephews. They were lovely little boys - Chris was still a toddler, and Peter was just a baby.

·We went for lots of long walks, myself, Pip and the boys, taking it in turn to push the pram, or carry Christopher when he got tired. The sun shone for most of my time there, and a couple of times we went into the grounds of Stowe School, and I remember walking along this long tree lined avenue, with that beautiful building at the end of it. It was during a school holiday, and we had the whole place to ourselves, and we went swimming in the lake, which was in the school grounds. That's always stayed with me, the feel of that smooth cool water, so very different to a swimming baths or the sea. I always loved swimming in fresh water - lakes, rivers and canals. Nothing like it. That was long before it got to be very unhealthy because of that bloody Wyle's disease and pollution. But I'll always remember Stowe lake with Pip and the boys, and that silky water....... Magic.

Pip and I talked for hours, and I told her all my troubles and feelings about things in general, and she was very kind and understanding. It was so refreshing to be with an intelligent adult who actually listened. A very new experience for me, and a very valuable one, because that short time in Buckingham sort of re-charged my batteries, and I left there a much happier person, with a lot more confidence. I couldn't stay there on a permanent basis, because there wasn't the room, so Pip had written to Ivy and arranged for me to go there. But dear Pip earned my eternal gratitude.

Pip

Frank

Pip became an authoress, writing under her maiden name -..Pip Beck. She wrote - 'A WAAF IN BOMBER COMMAND' - about her experiences as an R/T operator during the war, and if you want to see what she looked like, the book has her picture on the back cover. 'Leo' is my brother Frank by the way. His second name is Leonard, and whilst in the RAF, where they met, he was known as Leo. I've never heard Pip call him anything else but 'Brim'.

. . . .

LICHFIELD

Ivy and Tiny lived in a farmhouse just outside Shenstone, a little village between Lichfield and Walsall. When I got there, just a couple of fields away, the Midlands television transmitter mast was being built - the very first one since Alexandra Palace. Their's was the nearest house to it, and over the next few months we watched it climbing, pencil slim, up into the sky, higher and higher. Tiny explained that they wouldn't finish it until it would be possible to see the top of the Ally Pally mast over the curve of the earth, as television waves travel in a straight line and don't bounce back down from the Heaviside Layer like radio waves do. I told him about that conversation years before, when we were queuing up to see 'The Sea Hawk', and imagining how good it would be to all have our own little cinema. It was all coming true.

Ivy and I had always been very close and Tiny was an absolute diamond, so I was very happy to be there, and they made me very welcome. Their first child, my little niece Jenny, was brand new then, just a few weeks old, and I remember that she used to howl all day, and most of the night - at least for the few weeks I was there.

My sister had met Tiny during her service in the Land Army. He was working as a labourer on the same farm, although he came from a very good family, and was very well educated. The reason for him being there was that he was a conscientious objector, which in the climate of attitudes in those days meant the lowest of the low. They had to put up with an awful lot, despite even the more intelligent knowing full well that it took enormous courage and will for them to follow their convictions.

Howard Bailey was my brother-in-law's name, and he was a very big, well built and handsome bloke - hence his nick-name - Tiny. He was a lovely man who exuded a quiet strength and dignity, and I never heard him say a bad word about anybody or anything. He was a Christadelphian, as were all his family. Every conscientious objector had to be examined by a tribunal during the war, interrogated at great length as to their reasons for not being prepared to fight, and a very tough tribunal it was, with many of the objectors being treated very harshly, quite a few of them ending up in prison. In Tiny's case however, it just meant establishing the fact that he was a Christadelphian, and had been one all his life. Pacifism is one of the most important aspects of their faith, and the tribunal knew it, so all lifelong members of the sect weren't treated too badly, nearly all of them being directed to work on the land, albeit in very menial occupations. That's how he and Ivy met, when he used to pick her and the other land girls up to take them to work.

Apparently, all the girls used to fancy him no end, and there was great competition every morning to be the one sitting next to him in the cab. Ivy said that they used to drive him mad, as he was very straight-laced and English, and all the flirting used to frighten the life out of him. At that time, she was eighteen and he was twenty-four. She told me that because she didn't come on too strong, like all the others, they became friends - nothing more, because she was otherwise enamoured. She broke her engagement with Kinney just after the war, and eventually, she and Tiny got it together, and they married in 1948. After the war, he went back to his very good executive position with the 'Farmer and Stockbreeder' magazine, and had a very successful career.

I had to watch my language during my stay there, having to very quickly drop my habit of saying 'Christ Almighty', as the old bit about taking the Lords name in vain was very strictly adhered to. But Tiny was not what you'd call a 'Holy Joe', and never tried to preach or 'give me the word'. Great bloke to talk to, with a lovely sense of humour. It was curious that although he was deeply religious, he told me once that he thought that Easter was a load of cobblers. I don't mean the Resurrection and all that - of course he a great believer in the biblical version. He meant the word 'Easter' and the Easter egg, and the Easter bunny and the rest of it. He told me that it came from the old pagan times, and that Astarte was the goddess of fertility, and those randy old priests weren't going to give all that up just because they had embraced Christianity. That's why Easter is celebrated in the Spring, the same time as the old feast of Astarte.

You live and learn.

. . . .

The first job I had up there was in a laundry in Lichfield. To tell you the truth, I went there because that was where all the girls worked. I stuck out like a sore thumb, because I was the only cockney in the town, and immediately acquired the nick-name 'Smoky'. They used to crack up at my accent, and I like to think that I was quite popular with everyone, and for my part, I liked all of them, especially the girls. I was quite happy for the couple of months I was there, but I'm afraid the old dislike of authority once more led to the inevitable clash followed by departure.

It was quite a big laundry, employing about a hundred people, and it was owned by this little fat, bald bloke who used to strut about the place in a purple boilersuit. I'm not making it up. A purple boilersuit for Christ sake! He'd change out of his suit twice a day, each morning and afternoon and do his rounds. He was such a pompous little sod too, a city alderman and ex-mayor. Talk about drunk with power. I thought it was hilarious. But they all seemed to be in awe of him, and some of them would actually go as far as touching their forelocks, straightening up and shouting 'Good morning Mr ---' as he went by. It's hard to imagine now, but out in the shires, the old class structure was still very much intact, and they deferred to their 'betters' without question. They regarded him as their superior, and he definitely treated all of us as inferiors. But not me matey. Londoners are as good as any bugger, and all that bowing and scraping had long gone as far as we were concerned. He cut such a ridiculous figure in that bloody get up, and I christened him 'The Plum'. I'd say - "Look out Harry - put yer cap on straight - here comes 'the Plum", and they would be doing their best not to laugh as they touched their fore-locks, because I would be behind him pulling faces and making rude gestures. They all called him 'Sir' as well, as a matter of course. Amazing.

I think I can say that I was an observer of the very last vestiges of feudal England.

I'd been there a couple of months or so, and had settled into the teenage society in Lichfield, and made some good mates at the youth club, as well as becoming quite popular with a few of the prettier girls. I missed my pals in London of course, but I was not at all homesick, and I enjoyed my time in the Midlands. I can say that in my opinion, based at the time of writing, on thirty years of continual travel around Britain, that the nicest, warmest and most friendly people in the country are those that live within about a twenty mile radius of Birmingham. I did my various jobs at the laundry quite willingly and well, and would have been quite content to stay there, but one afternoon, I was busy helping Harry loading up one of the huge dryers, when along came 'the Plum'. I grinned and said - "TenSHUN" as Harry automatically straightened up, and carried on working. The Plum tapped me on the shoulder and said all tight-lipped -

"Ah want a word with thee". I answered -

"What can I do for you mate?".

"Never moind about mate. Yow want to start showin' a bit of respect yow do. Now look 'ere. Ah want yow to start havin' a bit less to do with the lasses. D'y'ear?".

I thought he meant the girls in the laundry, as the foreman had already had a go at me for chatting them up while I was working. So I said

"Fair enough", but then the clown started on all to the effect that he meant not just in the laundry, but in the town as well. Being an alderman, and a figure of importance, and such was the old fashioned attitudes at that time and place, he thought that it was his duty to keep a patriarchal eye on the youth of the town. I couldn't believe what he was on about at first, and said -

"You what?". I must tell you that I had taken one of his nieces out a couple of times, but ditched her for someone else. Just normal teenage stuff.

"Yow 'eard me mister", he says and goes rambling on with more of the same, but I wasn't having any more of that and said -

"What I do in my own time has got fuck all to do with you mate". He spluttered and shouted -

"Down't yow swear at me. Yow may carry on loik yow are still in that Loondon sloom yow coom from, but yow ain't goin' to get away with it 'ere. Now go and git yow cards yow bloody gootersnipe!".

I hadn't lost my temper, in fact I thought it was really funny, and dropped the bundle of sheets I had been holding, and said -

"Open that lid Harry, I'm going to put him in - I'll give 'im bloody guttersnipe", and made a grab at him. I meant it too. He jumped back, and I actually chased him out of the drying room. Harry and the others in the room were crying with laughter, and one of them said -

"Oh moi Gawd - yow've doon it now Smoky". They were sorry to see me go, but I'm sure I made their day for them. And, I'm happy to say, he was ever afterwards known as 'the Plum'.

I wasn't worried about getting the tin tack, as I was getting a bit fed up and bored at the laundry, and anyway, there were plenty of jobs about. I used to pass the Lichfield Iron Foundry on my way to work, and for the past few days I had noticed this sign - 'Lad wanted - good wages'. 'That'll do me' I thought, and that's where I worked for the rest of my time in Lichfield.

. . . .

It was about the scruffiest, most run down old foundry in the Midlands - and the work was hard and dirty, but I loved it. It was like a big long corrugated iron shed, with the floor covered in a foot of black sand, which they used for making the moulds. Up one end was this ancient blast furnace - which I'm sure must have been there since the industrial revolution. I was put to work with this little chunky bloke called Harry Kedge, who was to become a great pal. He was only about five feet four tall, but he had muscles in his spit and shoulders like a barn door, and spoke with a black country accent so thick that I had a job to understand him for the first few days. His favourite expression was "Oo aw", which roughly translated means 'Oh yes'.

Our morning job was to break up scrap iron into pieces small enough to go into the furnace, as well as separating the pig iron ingots, and it all had to be done with sledge hammers. Luckily, I was very strong for my age because of all the weight training, but I could hardly lift my arms at the end of that first morning, as I'd never used a sledge hammer before. We then had to get inside the furnace and bust off all the slag from the walls, and then line it with about an inch of gannister clay. It was only a little furnace, like an upright cylinder, inside about six feet across and twelve feet high. All this time, the moulders - about a dozen of them - were busy making the actual moulds from wooden templates - all sorts of things, from big manhole covers to much smaller, more intricate castings. We would then fill the furnace with coke and fire up the gas jets till it was alight, then turn on the blast.

After about an hour or so, when it was white hot, Harry and I would start loading the little hoist with scrap and pig iron, and now and again, a shovelful of limestone, then press the button and watch it clamber up the side and drop the lot into the top. It was all really bloody hard work, but I used to treat it as though I was doing a training session, just as though I was in a gym, so the day used to go very quickly, more so because Harry Kedge and the moulders were all smashing blokes, every one of them a comic, so I fitted in very well, as I wasn't too bad in that department myself. It was a very happy place altogether, despite being so old and run down, with lots of holes in the roof, where the corrugated iron had rusted through.

The last hour of every day was the most interesting, and I never ever got tired of it. The furnace would be roaring away, with a blast of fire coming out of a hole in it's side, about six feet up, and after a time, it would start spitting out this white molten stuff. This was the slag, which was all the gunge and rust and stuff that had melted, and was actually floating on top of the pure molten iron, which had sunk to the bottom of the furnace. It looked like black glass when it cooled, and the whole area around the blast hole would look as though it was covered in cob-webs where the flying sparks of slag would stretch into threads. By this time, all the moulds would be ready, dotted all over the floor - various sized iron hoops filled with black sand, with holes in the top, waiting for the iron to be poured in. Up would trundle the one big cauldron, suspended on chains which ran along a girder in the ceiling, with a big crank wheel on the side, and that held about two tons of iron. It would be manoeuvred into the proper place, and then came the good part, and I'll never forget the first time I saw it.

The foreman, who all this time had been watching the slag hole and peering into the furnace through this little black glass window would get his long steel poker and dig out the plug, and a brilliant white stream of pure iron would cascade down the shoot and pour into the cauldron. When it was about half full, he would ram a plug of wet clay into the hole and the cauldron would rumble off along it's track, every so often stopping over one of the big moulds, while the wheel was spun, tipping it slowly over until the iron poured out into the mould, then on to the next one. The rest of the moulds would be filled from hand held pots - some big ones with the moulder on one side holding a double handle, because pouring was quite a skilled business on some of the moulds, and another bloke opposite holding the single bar. After a few weeks, I'd often be holding the single shank, and I used to love it - the blast of heat when we were catching the iron, then watching it being tipped very carefully, a drop in one hole and the smoke flying out of the others, then some in another hole, then back to the first, and so on, till the mould was full. The heat would be searing, even though your face would be about four feet from the pot because of the length of the handles, but it was all part of it, and somehow, it was very satisfying, like you were doing something very real and worth-while. I never got tired of it. When all the moulds were filled, the remaining iron was just tipped out of the furnace onto the floor, and we'd just break it up the next morning and mix it with the scrap, so nothing was ever wasted.

Of all the many jobs that I had, before I eventually found my raison d'etre as a folk singer, that was the one that I enjoyed the most. Dirty, hot, noisy and back-breaking as it was, there was something about it - difficult to explain - that made me feel good, finishing every day tired and dirty, but with a sense of having achieved something. I was fit and strong when I started there, but the first few days nearly killed me. I'm glad that I stuck it out, because soon, the blisters on my hands turned into callouses, and the stiff muscles eased, and I got even fitter and stronger. I used to eat like a horse, and sleep like a log, and I revelled in it. The day never seemed to drag, and the wit and humour flying about when we drank our tea - brewed up in tin cans on a coke fire, was a joy.

"What's black wi' a big white nob?". "What?". "A moulder oo's joost bin 'ome fer 'is dinner!".

Marvellous blokes.

It could also be a bit dangerous if you got careless. There were always sparks flying around when the furnace was tapped, and we all wore goggles. Molten iron just bounces off of you, but very occasionally, a bit will stick. I still have a scar on my right hand where a little globule popped up and landed on it while I was holding a shank. I was hopping up and down effing and blinding, much to the amusement of all present.

"Is that one of them Loondon dances then Smoky?".

Any iron left in the big cauldron was always tipped onto the floor. I'd been there a few weeks, and one of the moulders had just finished filling the last of the big moulds.

"Now then Smoky, tek it down to the end, and tip it oop", he says. So I start turning the chain that moved it along the girder, slowly walking along beside it till I got to the end of the shed, then spun the wheel and walked away. Now as I've mentioned, there were quite a few holes in the roof, and it had been raining, and there was this bloody great puddle right under the cauldron. Harry Kedge spotted this and yelled -

"Aw fook. LOOK AHT!!", and dived for cover dragging me with him. The rest followed suit while the giant pot slowly tipped over, no-one being brave enough to chance running over and grabbing the wheel. The molten iron started to drip out, then flow, down into the puddle. Jesus, what a performance! It was one of the best displays of pyrotechnics that you could ever wish to see, like a giant rocket, but upside down, with showers of molten iron sparks filling the foundry, and a banging and cracking like you've never heard. Really spectacular, and very noisy. When the last of the iron had gone, and the display was over, we all stood there, in the smoke and steam, laughing, more so because one of the older blokes who'd been in France in the '14 -'18 war said,

"Booger me, for a minute theer, I thought I woz back on the fookin' Salient!".

"Now thah won't be doin' that again will thah Smoky", the foreman said afterwards.

"Sorry, I didn't know Sam". He replied -

"That's O.K. No 'arm done". As he walked away he turned and grinned then said,

"It were good tho', wa'nt it".

. . . .

Soon after starting at the foundry, I moved into lodgings in Lichfield, to save on the travelling, although I always spent the weekends back in Shenstone. The couple who owned the house were called Rhoda and Len, quite cheerful, good natured people, but it can be said that Rhoda was not really much of a one for housework. In fact, the place was a bit of a slum, but none-the-less it was comfortable enough, and I settled in quite well.

I liked Rhoda and Len. She was a very chubby, scruffy lady and she wore the trousers without a doubt. Len was tall and skinny, with black hair and a moustache, and never went to work for all the time that I was staying with them. If they had been around twenty years later, I'm sure that they would have been beatniks. They both had a very ribald sense of humour, she having the dirtiest laugh that I've ever heard, and were forever asking me about my sex life. I'd get all spruced up to take a girl to the pictures, and Len would say -

"Now thah make sure ya give 'er one lad. Ah'm countin' on ya", and Rhoda would squawk out that laugh of hers. On my return I would be quizzed mercilessly -

"Did ya do it - coom on yer dirty little 'ound", and I'd laugh and say -
"Certainly not, she was a good gel".

"Ya lyin' booger. Look Rhoda - 'e's goin' all red!", and she'd start braying
and joining in the kidding. I'd be telling the truth though because those were
far more moral times, at least for teenagers.

There were three other lodgers, all Irish, and I had to share a room with
one of them, a quiet old fellow who never used two words when one would
do. He worked on the building, and was always in the boozer when it
opened, and stayed there till it shut. He'd come in, always unsteady, say
"God bless all here" and stagger up stairs. He used to wake up a couple of
times a night, and piddle into a quart beer bottle that he always kept under
the bed. He was harmless enough though. I don't remember much about the
other two.

. . . .

PADDY

We all meet people during our lives, who we are never going to forget. People
that enrich our time on this earth, and who will always be remembered with
real affection. I don't mean just good friends, although they certainly fall
into that category, I mean real characters. I'm consider myself very lucky, as
in my time, I've met about a dozen, and the first was Paddy.

Rhoda and Len were always on about him. This mad Irishmen who used to
appear out of nowhere every two years or so, and always stayed with them.
He was a merchant seamen, and they used to get postcards from him
occasionally, from all over the world. He was a legend in the town, always in
trouble, mostly for fighting, his opponents more often than not being irate
husbands or boyfriends. But everybody seemed to have a smile on their face
when he came up in the conversation, and he was obviously well liked by all
and sundry. He'd left Lichfield a bit sharpish at the end of his last visit, as
he'd hit a policeman, and he knew that there was a warrant out for his arrest.

I was having my tea when he turned up. He walked into the room, carrying a kitbag, dumped it on the floor, smiled and roared - "Well now me
lovely Len - how's de form?", this followed by a squawk of delight from
Rhoda, and lots of hugging and jumping around.

The best way to describe Paddy is to tell you that he was the dead spit of Brendan Behan, only bigger. He really was like the archetypal stage Irishman, with a beautiful Cork accent, and that charm and funny turn of speech that is peculiar to the Irish. He was something else, a fabulous character.

"And who's dis den?", meaning me. Len introduced us, and when he heard my accent he said - "Jasus, a cockney. How in the name of God did you end up here?". We hit it off very quickly, and he sat talking with us for about an hour, telling us about Canada where he'd just been, keeping us in stitches. Then he stood up and announced - "Ah well. Time to face the music". He meant that he had to go round the police station and sort out the business of his previous departure.

"Don't worry me love" he said to Rhoda who was very concerned - "It was ahl a mithundersthanding", went to the window, opened it, and yelled out into the street - "Come and git me coppers!", and roared with laughter, and walked out singing. He never took anything seriously. He spent that night in the nick, but was let out on bail the next day. He eventually got away with a fine and a binding over to keep the peace. I wasn't in the court, but I heard that he even had the magistrate smiling as he explained that he hadn't meant to hit the copper.

"I was meaning to tump another feller, but the silly sod got in the way, beggin' yer pardon yer honour, and any-way I didn't know he was a copper. He wasn't wearing his hat".

He disappeared after about six weeks, back to sea, but although I was only sixteen, he took a real shine to me, and we had some great times, and I learnt a lot from Paddy. He was very bright indeed, surprisingly well read, and a great talker, and I can tell you, he had a lot to talk about, having travelled such a lot. He had marvellous descriptive powers, and I never tired of listening to him. Mind you, he had that effect on everyone, especially the ladies. In all my life, I've never met anyone who could pull as good as Paddy, more often that not, other blokes wives, which was the cause of most of the trouble he was always in. He managed to avoid any strife in the six weeks or so that I knew him, mainly because of the binding over I suppose, although he sailed pretty close to the wind on a few occasions.

One evening, shortly after his arrival, he said to me - "I hear you're a bit of a swimmer Henry". He called me Henry, my second name, because he didn't like my first name. "Derek? God almighty what sort of a handle is dat.

Christ, yer parents must a' hated ya!'". I said that yes, I loved swimming, but that there was no pool in Lichfield.

"Ah, you're wrong there Henry". Now before he came, I'd heard Len mention that he would often go swimming in the canal, even in the winter. The upshot of it was that he talked me into going with him the very next morning. At first I said -

"Bugger that Paddy, it'll kill us", as it was by then winter. He laughed and said -

"Kill us my arse. It'll do yer good. You'll feel like a million dollars I'm tellin' ya". He woke me up at seven o'clock the next morning, and despite my protestations said - "Come on. Get your cossie", and turfed me out of bed. It was still dark, and bloody freezing, and there we were, walking to the canal with our cossies on under our overcoats, and there was actually hoar frost on the hedges and grass as we peeled off on the towpath. Paddy let out a whoop, ran and dived straight in, and came up with another shout of - "Jasus God almighty!" turned on his back and yelled - "Come on - it's lovely!". But I'm ashamed to say, that try as I might, I just couldn't do it, and stood there, blue with the cold, knees knocking and teeth chattering. He was only in the water for a minute or so, but I had already dressed by the time he came out. He towelled himself down saying -

"Ah Henry, ya don't know what yer missin'", laughing at my embarrassment. I laughed with him and said - "Sod that Paddy. You're a bloody lunatic". When we walked back over the fields, it was only just getting light, and I remember that we left a trail of footprints in the frost on the grass.

I've always regretted not doing it.

After a couple of weeks, Paddy ran out of money, so he did what he always did. Again, I'd heard about it from Rhoda and Len. It was quite simple really, so simple that very few people would have thought about it, but Paddy was the resourceful type who could find the simplest solutions to any problem. There was no way that he would ever work for anybody else, except on a ship, but he told me that there was always ways of making money honestly; it was just a question of using your loaf.   So he sold firewood.

There was a big furniture factory just outside Lichfield, always with a mountain of offcuts stacked up in the yard, which every now and again, they used to burn. So Paddy would hire a horse and cart from this bloke he knew, go round to the factory and fill up all these sacks he'd borrowed, also from a bloke he knew, and go round the street flogging the wood to the housewives, half a crown a sack. He used to make a fortune, about five pounds a day. He'd carry on until all the mountain of offcuts had disappeared and then turn it in, loaded with gold. Crafty bugger. It used to take him about a fortnight to clear the yard, ending up making about fifty quid, which was a lot of money in those days. It's a wonder that nobody else ever tried it, but nobody ever did, I suppose because of the fact that there were plenty of jobs about, coupled with the fact that few people had the nerve and cheek that Paddy had.

"Ya can give us a hand if yer loik Henry" he said to me one day, so I took a few days off, with the pretence of having the flu, (Paddy's idea), and went with him. I don't think I stopped laughing all the time I was helping him. Had a marvellous time. He very rarely failed to sell a sack of wood at any of the houses and it was an education to hear him get round the housewives.

"Missus, could you see yer way round to puttin' on da kittle and making a cup of tay. It's not for me you understand, but for dis poor boy here who's faint wid de cold, and mebbe you could make another cup for me auld horse, him bein' on his last legs. He was in de Grand National once ye know - came fifth!". Christ he had the blarney.

Of course, most of them knew him already, some of them rather well I noticed, and more than once I was left outside holding the horse for a half an hour or so. You know how most totters ring a bell when they go round the streets? Well, Paddy used to sing. I can still hear him ...
    "And the Auld Triangle - went jingle jangle -
    All along the banks - of the Royal Canal".

He had a terrific voice, and knew so many Irish songs, some of them really funny. Used to crack me up. It was that accent, and those sayings he used to come out with as well, but for my part, I used to make him laugh with my cockney accent, and I could hold my own at the joke telling. He went into hysterics once, when sitting on the cart, looking at the old horse's rear, I told him the one about the old Hansome cab driver in London, whose posh passenger was in a hurry.

"Use the whip driver" he says, "There's an extra sixpence if we get to my club in time for lunch".

"'E'll get you there guvnor, don't worry - no need for no whip". Half an hour later, the old horse is still plodding along.

"Use the whip driver - I'm in a hurry!". Same reply.

"For God's sake use the whip driver. Go on. Stick it up his arse!"

"I can't do that guvnor - oh no".

"Why not you fool?".

"Well, I'm saving that for Ludgate Hill!". He was giggling about that one all day.

"Ah Jasus Henry - where d'ya get 'em?".

He had his serious side too. For instance, when I told him about my mother, and how horrible she was, he said - "Now then, that's no way to talk. Ye should respect yer parents, especially your mother", and more to that effect, and that if she was touchy, then there was probably a reason for it.

"You see Henry, you've got to use your loaf. Bad tempered people are always unhappy people. D'ya have me now?" (He was always saying 'D'ya have me now'. It meant, 'do you understand'). Then he went on -

"People are unhappy because of circumstances ya see - things that have happened to them". I told him that yes, my mother had had a very hard life as a girl, but so had a lot of people, and they weren't all grumpy.

"Ah well, you're not talking about lots of other people are ye. You're talking about your own mother. Fock 'lots of other people'. They don't count. Just t'ink, and have a little bit of understanding Henry".

He was right of course. He went on to tell me that people are like mirrors - they react to how you treat them.

"Listen. Ya pass two fellers in the street. You smile at them and say 'Good day to ye mate'. The first one smiles back, and says 'And to you friend '. The second one looks at you as if ye was a bloody lunatic, then walks on without a word. Now then Henry. Which one would you choose to sit and have a drink with. Eh?. D'ya have me now?".

Quite a philosopher was Paddy, and I learnt such a lot from him. All of our characters are shaped by other people, initially our families, and then by acquaintances, and I know that he had a lot to do with shaping mine, despite knowing him for such a short time. Looking back, I think that one of the reasons he was so well liked, looking past all the charm and blarney, was that he was such a free spirit, avoiding any responsibility, going where he liked and doing what he liked, filling his life up and living it to the full. Ideally, that's how we'd all like to be, at least when we're young.

I asked him once - "You come out with all this stuff Paddy, always look at the other fellers point of view, never look for trouble, a koind werd is better'n a curse (taking off his accent) and all the rest of it. Well, how come you're always in the shit?". He considered the question for a moment or two, then grinned and said -

"Ah well now Henry, no-ones perfect. God knows, I've got me faults. I do like to follow the little major into battle (he meant shagging), and I must confess to a weakness for the odd drop of the auld electric soup (drinking), but I bear no malice to any creature for all that".

After spending a weekend at Shenstone, I went to work on the Monday morning, got back to the lodgings at teatime and Paddy had gone. I never saw him again. I'll never forget him, and he still pops into my head now and again, and I wonder what he's doing. Maybe holding court in a bar in Dallas, or perhaps Hong Kong, telling the tale, or just as likely shinning down a drainpipe with his trousers in his hand, or even flogging sacks of firewood in Murmansk.   I wouldn't put it past him.

"And de auld triangle - went jingle jangle -
Ahl along the banks - of the Royal Canal".

. . . .

I'd been away almost a year, just turned seventeen, and I had started to miss my mates and London. I wasn't exactly homesick - just at the stage where I fancied a change of scenery. My parents had been in touch with Ivy, and told her that I could go back if I wanted. I was in no hurry to do so to tell you the truth, but there occurred a sequence of events which made me decide that it would be best for me if I left Lichfield. I'd been happy at the foundry, enjoying the work, earning not a bad weekly wage, and as previously stated, I could not have been with a nicer set of work mates. Then, inevitably, came the fly in the ointment.

I don't remember his name, but he'd served his apprenticeship as a moulder at the foundry, and had just come back to work there after completing his National Service. He was a nasty, sarcastic big sod, very cocky and sure of himself, and he hated cockneys. Guess who he started to pick on? I'm glad to say that I was very popular with all the blokes, and Harry Kedge had become a really good pal, so he didn't have any allies, and being a good natured sort of bloke, I just rode all the piss taking, and the comments about all Londoners being crafty, slimy lowlifes, and gave as good as I got in the verbal department. After one exchange of pleasantries, he went so far as to threaten to punch my head in, to which I just replied "Yeah, I bet you would", and walked away, but I noticed Harry talking to him rather urgently afterwards. He'd said something to the effect that he should try picking on someone his own size, which I found quite amusing as Harry was a good foot shorter than him, but nobody, and I mean nobody would have been stupid enough to mix it with Mr Kedge. I told Harry that it was very nice of him, but I could fight my own battles thank you very much, although that was the last thing I wanted.

Well, came the day when it did boil over. I accidentally kicked his tea over while we were sitting around having a break, and he just lost it and went for me like a lunatic. He aimed a punch at me, which I dodged whereupon he grabbed me and tried to wrestle me to the floor. It wasn't a fight, more of a scuffle, as you can't exactly use good footwork when the floors covered in a foot of black sand. No actual punches were exchanged, we were just in this sort of clinch, then just as a couple of the blokes moved over to break it up, we sort of toppled over, me on top, and I heard this awful thud as his head hit the edge of one of the big steel moulding rings. He was out cold, with blood gushing out, obviously in a very bad way, and ten minutes later, he was in an ambulance. I was terrified, more so when I was sitting in a police car on my way to the nick very shortly afterwards. It had been reported as a matter of course, and as it had been a fight, I was being taken in for questioning.

They were two of the worst hours in my life. I was quaking, wondering if I'd get charged with GBH, or even manslaughter, sitting in this cell, with nobody bothering to tell me what was happening. It was a great relief when Sam, the foreman turned up. He had been in the hospital all that time, but had come straight round the nick on hearing I was there. He quickly sorted it, telling the inspector that it had been an accident, and that the other bloke had started it, and all to that effect. Also, the other fellow had come round in the hospital, and was just suffering from severe concussion, and was going to be OK. No fracture or anything, just a few stitches and a bad headache. He was back at work a week later, so I heard, but I'd left by then. I went to work the next day, and everybody was on my side, and said that it served him right. (Harry said - "It's a pity yow never killed the coont"), but never-the-less, I wasn't very happy about the situation, and would have given anything for it not to have happened.

That was one of the events that made up my mind to go home, but there was another.

Chapter 9

BACK TO TOTTENHAM

A few weeks before the disagreement in the foundry, I had left Rhoda and Len's, and moved into another digs. I had met my new landlady some time before, when I had a cup of tea in her house while helping Paddy sell his firewood, and although she was nearly twice my age, we had immediately struck up a friendship. She was a great laugh, and quite pretty, and I had met her a few times since when Paddy had taken me boozing, and on numerous occasions in the town. She was separated from her husband, waiting on a divorce, and had a steady boyfriend. She also took in lodgers, and one day told me that one of them was leaving, and that I could move in if I liked. Well, a change is as good as a rest, and it was much cleaner and more comfortable than Rhoda's, so I didn't have to be asked twice.

I won't go into any detail of my stay there. Suffice to say that my new landlady and I got on very well indeed, and even better after the other two lodgers had left, which was quite soon after I arrived. Her boyfriend was still in attendance, but he didn't live with her, as in those days, it just was not done for unmarried couples to co-habit. It was just about acceptable for me to live there, because I was a lodger, and not quite an adult, but there were still a few raised eyebrows and not a little gossip.

I didn't give a sod about that, and neither did she.

So that was the situation when this welfare bloke called round. I can't remember what his official function was, but because of the business with the police, and me being still a minor, a report had gone in and the wheels of bureaucracy had turned, and there was this nosey sod asking all these questions about why I had left home, and what the circumstances were, what were my intentions and all the rest of it. It probably wouldn't have happened in London, but Lichfield was only a little place, and like I have mentioned, I did rather stand out, especially now, and I've no doubt the business with 'the Plum' had not been forgotten, as well as being seen in the company of a reprobate like Paddy.

The man then starts giving me advice, really talking down to me as though I was some sort of naughty boy, but I cut him short, and reminded him that I had never been in any real trouble since I'd been in the town, and that the incident at the foundry had been a pure accident. I told him to stop talking down to me, and asked him what the fuck he was doing here anyway. I had started to get very annoyed, especially when he asked me if I realised how it must look, living alone in a house with a married woman at my age. Cheeky bastard. I got right up on my high horse and indignantly asked him what he was implying, and how dare he insult a lady's reputation like that?. This took him aback a bit, so much so that he actually apologised, and lamely explained that he was only doing his job, and that he only had my welfare in mind.

I finally got rid of him, and there was my landlady in the kitchen looking as though she'd been crying, holding a handkerchief to her eyes, but she had been listening at the door, all the while with the hanky stuck in her mouth to suppress her giggling. I put my arms round her and whispered in her ear -

"I'll have to watch myself with you - he reckons I'm in moral danger", and that started her off again, and then we both cracked up laughing.

She really was a great girl.

I've purposefully not mentioned her name, as it wouldn't be fair, but I remember her with affection, and I'm sure she'll always think kindly of me. All part of my growing up, and no harm done to anyone.

So, what with one thing and another; the foundry business, my landlady's increasingly suspicious boyfriend, plus the parochial attitudes of the time and place, I decided to end my exile. I'd enjoyed my time away from home. I like to think that I had left as a boy, and returned as a young man. It did me good.

. . . .

I've no clear recollections of my return to Tottenham. I've racked my brains, trying to think back, to no avail. I know that I did start to get on much better with my parents, but just as before, I very rarely spent any evenings at home. I even began to have the odd short conversation with June, but they were more polite than friendly. She was the same as me - always out, and she had become engaged to one of the acting set - a fellow called Ron Walsby, later to become well known as a T.V. producer.

Perhaps I can interrupt my narrative to tell you that despite all that I've told you about her, June and I, incredible as it may seem, became very close friends. This was a good few years later mind.

June married Ron Walsby, one of the show-biz set she mixed with. He did very well on the administrative side of things. She got to know all of the 'Goons', because he had a lot to do with their early television shows. 'A Show called Fred', and 'Idiot Weekly - Price Twopence'. She became Peter Sellar's private secretary, and did that job for four years. Liz Frazer was June's best friend, and it was due to her influence that Liz launched her career in the early Sellars films. It was my sister who persuaded Sellars to do his first big film - 'Up the Creek'. He had no interest in doing films, because, at that time, most people thought that the cinema would be extinct in the near future, as everybody had started buying T.V. sets, and it was very definitely here to stay. All this was in the early fifties. She'd read the script, after he'd binned it without even looking at it, and told him that it would be perfect for him. She actually had to talk him into reading it, but eventually he did. She told us that he started reading the part out loud and had the office in hysterics, and got more and more into it, and of course, the rest is history.

She eventually divorced Walsby, (citing a very famous lady as co-respondent), and remarried to Clive Davies, who was eight years younger than her, and they had her only child, Dilwyn. June seemed to undergo a complete personality change once she got away from the Luvvies, and lost all her snobbishness, and we eventually came to realise how alike we were, sharing the same irreverent sense of humour and an outlook of things in general. Of course, I had also altered by then, and wasn't that horrible little yob of a brother that I used to be, and I was a lot more responsible and adult by this time.

So, I grew to love my sister dearly, and we became close pals, and had some great laughs.

Who would have thought it?

. . . .

1950. Austerity was still around, but things had started to ease. The Welfare State was starting to work, rationing had all but disappeared, and there was a noticeable increase in the traffic, and the odd motor car parked in the side streets. Clothes were just as expensive, but a little less shoddy, and there was also a few extra spare bob in our pockets. We had two or three decent shirts instead of just the one. And if you wore a pair of brown suede shoes, people didn't necessarily call you a poof. I was re-united with my previous circle of friends, and it was a joy to be surrounded by the old cockney accent again -

back to the old familiar haunts - and that familiar smoky smell that was peculiar to London that I had never noticed before. It was nice to be called 'Del' or 'Brimo' again instead of 'Smokey', and to share in the relentless humour and street-wise ambience with mates that I had spent my childhood with.

It was good to be back.

Kenny, Alby, Billy and Freddy were all still at the same jobs. They thought it amazing that I had only had two in one year - "Bloody 'ell, you'll be going to church next!". There is however, the one big motivating reason for regular graft, and that is wages. I was as strong as a bull, and well used to hard physical work by now, so I spent the year before I went in the army labouring on building sites. Up and down ladders with a hod, shovelling sand and cement into the mixer - all of that, and I loved it, more so because the money was very good. I had no ambitions of any kind at the time - none of us had really, the reason being that, like all youths of our age, we knew that we would soon be spending two years in the forces. For my own part, I had this vague idea that I would start making my way in life when I'd finished my National Service, so sod it, I didn't mind what I did as long as the money was good. It wasn't exactly the right time to embark on a career was it? I think that most youths of my age shared that attitude, at least, those of us who had not stayed on at school.

All my friends had left the army cadets, but we still attended the youth clubs if we had nothing better to do - good places to hang out and have the odd game of snooker and table tennis. None of us played football or cricket, although we were all still ardent Spurs fans.

There was to be a big change in our leisure time however. All being healthy young seventeen year olds, and all being possessed of vigorous libidos, we quickly realised that the best place to meet girls was the dance hall.

And that meant 'The Royal'.

I came across a very accurate description of the Royal in a book called 'The Profession of Violence' by John Pearson. It's the story of the Kray twins, an excellent work, not only for the story of the twins rise and fall, but also for it's portrayal of the East End in those years. Let me quote:

'The Royal is still the one place in the East End where the young can meet, pick each other up and show off with impunity. A great barn of a place off the Kingsland Road, with brass and mahogany swing doors, and a facade that looks like mouldy marzipan, it usually boasts two separate bands, and the noise inside is deafening. In the early evening it is a ballroom, pure and simple, but when the pubs close it becomes something more. The noise increases, coloured spotlights flicker high above the crowd, and on hot, early summer nights, the Royal becomes a living showcase of the East End.'

The rest of Pearson's descriptions concerns the Krays, and how they took Dicky Morgan there when they went on the trot from the Army, but he also writes very accurately of the Royal being a 'tribal proving ground, where the self-appointed 'rulers' of the neighbourhood would make a ritual appearance like the young bloods of some primitive society', and 'sharp-eyed youths round the bar'.

Very good. Yes, if you were after a punch-up, the Royal was the place to go all right, and they usually broke out just as the place was closing, but you could just as easily stay out of them, and the very large majority of us did, and were quite content to be merely interested spectators. Girls were much more fun than fighting. None of our set were aggressive, (although we were just as 'sharp-eyed' as all those other nutters), and we steered clear of bother that year, except for the occasional barny at a party when we'd had too much to drink, but nothing serious, although for my part, I must confess to one notable encounter at the Wood Green Jazz club, but I didn't start that.

The Kray twins were a year younger than me, and were born in Hoxton, but moved to Bethnal Green, about half a mile away when they were little. I first came across them when I was about twelve, at the Repton boxing club, and knew them well enough to nod to. They were hard buggers when they were sixteen, but no harder than many others around at the time, this being before they became the hardest villains that the East End has ever known. In fact, as far as I remember, they were quite cheerful, always pulling strokes and playing tricks on people. They were always over the other side of the dance floor from us, with all the Jewish kids, and you'd often hear a loud out-break of laughter from that direction, and it was nearly always down to the twins. They had their own little team even then though, and one of them, a kid called Checker Berry, was a good friend of ours.

Here's a curious little fact: It was my wife Jeanny who, in 1992 said to me -

"Do you remember when I was sixteen, and we'd just met, and we used to all be sitting over one side of the Royal, and the Krays and their mates would all be over the other side by the bar. Well supposing someone had come and tapped us on the shoulder and said - 'Excuse me, this might surprise you, but one day, forty two years from now, you'll be sitting in a cinema, watching one of your children acting the part of one of those blokes over by the bar?'".

That's exactly what happened. Our Bobby was one of the gang in 'The Kray Twins' film. He acted the part of Gray, which is a fictitious name, the same as the Richardsons being called Mathiesons. I expect that was all done to avoid lawsuits, but we're fairly sure that our Bob was Checker.

What about that then?.

The Royal became almost the centre of our existence. We had been there before a few times, when we were fifteen, as they used to have dances for the younger fraternity on Saturday afternoons, but now we were fledgling adults, finally joining the grown-ups. We had some absolutely marvellous times there, learning the quickstep, fox-trot and waltz, then jiving, all to great music - Ted Heath, Ivor Kirchin, Matt Moore - big swing bands. Then the giant stage would revolve, and a smaller outfit would appear, the best of these being the Ray Ellington Quartet. Fabulous - like another world, a wonderland. All ponced up in our very best gear - drape jackets, peg-bottomed trousers, kipper ties, with brylcreamed hair, and reeking of after shave, sorting out the prettiest girls. It was so easy -

"Wanna dance love?", then that look you got from the girl, more often than not as if wondering where the psychiatric nurse that had brought you was, then the condescending nod as though she was doing you a big favour, and off you'd go, trying up your chat up lines, then getting the first smile. It was marvellous, and the youngsters of today - (sorry, I don't mean to seem like an old fart), who hop up and down with their partner three feet away to crap disco noise up near the pain level, will never know just how marvellous it all was.

It was a great learning process. The first time we got knocked back - the sniff, nose in the air and 'No thank you', and that accompanying giggle from the girl's friends was so embarrassing, and we'd stumble away, red faced and crushed.

"'Ow'd ya get on Del?".

"Daft cow - didn't reckon her much anyway".

Ken Handley

Terry Guyatt

Alby Dines

But we learned quickly and found that it always paid to be polite, and a refusal would be followed by a smile and a polite nod, and a wink at the gigglers, then an unhurried nonchalant departure, as though it was her hard luck.

We used to go every Friday and Saturday, and sometimes Sunday. Lots of little romances, because that was our main preoccupation, and I'd like a pound for every mile I've walked, taking girls home. The snogging on the doorsteps and the knee trembles, making dates for the pictures later next week.

Great times.

. . . .

There was a big jazz scene going on in the post war years. The best club in the neighbourhood was the Wood Green Jazz club, and we spent some enjoyable evenings there, listening and jiving to some of the best traditional bands in the world - Mick Mulligan, Humphry Lyttleton and Freddy Randall. Good trad jazz is just about the happiest, most foot stomping music in existence, and those days were the beginning of a life long love of it. I had an excellent collection of records by the time I went into the army: Turk Murphy, the Firehouse Five Plus Two, Kid Orey, Louis Armstrong, as well as the British bands. I never tired of them. Still haven't.

Bebop came on the scene at that time, and we sometimes went to a club in Tottenham and listen to Leon Roy. I never became a big fan of any modern jazz, except for the pianists, like Art Tatum and George Shearing, and I expect that was because I played piano myself. But we all liked listening to Leon Roy, and I can tell you that it was not his real name. I tried very hard to get off with his young sister, and had quite a few dances with her and I know I would have been all right, but for the fact that she already had a boy friend. Nice little girl she was.

Her name was Shani Wallace.

We had another soldier in our little platoon. His name was Terry Guyatt. I can't remember actually meeting Terry, although he assures me that it was at Risley Youth club when we were fifteen. He became a close friend, I think because we were very much on the same wavelength. A great comedian - he knew more jokes than any of us, and could see the funny side of everything, and he was very bright, and a great talker. Mind you, we were all like that come to think of it, so he fitted in quite well, but he was like me in that he used to have these crazes. When I first got to know him, he was a fanatical cyclist, and used to go on and on about gears and frames and time trials and the Tour de France with enormous enthusiasm. Then he took up Judo, and was just as enthusiastic about that, and it was all Koizumi, Yokotani and Eric Domini. Then it was something else, and so on, but I like people like that because that's the best way to fill your life up. Have a go at everything yourself. Do it.

Terry was also a good pianist, and the lucky sod had learned it properly, and could read music. He shared my love of Fats Waller, and taught me to play 'Ain't Misbehavin'' and 'Mean to me', also teaching me all about tenths with the left hand, but I really envied him, as it was a painstaking business learning those tunes parrot fashion, whereas he just had to go and buy the music. He is Godfather to my eldest son, Steve, and like Roy Sutton, is at the time of writing a retired headmaster, which again is to me, incredible, knowing what a scatty bugger he used to be when we were young. He is also a member of the Magic Circle.

Typical of Terry. Magic started as one of his crazes I've no doubt, but he must have worked at it with that enthusiasm of his until he reached a professional standard. Just like me with my guitar. So that's a good bit of advice for anyone. Don't just think - 'I wish I could do that'.

Do it.

. . . .

There must be many thousands of married couples who first met at the Tottenham Royal. Among these are Kenneth Handley, Albert Dines, Kenneth Goldstein, George Lemon, and - myself.

We were all standing on the edge of the dance floor, eyeing up the passing talent, when I spotted this gorgeous little bird with lovely curly red hair.

"Nice", I said.

"'Oo?", asked Alby. She'd disappeared in a clockwise direction by then, but when I spotted her as she came up our end again, I said -

"Her - the ginger one. Ain't she lovely?".

"Yeah - very nice".

"Must have some of that sir", says I, which was an expression current at the time, and meant that I would be doing my best to make her acquain-

Jeanny - aged 16

tance. One of the boys remarked to the effect that he knew her slightly. "Mystery, ain't she", he said. That wasn't a question, it was a statement. Now a mystery is a nice girl - nice in the sense that if you were after anything more than a kiss on her doorstep, then you would be very much out of luck.

"We'll see about that my old son", says I, cocky young sod that I was.

So, there was I, ten minutes later, dancing with this very pretty, quiet little number, chatting away like a good'un, and making her smile. I took her home that night and in the doorway of number 111, Love Lane, I must confess that I did try it on. Nothing too heavy, just a teenage fumble, which earned me a firm little knee in the nuts and a door slammed in my face. I remember walking home, bent slightly forward for the first few hundred yards thinking 'Bloody stroll on, there wasn't any need for that. Soddin' women'.

I don't think that anybody could have convinced me that one day, we would celebrate our ruby wedding.

I saw her a week later, and after a profuse apology, was grudgingly forgiven, and after a lot of hard work, persuaded her to let me walk her home again. ('Only if you keep your hands to yourself mate', which I did). So that was how I met Jeanny.

It was about this time that Alby had also got a fairly regular girlfriend, a cheerful forthright girl called Pamela Humphries, and their's was, to put it mildly, a very stormy relationship, and the cause of lots of mirth among the rest of us. Pam was very jealous, and Alby was always winding her up, dancing with other girls. He'd dance past us, with his hands firmly on the other girls bum, and give us his best sexual maniac's leer over her shoulder. Pam would just not see the joke, and the more we laughed, the more she got the hump, and on Alby's return, despite his cheerful grin, the sparks would really fly. They were always at it.

Poor old Pam was somewhat accident prone. For instance; she was a very good ballroom dancer, by far the best amongst our clique, and it was her ambition to dance with this heartthrob character who was just about the best dancer in the Royal. We used to call him 'The Wop'. She didn't know the bloke, but if she saw him while she was dancing, she'd really turn it on, trying to impress him. So one day, in between dances, here comes Rudolph Valentino, striding purposefully towards our little gathering. Pam gave a little squeak, and whispered to Jeanny -

"I think he's going to ask me to dance". Sure enough he did, and Pam rose to her feet, arm outstretched to our hero in the classical 'Come Dancing' pose, and off they swept with great style. They made four complete circuits of the Royal's huge dance floor, perfectly together, with all those complicated twiddles and hops. It was so beautiful. The trouble was, that the back of Pam's dress had got caught up in her knickers, and she was showing all her stocking tops and suspenders. We very nearly did ourselves injuries laughing, but she was so intent on what she was doing that she didn't notice. We could hear the cackles all round the floor as they twinkled past. On the fifth circuit, her dress had dropped down and everything was in order, and she returned breathless and happy at the end of the dance to find all of us red-eyed with laughing. The more she asked what the joke was, the more we giggled. No-one had the heart to tell her till later in the evening, and guess who told her? Yes, Alby, with great relish. Vesuvius wasn't in it.

I recall an occasion when Alby Dines announced that he'd learnt a new trick.

"Go on then", said Terry. Alby took a deep drag of his cigarette, then blew a thick stream of smoke out of just his right nostril.

"See - magic", he said smiling.

"That's brilliant - how d'ya do it" says Terry in astonishment.

"Ah've got a cold", says Alby.

It does me good to think back to those times, because it always makes me realise how lucky we are today. We were happy enough at the time mind, as all things are relative and it was much better than it had been. For instance, one of our mates, Billy Martin, had parents who were quite well off. We were round his house once, and he says - "Come and look at this". We followed him into the kitchen and there was this fridge, a huge great ivory coloured job with rounded edges, just like we'd seen in American films. We were awe-struck believe it or not, as it was the first one we'd ever seen. We raided it and scoffed a whole bowl of ice-cold stewed apple and custard. Don't suppose his mum was very pleased. We'd never tasted anything like it! I remember that we talked about it for weeks and told our other mates - "'Ere. Billy Martin's mum's only got a fridge ain't she! Just like in the pictures!".

I realise that this may seem a little trivial, but things like fridges are taken for granted now, and not even noticed. But I well remember how impressed we were at the time. Another instance - telephones. No-body had one - I mean nobody that we knew. Yet recently I was in Central Park in New York, and my son Bobby, when he fished his mobile out of his pocket, tapped a few buttons and was then talking to someone in his office in London. Ridiculous. Dick Tracey stuff.

These are just two instances, and there are many many more of course, but to repeat myself, thinking back to the old times does you good. Puts things in perspective.

. . . .

I often wonder what my grandchildren would think of 1950. I suppose it would be like us at the time being told about 1900. Hard to imagine those times - no cars, no aeroplanes, blokes still around who had fought in the Crimea and the Indian Mutiny. It's amazing how recent history appears when I can tell you that it is entirely possible for a veteran of the battle of Waterloo to have still been alive when my mother was a baby.

So, 1950..... For us working classes - no telephones, cars, TVs, washing machines, fridges. Our mothers still queued up at all the different counters for the weeks food. No supermarkets yet. No Chinese or Indian restaurants, no hot dogs, hamburgers or pizza, just fish and chips. Coffee was a dreadful concoction made from a spoonful of 'Camp', which very few people drank. Gay still meant happy, and homosexuality was still very much on the back burner, to us a rarity, and only ever cropping up in jokes. We all stood up at the end of the film when they always played 'God Save The King', and none of us would dream of not giving up our seat on the bus to a woman. That was automatic. No women's lib yet. Whenever there was a murder, it was a headline in the national papers. No drugs. None at all. Rape was extremely rare. I never met anyone who had been burgled or mugged. Children were sacred, and were perfectly safe playing in the parks, unsupervised.

A shirt still cost half a weeks wages, and when the collars frayed, we'd turn them. A suit was a hire purchase job, always carefully sponged and pressed, and hung up with mothballs in the pockets. Shoes still went to the cobblers. We all wore ties, and owned either an overcoat or a mackintosh. We all used either Brilliantine or Brylcream. Smartness was the fashion, for the girls too. The New Look was in vogue with skirts down to near the ankle, often worn with a drape jacket and platform shoes. No tights yet, and stockings were very expensive, ladders being carefully mended. They often set their hair with sugary water - no mousse or gel in those days, yet they invariably managed to look well groomed and smart.

No pop music or top twenty, and all the popular tunes of the day were sung and played by adults, and the explosion of teenage rock and roll, triggered off by Lonny Donnegan and Bill Haley was still a few years in the future. The only guitars we ever heard were Elton Hayes when he sang 'The Owl and the Pussycat', or Burl Ives doing 'Jimmy Crack Corn'.

The radio was still the main topic of conversation in the workplace at the morning tea break. The jokes from 'Educating Archy', (yes, a ventriloquist on the radio!), 'Take it from Here', and how was Dick Barton going to get out of his latest perilous situation, and the streets were nearly all empty during the weekly episode of 'Appointment with Fear'. Most people went to the cinema at least once a week, and more than half of the new films that we saw were still being made in black and white. Great films too, that have stood the test of time, and are still being shown today. The criminals never ever got away with it, and if a couple were seen in bed together, one of them had to have a foot touching the floor.

All that may sound a bit grey and cheerless, but it wasn't. Far from it. Things really were improving at quite a rapid pace, and the war had started to recede into the past, despite all the bomb sites, and so many men still wearing their old battledress blouses to work, often with a light patch where their stripes had been. The war clouds were gathering again however, as North Korea had invaded South Korea, and the embryonic United Nations had weighed in against the aggressor.

They had no choice.

Believe it or not, we couldn't wait to go into the forces. We were really looking forward to it, so much so, that Ken Handley, Alby and myself decided to join the Army as regulars. We wanted to be bandsmen, obviously, and it was our ambition to get into a Scots regiment, as drummers in a pipe band. So we set off for the recruiting office in Whitehall in great spirits, and returned a couple of hours later utterly dejected.

My bloody eye again. One of the many questions on the application form was about my eyesight, and I had to be truthful. So, there I am, sitting in the interview room with this recruiting officer, waiting patiently as he perused my application form. He finally looked up and said -

"Yes, everything seems to be in order, but you do realise that you won't be able to enlist in an infantry regiment don't you?".

He saw my look of disappointment and continued -

"Your eyesight son. Need two good eyes for the infantry. No problem though, if the rest of your medical is OK you'll be 2A (vision), and you'll be eligible to join any of the Corps, or the Royal Artillery".

That was that then. Just like that day when I tried to join the Merchant Navy, only worse. Alby and Ken were eligible, but they were as pissed off as I was because we didn't want to be split up. So during the miserable ride home, it was decided that they would enlist for five years, and I would do my two years National Service.

Shortly after all that, my two mates joined the Royal Fusiliers, by tradition, a cockney regiment, and a few months later were off to Korea, where they served for two years, and saw a lot of action. (Incidentally, Michael Caine, the actor was in their platoon). They say 'it's an ill wind etc.', and who knows?, my dodgy eye might well have saved me from getting my arse shot off, but I swear to God, I'd have given anything to have been with them.

We all remember our youth with nostalgia. I certainly do. We made the most of that year and had some great times, but I think that my memories are coloured by the fact that for all three of us, it was to be the last period of our lives when we would be single and free, with no responsibilities, although we didn't realise it at the time.

Just before Christmas, a brown envelope came through the letter box, addressed to me. Inside it was a railway warrant, and a letter telling me to report to Catterick Camp, Yorks, on the 18th January, 1951, to enlist in the Royal Corps of Signals.

'Could be worse' I thought.

. . . .

Ken and Alby embarking for Korea with The Royal Fusileers.
(Alby is third from the right in the top row. Kenny is immediately in front of him).

Chapter 10

THE ARMY RECRUIT

Catterick camp, North Yorkshire, sprawled over a huge area of moorland, and in 1951 was the training depot for the Royal Corps of Signals. Also here were squadrons of the Royal Tank Regiment, and the 17/21st Lancers, also an armoured regiment.

At that time, there were about twenty thousand living in the camp, the large majority of whom were trainee National Servicemen. For three horrible months, I was one of them.

I had been really looking forward to joining the Army. A good pal of mine, Ronny Rosher, an old schoolmate, was also joining the Signals, and I remember us being very happy as our train sped north, with me having been a cadet, reassuring Ronny that it would be a doddle, and excitedly discussing the possibility of ending up in Hong Kong or Egypt, or some such exotic location, as at that time the British Army was spread all over the world. It was a nice knowing that we'd each be doing our square-bashing with a mate - bit of luck that - and for me it certainly was lucky, as I couldn't have had a better friend to share that time with. Ronny was one of those calm placid types, who rarely let anything bother him, the opposite to me, and he was responsible for keeping me out of a lot more trouble than I was to get in. I like to think that I repaid him by helping him through his training, as I was already very fit, and as good at drill as most of the instructors, whereas Ronny was very soft when we first joined, and it came quite hard to him initially, but he finished up as good as anyone in the company.

Most ex-servicemen like to go on about how hard their training was, but I never do. It was hard all right, but to tell you the truth, I enjoyed the actual training, and I think that most of us did. We moaned about it of course, but that's a tradition, ingrained in the British soldier's character, but to tell you the truth, the parade ground and the assault course, the rifle range, route marching and the gymnasium, when we were actually training, doing something, was the best part of it. For one thing, it was the only time that we were ever warm.

I can't stand the bloody cold - never could, and that was one very hard winter, and the Yorkshire Moors are definitely not the place to be in those conditions. There was an intake of recruits every two weeks, and depending on your luck, you were either in a Vimy block, which were brick, three story buildings which were centrally heated, or the pre 1914 wooden annex huts - H shaped single story affairs - two long barrack rooms joined by the ablutions area. Each room had one single coke burning stove in the centre, and that was it. Central heating of a sort. Needless to say, we were in the latter for all the time that I was at Catterick.

That first evening found about thirty of us eighteen year olds in the barrack room, all gathered round a fierce looking Scots lance corporal, having our induction lecture. Earlier, we had been driven into the camp in a convoy of lorries, and clambered off and been chivvied into three ranks, about a hundred and fifty of us, and stood there for half an hour listening to the screaming drill instructors and the crash of boots, watching the squads of recruits being put through it.

"Sod this", whispered Ronny nervously, but I told him through the side of my mouth not to worry, as it was all familiar to me. We had our first Army meal, drew our bedding, and were taken to our billets, Ronny and I making sure we kept together. I recall that the sun was shining, and I'm pretty sure that was the last time it did while we were at Catterick.

We were a very mixed bunch. About half were Jocks, mostly from Glasgow, the rest from all parts of England, and Ronny and I were the only two from London. So there we were, still in our civilian clothes, some with drape jackets and peg bottom trousers, some with sports jackets and flannels, and a few very scruffy dosser types, all gathered round to hear the words of L/Cpl Buchanan.

Buchanan looked quite old to us. I suppose he must have been at least forty, and I wondered why he was still only a Lance Jack, as he was obviously an old soldier, with two rows of medal ribbons, but subsequently was to learn that he had once been a Company Sergeant Major in a Highland regiment, but had performed some dark deed or other in Egypt, been given eighteen months in the glass house and busted down to private, and transferred the Signals. He talked to us for about half an hour, giving us the form, telling us what we would be doing for the next three months, and he spoke in quite a kindly fashion. He then told us to ask him anything that we wanted to know, and chatted to us for about an hour or so, asking where we were from and our names and so on. 'What a nice bloke' we thought. Then he stood up and told us to stand by our beds.

"Right chaps. A couple more things. Ye'll be meeting your troop Sergeant and the company commander tomorrow. They are both evil bastards, and ah'm even WORSE!" - the last with a shout that made a few of the blokes visibly hop in the air an inch or two.

"Now get tae ATTENTION". He walked along the aisle pushing shoulders back and kicking heels together.

"Noo then. Tomorrow we start turning ye from a shower of shite intae SODJERS!. Ya Sergeant is Jesus, ya officer is God, and ah'm even fuckin' HIGHER!. Noo then. When ah say 'Guid Night', ah want yez all to shout 'Guid night Corporal'. OK?". There was a muted murmur of assent, and Buchanan strutted to the doorway of his little room at the end of the block. He turned and shouted - "GUID NIGHT". There was another muted murmur.

"WHIT THAE FUCK WAS THAT", he yelled. "AH SAID 'GUID NIGHT'!". There was a much louder response.

"Tha's better. Get yersel a guid nights sleep. Ye'll be needin' it. Lights oot in fifteen minutes. After that, no talkin', no smokin, and no pullin' yer puddin's. See ye in the morning. Guid night".

"GOOD NIGHT CORPORAL" we all shouted.

We made up our beds and smoked our final fags of the day, all chatting away about the days events, then 'pop' the lights went out and we slid between the sheets, listening to the mournful sound of the bugle playing the last call of the day.

Now it takes all sorts doesn't it, and naturally there was a diversity of characters laying there in the dark, wondering what the morrow would bring - streetwise lads from the Gorbals, London, Newcastle and Liverpool, country boys from the various Shires, as well as two ex public schoolboys. Most of them had never been away from home before, and I had already noticed that a few of them winced every time that they heard the 'F' word. So I shouldn't have been all that surprised when, after hearing a sort of urgent whispering, I sat up and saw, lit up by a faint shaft of moonlight coming through the window, a youth kneeling beside his bed saying his prayers.

Buchanan's door opened and there he stood, in pyjama bottoms and singlet, a paperback clutched in his hand, giving us one final look round. He spotted the kneeling supplicant.

"Hey yew - Christopher Robin. Get tae fuck intae yer pit, afore ah skelp ye!".

We were very lucky in having Buchanan as our instructor. Most of the instructors at Catterick were regular soldiers, who had been through the war, and they all seemed to have a vitriolic hatred of National Servicemen, and were all utter bastards, and that included our troop sergeant. Buchanan was also a bastard, and there were times in the next few weeks when we hated his guts, and would have cheerfully killed him, but he did have a sense of humour, unlike the sergeant, and he knew his job, and was more like a very strict uncle to us all, being so much older, and most of us actually liked him by the time we left basic training. A lance corporal is the lowest rank of NCO, just one up from a private, or in our case, signalman, but in a training regiment as an instructor, he is very powerful. He lives with you, and is constantly present, on your back all the time. Buchanan was hard on us all right, and would stand no nonsense, but he wasn't a nasty sadistic bastard like some of the other lads had to put up with. The worst of all these strangely enough, were the young National Service lance jacks.

The first day wasn't too bad, just frenetic. Drawing our kit, and there seemed to be an awful lot of it, getting our hair cut, (a traumatic experience for most of us), having another medical, being shown how to fold our blankets and lay out everything for inspection - all that sort of thing. All this after being woken up at 5.30 by Buchanan screaming - "GEDDUP GEDDUP GEDDUP" while smashing the metal lockers with a stick. A few were a bit too slow for his liking, and they were unceremoniously tipped neck and crop onto the floor, mattress and all. I was one of these.

It was a very long day, with no rest in the evening as we were put to shining our brasses and boots, and being shown how to apply khaki blanco to our webbing and packs. We met our bastard of a sergeant in the afternoon, paraded in three ranks in our brand new denims, standing there in a freezing drizzle while we were given a far less kindly induction lecture than the one we'd had the previous evening. He gave us our first drill, which was no more than standing to attention, stand at ease and stand easy.

"TEEEEN-SHUN" he screamed. This was followed by a desultory and spasmodic clatter of boots on tarmac. He stood there, ramrod straight with his pace stick under his arm, threw back his head shut his eyes and screamed - "AAAAAAAAARGH!!". It was obvious to all that he wasn't pleased.

"STAND AT - EASE!", the last word a yelp like a dog when it's paw's been trodden on. Again that dreadful pitter patter, and a repeat of that howl of anguish.

"Oh, I do hope you're not all taking the piss. Let's try again shall we -

TEEEEN - SHUN!".

It improved a little after about a quarter of an hour, after which he favoured us all with a withering sneer, turned on his heels and strode off, shouting over his shoulder -

"Take them away Jock for fucks sake". Do you know, I can't for the life of me remember his name, but there you are, they say that the mind blanks out painful memories. We were to see a lot more of that gentleman during the next few weeks.

For all that, I've had worse days, and I was better equipped than most, as I was used to blancoing and polishing, as were a few others who had been Army cadets. Buchanan had sorted that out from the beginning, and got us to help him show the others. All that first evening was spent in showing them how to use a button stick, and burning the toe caps with lighted polish to get rid of the bumps, then rubbing spit and polish in with a tooth brush handle. Also, some of the lads had never used an iron in their lives. "Ye've not got yer wee Mammy here with ye noo son", said Buchanan. Just before lights out, one of the boys asked if he could have another blanket.

"Oh, are ye cold son?" asked Buchanan, in quite a concerned kindly manner. It was bloody cold too, even for those lucky enough to be next to the stove. The lad replied in the affirmative, whereupon Buchanan, addressing us all in the same pleasant way, asked if anyone else was cold. There was a chorus of assent from all corners of the barrack room, whereupon in the same quiet nice way, our corporal requested us to get into our PT kit, as quickly as possible.

"Cold are ye?. Right, ah'll warm yez all up. OOTSIDE - THE SODDIN' LOT OF YA!"

He doubled us round that bloody parade ground till at least half a dozen had dropped out holding their sides with the stitch, then formed us all up and made us do twenty press-ups.

All by the light of the moon.   Bastard.

. . . .

I fell foul of authority the very next day. We'd had a very hectic time of it, drilling and PT, getting doubled around and shouted at - usual stuff, but the days training had at last come to an end, and I was walking back from the

mess at tea time, with just the evenings cleaning and polishing to look forward to. The novelty had already started to fade for all of us, and I was to
say the least, thoroughly pissed off. Then suddenly there was this short,
bespectacled lance jack, who only looked about sixteen, screaming at me.

"YOU - COME HERE ". I didn't think he meant me at first, and looked
round to see the object of his wrath, then there he was, his face about two
inches from mine yelling in my face.

"GET TO ATTENTION WHEN I'M TALKING TO YOU", - and pro-
ceeds to give me a dreadful mouthful, the reason being that I had one of my
hands in my pocket. He strutted round behind me, a favourite habit of drill
instructors, and shouted right in my ear to the effect that he would 'have me'
if ever he saw me doing it again. I said 'yeah, right', and walked away, which
rendered him into a state of incandescence, and it all started again.

"ONE OF THEM COCKNEY CLEVER DICK HARD CASES ARE
YOU? WELL, I'M HARDER THAN YOU ARE SON!". He called me son.
Well, I'd had enough of our dear Buchanan that day, and anyway, he was
nothing to do with our squad, so I told him "Bollocks" and walked away
again, with him snapping at my heels like a little dog.

"STAND STILL!" he's screamed, but I told him to piss off before he got
his arse kicked, and continued on my way. It was a very silly thing to do, but
one thing I did know was that they very rarely put anyone on a charge in the
first two weeks - you'd have to do something really bad like chinning an
NCO or going absent for them to go that far.

So I'm back in the barrack room for about five minutes, when in comes
that little bastard with Buchanan and two very large regimental policemen,
and I was doubled over to the guardroom and put in a cell. I got the mother and father of all bollockings from our sergeant, then another one from the
officer, all to the effect that my card was well and truly marked, and the
Army had ways of dealing with troublemakers and all the rest of it and then
they let me go back to the barrack room. I wasn't charged, but might just as
well have been, because I had to report to the guardroom in full FSMO at
five o'clock for the next three mornings, and again in the evenings. Field
Service Marching Order means everything - best uniform, greatcoat and
webbing, with all your kit in it. Everything, shirts, socks, underwear, all neatly folded, and every little bit of it was inspected by the Provost Sergeant. It
may not sound much, but it bloody well is, especially when your day is so full
anyway. I could never stand anyone shouting in my ear, but it is something
that you have to put up with in the Army. During the next two years, I was

to fill up two blue charge sheets, nearly all of my grief coming from insubordination. Me and my big mouth. But you'll never beat 'em.

Fortunately, I was a very good recruit, as far as drill, weapons training, PT and all the other things that are asked of us in training are concerned, and I have to thank my time in the cadets for that, plus being already very fit. Some of our squad, chaps who had come into the Army very unfit, or with two left feet, had a dreadful time of it, and Buchanan made their life hell. That first month was murder, but as I have previously stated, it wasn't the actual training that was the bad part of it. It was all the rest of it.

For a start there was the cold. We used to sit on our beds all evening, bulling our kit, which was inspected each morning, with a blanket round our shoulders trying to keep warm. We'd come off the assault course, or a route march, soaking wet, then change into PT kit for an hours hard physical training, then have to drag on our wet, freezing cold denims for more drill. Cold makes you miserable.

Then there was the queuing. For some reason or another, we were always queuing, meals, lectures, at the stores, the NAAFI, always in the bloody cold wind, and often in a drizzle or sleet. The mealtimes were the worst, standing in a queue which was sometimes fifty yards long, often for as long as a half an hour, waiting for the previous sitting to finish, then having to bolt our meal down quickly in time for the next parade.

The very worst thing of all was the food. Now I may seem to be coming across as a bit of a moaner, but before I go on, I can tell you that while I was at Catterick, there were three suicides, poor desperate bastards who could not take it, and the whole business came to a head because of a question that was addressed in the House of Commons, as to the severity of conditions at Catterick Camp.

There were two incidents that triggered this off. One of these became known as "The Jones Case".

If a soldier was really dirty, and it must be realised that in a camp holding twenty thousand, there were blokes pulled into the Army who had never had a bath in their lives. It takes all sorts, and it was just the way the poor buggers had been brought up, be it on a remote farm, or an urban slum, with unhygenic parents. Not their fault really. But if one of these boys persisted in being manky, he was given just so many warnings, and if these were ignored he was scrubbed. Outside, stripped naked, with two NCOs using a hose pipe and yard-brooms. It was an old Army custom, rarely employed, but never-the-less still practised in some training camps, and then only if the NCOs were really nasty bastards. That's what happened to that poor Jones fellow - in midwinter. He caught pneumonia and died. It had happened, as far as I remember, just before I got there. Naturally, there was an awful stink, and people had started to ask questions about Catterick.

The second incident concerned the food, and I was there when it happened.

Being all young healthy lads, and expending an enormous amount of energy, it will come as no surprise when I tell you that we were always ravenously hungry. We'd eat anything that was edible. The trouble was, that often, the food was so bad, that - hungry as we were, we couldn't eat it. Breakfast wasn't too bad, it would take a genius to ruin porridge, but often the rest of it was half cooked, but we'd still wolf it down. The dinners however, were dreadful, barely edible most of the time. At least once a day, the orderly officer inspected the mess at mealtimes, with the R.S.M. and the orderly sergeant in tow, stopping at the end of every table and asking "Any complaints". But we soon learned that it was best to keep our mouths shut, otherwise you'd be peeling spuds all that evening. This particular day, we were surprised to find that there was no queue outside the mess at dinnertime. We soon found out why. The dinner consisted of boiled fish, potatoes and greens. The fish was half raw, and cold, the potatoes had been boiled without any salt, but worst of all was the greens, which had not been washed, and we could feel the dirt scrunching in our teeth. The buzz had already gone round that nobody was going to eat that shit, and everybody had dumped it, so we did the same.

Outside every Army mess, there used to be three large metal basins full of boiling water. Wash, rinse and sterilise. In training, we were all issued with our own tin plates. There were also the dustbins for any unfinished food. When we got outside, these were all full and overflowing where everyone had dumped that awful dinner, and all round them was a growing mountain of fish, spuds and greens. And dirt. We just slung ours on top of it, washed, rinsed and sterilised our plates, and went back to our barrack room. And so did everybody else in our battalion that day. We heard that the sergeant cook got busted to private, and posted, and all the other cooks were charged, and after that, there was a definite improvement, but even so, it was still nothing to write home about. But at least you could eat it. Word got out however, and what with that, and the Jones incident, and the suicides, they did lighten up a little bit, but unfortunately, that was after I had left Catterick.

We were unlucky, being there through the worst part of the winter. I dare say it would not have been half so bad if we'd done our training in the sunshine. It got dark so early too, about four o'clock, which somehow made the days seem endless. After a couple of weeks, it seemed as though we'd been there for months, and all memory of home had started to fade. Two more bloody years to go.

Fortunately, they were a good bunch of blokes in our hut, and there was very little friction. All in the shit together with a common enemy - the Army - has that effect. We started to harden up, physically and mentally, and those boys who went scarlet if they heard any naughty words were soon effing and blinding with the rest of us. We had good reason to, on many occasions, such as being woken up at three o'clock in the morning, all the lights going on, and Buchanan bashing the lockers with his stick, then being made to stand by our beds, sometimes in battledress, sometimes PT kit, all to shouts of "COME ON - COME ON, MOVE YERSELVES", then after a cursory inspection being allowed to get back into our nice warm pits. For no reason. In fact there were many times when we had to do really stupid unnecessary things for no reason, but that is the way of the British Army. They make life very uncomfortable for recruits.

But there is a reason.

None of us realised it at the time. Remember, we were all conscripts, not volunteers, which added to our resentment, but I eventually came to see, a good few years on, that all that relentless bullshit and discomfort is what makes the British Army so effective when it has to come down to the nitty gritty. The American Army for instance, went through a really savage indoctrination as far as the actual training went. Their NCOs were worse than ours, real brutal bastards. But they always had the best food and living conditions. They knew they'd be going back to steaks and ice cream, hot showers and comfortable living conditions, and had plenty of money for cigarettes and other small luxuries. Like training for a football match. But when it comes down to it they always seem to fuck up, because the real thing is not like that.

It's nothing to do with guts. The average Yank has got as much courage as anyone, but because of the aforementioned reasons, plus a poor relationship between the men and their officers and NCOs, the whole thing so often goes dreadfully wrong, Vietnam being the prime example. Superbly fit blokes, plenty of guts, with the very best equipment, plus armour and a very good air force get their arses kicked by a lot of little brown blokes with little more than small arms, and shoes made out of old car tyres.

In Korea, Alby and Ken told me that if you were to see them at the leave centres, they all looked older, mean tough sods who you wouldn't like to get into a brawl with, all crew cuts and muscles, not to be trifled with. They also told me that they were the least effective of all the UN forces that were serving there. A division of Chinese went through an American Army as though they weren't there, but were stopped dead by a battalion of Gloucesters and a company of Argylls, mostly youngsters with pimples and bolt action rifles, which we were still using at the time. That was the battle of the Hook. It's hard to pin down the reasons. In the First World War, they were brilliant, luckily for us, but they didn't come into the actual fighting until the last few months. They were fresh, well trained and well equipped, did a great job, and fought very well, and really bailed us out, but could they have slogged it out in the trenches for four years, and undergone that awful privation and discomfort?. Forty years later, Patton's tanks did a great job, and they were superb against the Japanese in the Pacific, but they still lost far more men than was necessary. I think it's all summed up by what an ex-GI, a veteran of Vietnam told me, when he said that the most used phrase over there, a sort of Army motto was - 'Fuck you Captain'. In the British Army, you do what you're told, instantly, right or wrong. You may think it, but you would never say it. No-one likes being on the other end of that rigid discipline.

But it's the only way.

There were some lighter moments however. The most memorable of these occurred one morning at breakfast, which on this occasion consisted of porridge and kippers. Along came the orderly officer of the day, with the RSM and the duty sergeant.

"Any complaints chaps?" says this toffee-nosed young subaltern. A couple of tables away from us this squat hard looking little Jock shouts -

"Yeah - ah got one. Will ye look at this kipper. It's fuckin' winkin' at me"

"STAND UP - STAND UP - GET TO ATTENTION!" screams the sergeant and the officer, looking startled says -

"Take that man's name".

"GET TAE FUCK!" yells the Jock, and jumped up onto the table, wildly brandishing his kipper and began kicking the plates of porridge and kippers and mugs of tea in all directions. He really went into one, shouting and cursing, all to a cacophony of bellowing from the sergeant, and the sound of chairs crashing over as everyone ducked for cover, plus a concerted cheer of encouragement from the rest of us. The officer tried to retrieve the situation, walked up to the table and yelled -

"GET DOWN AT ONCE - YOU'RE UNDER CLOSE ARREST", whereupon the Jock swiped him across the face with his kipper!. It was the most amazing thing that I ever saw while I was in the Army.

Almost as amazing is the fact that I was to meet him over ten years later in Hemel Hempstead. I was doing a night shift in a factory, and during the meal break, I heard - coming from a noisy little pontoon school at the next table this guttural Glaswegian accent saying "Get tae fuck - ah've busted". I thought - 'I know that voice', and went over to him.

"Excuse me mate, this may sound a daft question, but where you at Catterick in 1951?".

"Thass right, ah wuz".

"You hit an officer with a kipper didn't you".

"Jeez, ah did. Wuz you there?". I told him that I was and learned that he got fifty six days in Colchester nick.

His name is Jock McArdle, and he became a good mate of mine. He still lives in Hemel Hempstead.

It's a small world.

Another incident concerns a character called Dozy Ward. I've no idea what his first name was, but the poor sod was the most hopeless member of our company, and was always in deep strife. Buchanan made his life a misery, trying to turn him into a soldier, all to no avail.

We were having an instruction which entailed describing a location on this large panoramic picture of a piece of countryside. It was about three feet high and about twelve feet wide, stretched right across the front of the room. Buchanan would point to one of us, and we would have to pinpoint a location as though we were talking on a transmitter to a Bren gun section in the vicinity. It's much harder than it sounds, but we gradually got the hang of it. "25 yards at two o'clock from the copse to the left of the red barn". That sort of thing. It was quite a laugh actually, as Buchanan could be a bit of a comedian when he was in the mood. So eventually, he points to Dozy. Dozy got to his feet and cleared his throat nervously, staring dumbly at the picture. After about twenty seconds Buchanan shouts -

"Come on - come on. The Germans are gettin' awa'!". Dozy cleared his throat again and said -

"There's an 'ill".

"Whitja mean there's a hill. Ah can see aboot twenty bloody hills. Which hill ya pudden?'. Dozy raised a trembling finger and pointed, but quickly put it down again at Buchanan's outraged yelp.

"It's a little 'ill", blurts Dozy.

"Sufferin' Christ" moans Buchanan gazing imploringly at the ceiling - "Issa little hill is it?". In desperation poor Dozy shouted -

"It's a little brown 'ill".....Buchanan strode across the room and grabbed Dozy's collar and dragged him to the front, then started to bang his head on the picture, all the while yelling -

"Where's this hill" - Bonk - "Where's this wee broon hill" - Bonk - "Ah canna see it" - Bonk - "Where the fuck's this wee broon hill" - Bonk - "It musta bin where someone shat!".

Poor old Dozy.

The first time you fired a rifle in the Army, it was at a large target no more than thirty yards away. Just five rounds each to get you used to the kick and the bang, which for some blokes was initially very frightening. All us ex cadets were already experienced on the range of course, so it was a doddle for us. Five at a time, laying prone, with Buchanan kneeling by each one in turn making sure that the rifle is pulled in tight to the shoulder, and not to shut the eyes when the trigger is pulled. "Right son. Now line up the sights. Now Squeeze". Bang. "Thassit. Guid". and on to the next. Then he'd stand back and say, "Right, in yer own time", and the other four rounds would be fired.

Among the last five to fire was Dozy Ward. We're all standing behind watching, and after they'd all shot the first round Buchanan joined us. Crack Crack go the rifles but then we saw that Dozy was kneeling up and turning towards us. He'd had a misfire. He was looking down, puzzled, at his rifle, which was pointing at us, pulling the trigger repeatedly, and calling in a plaintive voice -

"It won't go corporal"..... Christ, you've never seen anyone move as quickly as we did, flinging ourselves flat in all directions as Buchanan ran over and kicked the rifle up in the air. We were cursing Dozy for all we were worth, but we soon felt sorry for him as he had a very badly split lip and had to be helped away to the MO.

One thing about the British Army is that no NCO can lay a finger on you. Mind you, this doesn't always apply in the nicks, but in normal regimental life, it is unheard of. They do bend the rules a little bit with the odd kick in the ankle or whack with a pace stick to make you stand to attention properly, but never actually hit anyone. In this case however, Buchanan had no choice, as it could have been a life-saving situation. But that evening, Dozy was sitting on the side of his bed looking very miserable, face all swollen, and I saw hard man Buchanan sit down beside him, put his arm round his shoulders and say to him quietly and kindly -

"Y'alright son?".

Came the day when our initial training was finished and after the last severe kit inspection and parade, we said goodbye to L/Cpl Buchanan and Sgt Bastard and moved on to our further trades training. The Signals have quite a few trades - from radio mechanics to wireless operators, drivers to clerks, from linemen to OWLs, (Operator Wireless and Line), and we had all undergone aptitude tests. Being brainy, both Ronny and I were told that we would almost certainly be Radio Mechs, which we were very happy about, as it was a cushy old number, as well as being a very useful trade in civvy street. What we didn't want to be was linemen, as that was about the most dangerous job in the Army, and a lot of them were getting killed in Korea. At that time there were too many radio mechs already unfortunately, and both Ronny and I found that we were to be clerks. Actually, I might be wrong there, as I remember Ronny wearing a leather jerkin, which meant that he might have been trained as a linesman. No matter, we went to the same training battalion, and the same hut. We weren't too disappointed, as at least it meant spending the rest of our time in a nice warm office........... Or so we thought at the time.

. . . .

Chapter 11

CATTERICK Pt2.

We only moved about half a mile away, to 2TR, (number two training regiment), again into those bloody freezing annex huts, our room being full of trainee clerks and linemen. It wasn't much better than the first place, as half the time was still spent in normal basic training - harder physically than initial training, but at least the other half of our time was spent in the warm, learning typing and Army procedures and suchlike. The discipline was just as severe, and the NCOs were all bastards as usual, but we expected that and handled it better, by now being no longer raw recruits.

The Army, especially for the first few months, is about the worst place to be for someone of a rebellious nature, such as myself. Some people can accept authority and discipline quite cheerfully, but unfortunately, I'm not one of them. I did as I was told, and jumped about with the best of them, but it was when I was singled out by an irate NCO for some reason or other, and having my earhole screamed into, and being called names - well then, I had great difficulty keeping my temper, and my mouth shut. This led to a few spells of jankers, or Confinement to Barracks, for yours truly, which at Catterick was no joke. No recruit can leave the barracks anyway, but it also meant three visits to the guardroom every day, in full kit, and being inspected by the Provost Sergeant, a very nasty piece of work, and the slightest thing wrong could mean another charge, and another three days CB. It also meant three hours fatigues every evening. All this on top of a normal training day, and that's bad enough. This had the effect of making me even more pissed off, if that was possible. Ronny Rosher was of a much more placid nature, and took it all in his stride, and never got in any trouble at all. He was a great friend to me, and if it wasn't for him I think I'd have gone nuts.

A calming influence you might say.

Fortunately, I also happen to be very lucky. Not in little things mind - everything goes wrong in that department - but big things. I'll give you two instances when my lucky star shone during my time at Catterick:

The first of these concerned an occasion when I was being given a hard time by this Corporal when I had been sent to the stores for some reason or other. I can't remember exactly why he was having a go at me, but there was I, standing rigidly to attention with him yelling in my face. He was a big chubby sod, a regular and a permanent member of staff. I must have been looking sullen I suppose, because he said something like -

"You'd love to have a go at me wouldn't you. Well if I never had these - (pointing to his stripes) - I'd kick your arse for you". I answered -

"Oh would you? - It'd take more than you, you fat cunt".

I was so lucky. Just as he opened his mouth to shout for two men to double me away to the guardroom, and very big trouble, an officer, who had heard it all from the next room, walked in and snapped -

"You" - he meant me - "Out - get back to your squad".

I didn't need telling twice and scarpered, but I heard from a fellow who was doing fatigues in the stores that he overheard the officer giving the corporal a real bollocking for threatening a recruit.

The second incident I count as one of the greatest escapes of my life. When I look back on it now, I go cold thinking of what the consequences might have been.

Saturday morning inspections were the most severe of the week. They were conducted by our Company Commander, a Captain, the Company Sergeant Major, and our squad NCOs, and our kit was laid out on the bed, everything in it's exact place, blankets folded with knife edged creases (we used to iron then), the floor gleaming like glass, not a single speck of dust anywhere in the barrack room. And ourselves of course, at attention, in best battledress, blancoed and polished, shaved and shining. God help you if there was the slightest thing wrong. The officer and his entourage would slowly walk along the room examining everything minutely. The officer would just have to point at something and the sergeant would yell "DIRTY CAP BADGE - TAKE HIS NAME CORPORAL!" - and so on. We dreaded Saturday mornings. Occasionally, either the officer or the CSM would shove his stick under a mattress and heave the whole lot onto the floor, which meant another inspection that evening.

This particular morning I thought I'd got through, but the CSM, who was a very good-looking bloke, only in his late twenties, with prematurely grey hair, and one of the nastiest, most arrogant bastards I was ever to come across, lifted up my spare pair of boots with his stick, looked at them as though they were two turds, sneered at me and dropped them on the floor. The usual chorus started "FILTHY BOOTS!" etc etc, although they couldn't possibly have been any cleaner. I was seething as they continued their inspection, calling them all the bastards I could think of under my breath, and my temper was building up to exploding point. They had finished their inspection, and were disappearing through the door, the CSM taking up the rear, when I actually did explode. The red mist. I picked up my boots and flung them at the at the CSM with all my strength. They missed him as he went through the door and smacked into the wall. At that precise second, someone slammed a locker door and God Almighty, he just kept going. He didn't even notice!.

"You stupid bastard" said Ronny angrily, but with relief, then someone else said - "You mean you lucky bastard", and all the others who had been standing there with there mouths open all chorused their agreement in no uncertain terms.

My good fairy was working overtime that morning, because I could so easily have been spending the next six months in Colchester Detention barracks. If my aim had been better - if that locker door hadn't slammed, masking the sound of my boots hitting the wall. Well there you are. If Aunty Gertie had grown gonads, she'd have been me uncle.

. . . .

Came the day when we had our last parade, the big one - the passing out parade. Three hundred very happy young men, because it meant goodbye to that bloody hell hole, and all off home for our first seven day leave on the morrow. There was also a great feeling of being soldiers at last, fit and fast and fuck 'em all as we used to say. The day before, we had done a nine mile forced route march in full kit with rifles - half in fast paced marching - half at the double, up hill and down dale, with no stops. No-one dropped out. A couple of months before, that would have killed us.

There is a manoeuvre that every soldier does at his passing out parade called 'Regiment will advance in review order'. It's very rarely done again, except if you're in the Guards, and it takes many hours of practise to get it right. The battalion, in columns of three along the edge of the huge parade ground turn right into line abreast. After fixing bayonets and sloping arms comes the command, bellowed out by the RSM -
"REGIMENT WILL ADVANCE IN REVIEW ORDER - BY THE LEFT - QUICK MARCH", the battalion march for fifteen paces, accompanied by the regimental band playing the first fifteen beats of 'The British Grenadier',

and then halt, on the same beat that the band stops playing. That's the hard bit, because all three files, a hundred men across, have still to be in perfect line abreast. Then comes the command -
"GENERAL SALUTE - PRESENT.....ARMS!".... SLAP - SLAP - CRASH, and three hundred boots smash down in unison, and the band plays the General Salute while the officers salute and the Regimental flag is lowered. The band finishes.
"SLOPE....ARMS!". "BATTALION WILL MOVE TO THE LEFT IN THREES - LEFT....TURN!"..... Another concerted swish and crash of boots. "BY THE RIGHT - QUICK.....MARCH!", and we swing off to the regimental march - 'Begone Dull Care'.
Quite a thrilling occasion that was.

All through our training we had wondered where we would end up. Every two weeks, there would be a mob outside the regimental office waiting for the postings to be pinned up, because no-one except the higher ups had any idea until they saw that notice. We used to discuss it at length, and pray that we would not be sent to any of the German postings, especially Berlin Signal regiment, as they were reputed to be very hot on bullshit and discipline. We all hoped for somewhere exotic, like Hong Kong, or Singapore, but by the same token, didn't fancy the Middle East and all that sand and boredom. I well remember the intake before ours, who were all linemen, standing in the dinner queue with very long faces, because when their list was pinned up, beside every name was: FARELF (Far Eastern Land Forces) - Korea. None of us envied them. A lot of them would be right up the sharp end with the infantry, with very dangerous jobs to do. I expect a few of them are still there.
Two weeks later, a couple of days before our passing out parade, myself, Ronny and a dozen or so others gathered round the clerk as he pinned up the notice. All different - BAOR - (Germany), MELF - (Egypt), etc. Beside my name it said: 5 AA Mixed Signal Regiment - Scarborough.
I told you I was lucky. Not only was I staying in England, which is what I wanted, but I was going to the seaside, and a mixed regiment as well, which meant serving my time with the WRACs, - The Women's Royal Army Corps.
"Oh you jammy sod", said Ronny.

Civilian clothes felt very strange, and pleasant, after those months spent in khaki serge. Shoes felt like feathers after those ammunition boots. Now I could relax, just for a few days, laying in bed for as long as I liked, and not being shouted at. Christ I was happy. Lord knows why, but I'd been suffering badly from homesickness at Catterick - something I'd never felt when I was living in the Midlands, and it was great to be home. I felt as though I'd been away for ten years.

A big contribution to my unhappiness during the last few months was that I'd been sent a 'Dear John'. Perhaps I should explain that about a month before I went in the Army, I had split up with Jeanny Smyth. She was a lovely girl all right, and straight as a die, but a bit too straight, and after all I was only eighteen, with a very roving eye, and at that time, our relationship wasn't all that serious. So I told her that it wasn't fair to her to stay with me, as who knows?, I might be going abroad for a couple of years in the near future. Big of me wasn't it. Obviously, it was my excuse for a chance to play the field I'm ashamed to say, but there you are - no-ones perfect.

I'd very soon taken up with another girl, Pauline. It all got very intense, just as I went to Catterick. Given other circumstances, I would almost certainly have given her the elbow after a few weeks, but the romance was at it's height just as we had to part. It's happened to millions of blokes. Away from home, with all comforts removed, the feelings for the lady become heightened out of all proportion - she's all you can think about, and you get to wondering what she's doing, and what other feller is chatting her up, and all the rest of it. I'd been away about six weeks, writing every day, and getting a letter back daily, then the old story. Two or three days without a letter, then a week. That can drive a bloke up the wall - stupid as it may seem now - but very real at the time I recall. Then the 'Dear John' and the elbow. Suicidal. All this added to the cold, those maniacal NCOs, discipline and a horrible haircut!

But now it was all behind me - the daffodils were growing and the sun was shining. Things had started to look up.

What a favour that bloody Pauline did me. During that first leave, I met Jeanny again at the Royal and we danced all evening, and I started to realise what a stupid fool I'd been. I saw her a couple more times during that week, and although we weren't exactly together, we were good mates.

"I'll write to you if you like", she said on the last evening.

"Yeah - that'd be nice", says I.

. . . .

Chapter 12

SCARBOROUGH

Although it was close on forty-five years ago, at the time of writing, I have a very clear recollection of my first day at my new posting, because I had what you might call a bad start.

I was picked up at Scarborough station, and taken by lorry to the barracks, and on quizzing the driver was told that it was a good posting. "Lot different to Catterick mate", he said. I duly reported to the guard room, and was taken to my quarters, dumped my kit on the bed, then toddled off to the stores to collect my bedding. It was in the afternoon, and there was nobody about, as they were all at work, and I hadn't seen anyone except the blokes in the guard room. I turned the corner of the block, and there was this WRAC captain walking towards me. I said -
"Afternoon", and gave her a nod as I passed her.
"YOU - COME HYAH!!" she shouts. I knew she meant me, as we were the only two people in the vicinity, so I walked back to her, gave her a smile and said -
"Yes love, what have I done?".
"LOVE? LOVE? WHAT DO YOU MEAN LOVE? - AND GET TO ATTENTION WHEN YOU ADDRESS AN OFFICER!". Blimey she was angry. She gave me such a bollocking for not saluting, and all the rest of it, and I tried to interrupt and tell her that I'd never come across a WRAC officer before, and didn't know the form but she yelled -
"BE QUIET AND PLEASE DON'T INTERRUPT. I'LL TELL YOU WHEN YOU CAN SPEAK!", and continued on with more of the same, and made me salute about a dozen times. She finally calmed down a bit and asked me sternly if I'd just been posted in from training.
"Yeah, that's right. I'm sorry lady but....". Christ, off she went again.
"LADY? - LADY?... You address me as MA'AM, not bloody LADY!".
"Right" I said weakly.
"NOT RIGHT - YOU SAY 'YES MA'AM'!".
"Yes ma'am".
"That's better. Now what's your name?".
"Signalman Brimson"..... A raised eyebrow.
"Ma'am", I added hurriedly.

That was how I met Captain Franks. Actually, I was to find that she wasn't a bad sort at all, but she frightened the life out of me that first morning.

I once read a biography of the great war poet, Wilfred Owen. It was many years after I had left the Army, and I was surprised to learn that after leaving the convalescent home in Edinburgh and just prior to returning to France and his death in the last week of the Great War, he spent two weeks at an 'old red brick cavalry barracks at Burniston, just outside Scarborough'. Burniston Barracks was a very neat, well laid out little place, and was home for my regiment, 5AA (M) Signals, as well as the Northern Command PT School. The latter had a tiny staff of regular Army Physical Training Corps sergeants and WOs, and were nothing to do with us. The reason they were there was that the barracks had an enormous, well equipped gymnasium, which bordered one whole side of the parade ground. Their main function was administration, but they used to have occasional Conditioner courses. This was for National Servicemen who come into the army very under-weight and unfit. Obviously, there were many of these among the vast intakes, and it was most peculiar to see these little blokes, some of them only looking about fourteen. We used to call them 'Oliver Twists'. They'd stay at Burniston, working out and eating good healthy food until they had put on a certain amount of weight and passed the required fitness levels, and were then returned to their training regiments.

My regiment was quite small - if I remember rightly, about a hundred and fifty men and sixty or so women. To this day, I'm not very clear what it's function was. We had quite a few linemen who were always buggering off in lorries to 'wire up gunsites', what-ever that meant, and the rest of us, cooks, clerks, drivers, GDs, (General Duties, which meant chaps with no trade), switchboard operators, etc, were all employed to look after each other, or so it seemed to me. At the time, we never really thought about it.

Compared to Catterick, Burniston Barracks was a holiday camp. Mind you, so was anywhere else for that matter, but I can say that it must have been one of the cushiest postings in the British Army. The discipline was there all right, but nowhere near as harsh as in training, and by and large, the NCOs and officers were decent enough, although inevitably there were a few exceptions. The food was infinitely better, and the barrack rooms had radiators, Glory be, and constant hot water for showering and shaving. Luxury, until the novelty wore off that is.

. . . .

The next twenty months passed very very slowly. Ask any ex National Serviceman, and 99 per cent of them will tell you the same. We did not want to be in the Army, we wanted to be home in our old familiar streets, with our mates, coming and going as we pleased, and having the choice of telling people in authority to sod off if we didn't like them, or what they were ordering us to do. Quite natural at our age. It was different for regular soldiers, they were in from choice, and serving at least five years, as were all their comrades, and they were also imbued with esprit-de-corps and pride in their regiment. Kenny and Alby were exactly the same as me in temperament, but they enjoyed their time in the Royal Fusiliers, because they weren't counting the days till their release, as all of us were. I'd have been the same if I had been with them. Terry Guyatt enjoyed his time in the RAF, because the lucky bugger was aircrew, and consequently, automatically became a sergeant, which must have been very interesting and fulfilling, plus the fact that he was much better paid. But us squaddies were just bored shitless, and permanently skint. For all that though, I'm very glad that I did it - I wouldn't have missed it for the world.

It won't take long to tell you about the normal week at Burniston. Revielle seven o'clock. Breakfast. Works parade (the whole regiment) and inspection at eight o'clock. Work. Dinner. Work till 4.30. Tea. Finish for the day. Saturday morning room and kit inspection (very strict), and Commanding Officers parade and inspection (also very severe), one hours drill, work - then off duty from one o'clock till Monday morning. That was the pattern, although this was punctuated by the odd hour on the assault course, or PT, and a visit to the rifle range every so often. And guard duty of course, about once a fortnight.

Not exactly Beau Geste really.

I was luckier than most, because I did half a dozen detachments in various places, each of which meant two weeks away from Scarborough, which broke up my time quite nicely. I'll come to those later. To tell you the truth, when I look back, I had some very interesting times, and a lot of laughs. They say that you always remember the good times, and that has proved to be very true in my case. I find it an effort to remember the boring parts, the homesickness, the endless games of three card brag, gambling what few coppers we had left, sitting in the NAAFI with my mates, all of us bare-arsed skint, longing for Thursday and pay parade, when we could draw our twenty three shillings (five shillings of our twenty eight bob being stopped for compulsory savings), and buy some cigarettes. We all smoked and were all skint by Monday, and there was a constant cadging of fags and borrowing money. 'Knock knock' - 'Who's there?' - 'Godfrey' - 'Godfrey who?' - 'God three-ha'pence for a cup of tea?'. 'Gissa fag' - 'Bollocks' - 'Come on, gissa fag - I'll give you two back on Thursday', - 'Still bollocks'. Then when I started courting Jeanny, missing her so much and really suffering from the blues counting the days till my next leave. Crossing the days and weeks off from the calender stuck inside my locker. 'Christ, nine more months to go'.

Yes, the time passed very slowly.

The same as at Catterick, there was very little friction among us squaddies, which is quite surprising really, considering that we were for the most part still teenagers, and very pissed off ones for that matter. You get to know each other very well in a barrack room, and a strong camaraderie developes. You can't hide and pretend to be something you're not, and anyone who's a natural shit soon gets found out, but we had very few of those. In my barrack room, there was only one that I can recall, a Welshman who we caught cheating at cards, and he was on his own after that. The rest of us were all good mates I'm happy to say, and when one finished his time we were sorry to see him go, and new blokes who were posted in were soon part of us. Of course, there was the odd one who tried to throw his weight about, but that never lasted long.

The only time I ever came close to scrapping, outside the boxing ring, for the whole of my time in the Army, concerned one of these. He was a Jock from Glasgow called Shields, and at first sight, a really bad tempered nasty type. His first day at Burniston he threatened one of the boys for some reason or other, a mild inoffensive chap who was a good mate of mine. Gave him a right mouthful and shaped up to hit him. There was a chorus of 'Hey hey, pack that in mate' and he turned on us with his fists clenched and yelled - "Any o' youse bastards want to tak his part then?". I happened to be in a very bad mood myself at the time for some reason, and I cannot stand to see anyone frightened and bullied, so I found myself standing up and saying -

"Yeah - me". It seemed to take the wind out of his sails a bit, and he said -

"Any time ya like pal", but I somehow immediately saw through him. I knew all about that Glasgow accent. They all sound like hard men. A real hard man wouldn't have said that. I walked past him and said over my shoulder -

"Now. Outside".

I waited outside with my sleeves rolled up ready to do battle, working myself up into even more of a temper, but he didn't follow me out. I went back in and he told me how lucky I was, he'd have murdered me for sure, but that if he got caught fighting again he'd get twenty-eight days inside. It was a load of bollocks of course. Just saving face. Working in the office, I was able to take a look at his documents, and found that he'd never even been on a charge. For all that, it wasn't long before he started to fit in, and we soon straightened him out, and would you believe it? Jock Shields became one of my good mates.

You learn an awful lot about people in the services. It's inevitable, living in each other's pockets for months on end. The most valuable of these lessons as far as I was concerned, was never to trust first impressions. People you take an instant dislike to often turn out to be good friends, and conversley, nice chatty, hale-fellow-well-met types are found to be complete wankers. My two great buddies during my time in the Kate fall into the former category.

Jim Hanson got to Burniston just a couple of weeks before me. He was a miserable looking sod, and always looked unhappy. He occupied the next bed but one from mine. The first evening, on hearing his cockney accent, I said to him, quite cheerfully -

"Thank Christ, another towney. Where you from mate?".

"Cardiff".

"Leave off - you're a Londoner ain't you?".

"What you ask me for then?", and he turned back to his comic.

'Well sod you pal', I thought. Miserable bastard.

The next day, I had just sat down with my breakfast, and the chair next to mine scaped back, and he sat down beside me, plonked his plates down and said mournfully - "Stepney". We were more or less inseparable after that.

Jim only looked miserable. Actually, he was one of the most comical buggers you could wish to meet, with a beautiful laid back sense of humour. He could have us in hysterics, but still look as though he was about to be hung, which made it even funnier. He somehow gave the impression that he was a quiet sort of bloke, whereas actually, he'd rabbit away with the best of us, and had a very enquiring mind.

I was surprised when after knowing him for a few days, he asked me if I'd write a letter for him. He was totally illiterate. It didn't seem to bother him at all - "I was born fick wasn't I. I don't give a fuck. I'll still be earning a score a week down the docks , while you're taking 'ome a fiver from some poxy office".

Actually, he was very far from thick. There was an occasion when one of the boys was trying to work out his winnings from an each way treble that had come up. (One of our corporals ran a book). It was a very complicated affair, something like half a crown each way, with an eleven to two and five to one winners, and a third at five to four, (a quarter of the odds with no stake back). I worked it out with a pencil and paper, taking about five minutes and announced the result. "Wrong" - says Jim looking up from his comic, "You're threepence out". I did my sums again, and blimey he was right! Spot on. He'd done it in his head whilst looking at the pictures in 'Corky the Kat'. He was marvellous at mental arithmetic because his father had taught him how to work out his bets when he was a little kid. But try as I might, I was never able to persuade him to let me teach him to read and write. When I say that he was totally illiterate, I'm not being accurate, as he could read signs and place names and such, but he could not handle sentences. I doubt very much that he was dyslexic, and anyway, the word had not been invented at that time. He'd been told so often that he was thick that he'd come to believe it, and accepted it quite happily. He'd never tried to learn to read and write, because he was convinced that it was beyond him.

For some reaon or other, he always called me 'Uncle Del', and I always called him 'Uncle Jim'.

And then there was 'Uncle Arthur'.

Jim always looked unhappy. Arthur always looked angry. He came along about a month after me, and had been in the regiment for a few weeks before I got to know him, because he was in the other block. He was a real mean looking sod, built like a brick shithouse, with a blond crewcut, broken nose, and narrow eyes. All this with a permanent frown, as though he had the hump. Definitely not someone to get on the wrong side of, every inch a hard man. His name was Arthur Nutt. I remember thinking - 'Blimey - you've got to be hard with a name like that', and mentioned as much to Jim, who worked with him, as he was also a driver, but Jim laughed and said -

"Yeah right. He's a good bloke though. Comes from Dagenham. He's got a sister called Hazel". (That turned out to be true).

It's always stuck in my memory how I first spoke to him. I was about to go on guard, and had gone into his block to wait for one of the others. We inspected each other all over, because God help you if anything was wrong, and he says -

"You've got a bit of a stain on that tie Brimo". So I had, and there wasn't time to go back and get my spare. Mr Nutt was sitting on his bed darning a sock, and I said -

"Ain't got a tie I can borrow have you mate?". He looked up at me quizzically for a few seconds, then shut his eyes and said -

"Now let's 'ave a fink". He opened his eyes and said "Yeah", and dragged his kitbag out of the locker and proceeded to rummage, finally pulling out his spare tie.

"Here y'are. Gis it back tomorrow".

Arthur was just as tough as he looked. He'd been boxing since he was a little kid, and had a very good record, and had been asked to stay on at Catterick to box in the Signals team and train as a PTI. "Fuck that", he growled - "Best out of that bleedin' hole". My sentiments exactly. He'd never been knocked out or stopped, and when his nose had been broken, he had still won, even though he didn't remember the last two rounds afterwards. Hard as a rock. He always looked humpty, but it was just his way and actually he had a great sense of fun, and was always kidding and thinking up elaborate practical jokes - myself being on the end of quite a few of them. We were always fighting, all three of us, something like Inspector Clouseau and that Chinese bloke in the Pink Panther films. The cold wet flannel down the trousers was the usual aim, and we'd lie in wait for each other and then attack, usually two of us onto the other one, and wrestle around on the ground till the deed was accomplished. Jim and I once got Arthur when he was on guard at two o'clock in the morning.

Arm punching was another pastime, when least expected - wallop - Christ it did hurt, and then the chase to get one back. Sometimes we'd get one in, or receive one, when we were on parade when there was no means of retaliation - Whack - then a moan and an anguished whisper - "You cunt", and the Sergeant whipping round and yelling - "Silence in the Ranks!". I suppose we were like big kids really, but come to think of it, that is exactly what we were - big kids.

Anyone will tell you that your Service mates are the best you will ever have, and it was true in our case, and the three of us shared some great times, as well as helping each other through the bad. Like me, Arthur and Jim had that hatred of authority, and the same rebellious spirit. Mind you, so did quite a few of the lads at Burniston.

BOXING

If I had a pound for every round I sparred with Arthur, I'd be quite well off. We'd go at it for hours, open bare handed friendly sparring, just slapping and flicking and cuffing - but that's a very good exercise actually, the footwork and moves are the same as in the ring, and I could hold my own easily with Arthur, as I was faster. A few of us used to indulge in this, the best being Alan Haslam, our room Corporal, who had the beatings of all of us. Alan was a great mate of ours. He was mustard, quick as light, but then, he had had half a dozen pro fights when he'd been in the Merchant Navy.

But in the ring with the gloves on it was different. We were allowed unlimited use of the gym in the evenings, and we both decided to start training properly, together with a few of the others, and we used to get some coaching from one of the APTC sergeants, who really knew his job.

Arthur used to half kill me. I was a welterweight, and Arthur was a big middleweight, a real powerhouse, and he never used to hold back. He'd have the big sixteen ounce gloves on, and I'd be wearing the full headguard when I sparred with him, but he still used to try to knock the shit out of me, and I'd spend all my time on me bike defending, slipping and bobbing and countering. I did used to catch him really hard sometimes, but he simply marched right through everything. We'd be in a clinch after me catching him with my Sunday best, but he'd just grin and hiss in my ear - "My fuckin' sister 'its 'arder than that, you wimp", then push me away and come slamming in again. No friends in the ring.

Lucky I was fast, and my defence improved no end.

But came the day......

I was never a big puncher. I was strong and fast, and could string punches together, but I didn't have the big one that could put the other bloke to sleep. You've got to be born with that, and I wasn't, perhaps the reason being that I have very small girly hands. I won most of my bouts inside the distance, but only ever had two KOs to my name, and they were both from body punches. The others were stoppages, with the referee stepping in. But I'd like to tell you about the time I lowered the boom on Mr Nutt.

A lot of us have magic moments in sport, when everything goes right. Scoring a goal, hitting a six - whatever. Most of mine have been on the golf course, like the three iron carrying two hundred yards into the teeth of a gale, pitching and stopping two feet from the flag on the eighteenth at Stockwood Park. That five wood over the trees at Sandy Lodge....we never forget them, shots that Nicklaus would have been proud of. Mind you, they hit the ball like that all the time, and us fourteen handicappers do it about three times a year, but so what?. Every now and again, everything goes right, and that's what keeps us going, to try and do it again. Makes it all worthwhile. Such a moment occured when I was eighteen years old, in the gym at Burniston Barracks.

Arthur was committing his usual attempted manslaughter on me, his little cruel eyes alight with the joy of battle, and I was as usual running like a thief. I noticed that he was trying something new, a big swinging left hook while coming up from a crouch. No good trying to block it, it just swept my hands away, so I was moving inside it and clinching, or back-pedalling out of the way. But I noticed that he was pulling his right hand back, ready to throw a straight one after the big swipe, leaving a big hole in his guard. He kept trying it, but once to often, and I stepped in and hit him with a left hook that travelled about eighteen inches. Right on the button. I felt the shock of it right up to my shoulder, and Arthur went down like he'd been shot, like a puppet whose strings have been cut. I'd knocked him spark out. Our coach had been watching, leaning in the ropes. He smiled approvingly and said -
"Nice". We both thought that Arthur was buggering about at first, and I laughed and poked him with my foot and said -
"Get up you big tart", but he was out all right, listening to the birdies sing. The coach ducked under the ropes and got out the smelling salts and laughing said, "Christ, he's never going to live this down". Arthur had by now started to sit up, blinking, then screwed his face up as the ammonia fumes went up his nose. He pushed the coach's arm away and stood up shaking his head, and as realisation dawned he glared round with a furious look on his face, saw me, and shouted -
"YOU BASTARD - I'LL KILL YA - COME 'ERE!!" and proceeded to chase me all over the gym, much to the amusement of all present, who were

doubled up laughing, but he was in such a temper. He'd never even been decked before, let alone knocked out, and I'd ruined his record. He'd have done me serious damage if he'd have caught me, and I only escaped by locking myself in the bog. He calmed down just as quick though, and laughed with the rest of us, but I never let him forget it. It was worth all those drubbings he inflicted on me, and whenever we had a difference of opinion, I'd always say to him -

"Shut yer mouth you, or I'll knock you out". He'd go along with it, and pretend to look frightened and say nervously -

"Yeah - all right guv'nor".

My first official bout whilst in the Army was something that I'd like to forget. I entered for the annual Regimental championships, and when I climbed in the ring, it was the first time I had fought since I was fifteen. I was drawn against a L/Cpl Green, who I didn't know, as he'd only been recently posted in. He was and RP, (Regimental Policeman), a sturdy looking character, and from what I'd heard, quite a nice bloke. The list went up on the board the day before, and this character called Nosworthy buttonholed me in the mess and said -

"Tha's in big trooble Brimo". I didn't like Nosworthy, and nor did most of us. A mouthy big sod from Leeds, very flash and full of himself. He'd been at the same school as Green, and was a sort of mate of his. He cheerfully proceeds to tell me that Green was a great boxer, and had won all sorts of titles, Schoolboy ABA, National Youth ABA, and God knows what else. Arthur was with me, and on me remarking that it was just my bloody luck, he said -

"Let me fight 'im. I like 'itting coppers". He was a middleweight though, or I'd have let him.

Green climbed into the ring wearing shorts covered in badges, and a very well worn pair of boxing boots. Seeing them made me even more nervous, as the old wobblies had returned with a vengeance. I've started like a train, just as I used to do, and really clobbered him. He was so easy to hit, and I thought that I must have stunned him, and expected him to start repaying me at any moment, but I didn't give him a chance, and swarmed all over him. I felt great, everything was going well, except that the bugger wouldn't go down. One thing he did have was a cast iron jaw. He finally did go down, but got up again, looking very crestfallen. I suddenly realised that he was helpless, just covering up and not trying to fight back, and there were cries of "Stop it" from the audience. I grabbed him and spun him round, and looked appealingly over his shoulder at Colonel Sladen and the two other officers who were officiating.

"Box on" says Sladen. Poor old Green was in a mess, obviously out of it, so I eased right up for the few seconds of the round that remained. Sitting in my corner, I saw one of the APTC sergeants go and whisper in the colonel's ear, whereupon he rang the bell, and shouted,

"Cpl Green is unable to continue. Signalman BRIMSON IS THE WINNAH!". I was so relieved, and elated at blowing a champion away so easily...... Or so I thought.

Back in the dressing room I sat down on the bench next to Green and said -

"Hard luck mate - better luck next time". He grinned quite cheerfully although his face was very puffy, and said, -

"Fook that - there won't be no next time".

"Don't be daft. We all have off days - perhaps I was lucky to catch you early on".   He shook his head ruefully and said -

"Naw. Once is enough - never again".

"What do you mean - once is enough?"..... Jesus - he'd never been in a ring in his life before. He'd borrowed the shorts and boots from one of the cooks called Clark - a very useful lightweight. I'm not a bully, and I can't stand anyone who takes liberties. I told him about Nosworthy, and he said -

"Aw, he's a bit of a coont. He were joost kiddin' ya". I couldn't stop apologising, and I was so angry, as was Arthur, who'd been listening to all this. I went from being euphoric with the victory to being ashamed and angry, and I said -

"I'm gonna kill the bastard", but Arthur, who had earlier dispatched his opponent (a chap called Bowler I remember), in about ten seconds, was already changed, and heading out of the door.

"No you won't" he said, "I will".

Nosworthy was walking around, very shamefaced for the next few days, with a very fat lip and a black eye.

I had a few bouts while I was at Scarborough, and won them all, only one of them going the distance. How I got the decision in that one I'll never know; I was sure that I'd been beaten, and so did everyone watching, judging by the boos and whistles, but that's how it goes. You always get some very mysterious decisions in Amateur boxing. Another victory was even more lucky for me, as I was taking a bit of a hiding, and heading for certain defeat, when we had a bad clash of heads, and the other boy came out of it with a very bad cut, and as it was accidental, I got the nod. But there you are, it could just have easily been me. I realised however, that I was never going to get anywhere, as my hands were so weak. It never bothered me when I was a schoolboy, but you hit much harder of course when you're fully grown, and my hands were always swollen after any bout that went any distance, with one, or both of my thumbs knocked up. In the Northern Command preliminaries for instance, we had to box on consecutive days, (assuming we were winning), and both years I had to pull out, even though I had won quite handily. I really don't think I would have got very far though, because in those days, there were about ten times the number of amateur fighters that there are today, most of them in the Services, and my division, welter-weight, at ten stone six, was the most crowded, with dozens of very useful boys much better than me.

But I had a go, and like to think that I was at least average.

. . . .

Scarborough is a nice town, the Southend of the North as they used to say. We were allowed out whenever we were off duty, although we had to sign back in at the guardroom by midnight during our first year of service. After that, we had a Permanent Pass, which meant you could do what you liked as long as you were there for works parade in the morning. We spent many evenings mooching around the town, skint most of the time, looking for girls, especially those that smoked. A cafe on the seafront called Jaconelli's was our favourite hangout. Peter Jaconelli was a little chubby Scots/Italian, and I heard that many years later he became the Mayor of Scarborough. He was a good little bloke, especially putting up with us rowdy buggers, and we could always con a free coffee out of him if we were skint. I remember one particular night when there were about a hundred of us crammed in there listening to the Randolph Turpin - Sugar Ray Robinson fight, and how we went nuts when Randy won the World Middleweight title. Jim made the most of the confusion by lifting two pocketsful of cakes from the counter, so we had something to celebrate with on that long walk home along the seafront.

In those days, Yorkshire people were still very Yorkshire. I know that this may sound odd, but most people have forgotten, or have not even realised how much the advent of television, and the mass media culture have broken down many of the old barriers. The biggest of these is the matter of accents, as the whole nation is very familiar with Cockney, Scouse, Geordy, Brummy and Scots dialects, because of all the various soap operas. We're not as suspicious of each other as in those days. Yorkshire people were very prickly, and regarded their county as the centre of the universe, and every-one else as intruders. That included us, and I can tell you that the locals, during my time at Scarborough, did not like us in the least, and treated us accordingly. We used to have some fun with the situation sometimes, greet-ing middle-aged couples with a cheerful - "How ya doin' then? All right?", knowing that nine times out of ten, they would ignore us, and walk on with their noses in the air, at which we'd laugh and blow them a rasberry.

The girls were different of course, although they could be hard work, especially as they knew that squaddies were nearly always broke, but where there's a will there's a way. This led to resentment and many an altercation between the young blokes in Scarborough and members of the regiment, and we would never be fool enough to wander around in the evenings alone.

The WRACs, (Women's Royal Army Corps) were a nice bunch of girls. We were all told, when first joining the regiment, to 'treat these girls with respect, as you would your own sisters', and by and large, that is what we did. We worked with them, ate with them, shared many evenings in the NAAFI with them, and they became mates, just like the other blokes. There were countless romances naturally, and the assualt course, an area of bushes and long grass stretching from the games pitch down to the sea, was the scene of much nocturnal action. There were a few of them who would have nothing to do with us blokes though, and the prettier of these would fend off any chat up lines very quickly. They were very cliquey, and kept to each others company and we used to call them 'manhaters'. The word Lesbian was almost unknown to us, and at that time not in general usage, and I doubt whether it even crossed our minds, although looking back, that was obviously the case. I'm equally sure, that some of them didn't even consider it themselves, such were the attitudes of the time.

There was one big drawback however, when serving in a mixed regiment. The women NCOs have the same authority as the men, and being given a hard time by our own NCOs was bad enough, but we found it doubly irksome from a woman. I don't mean being told what to do by them, that was fair enough, and we wouldn't quibble at it - I mean being told off, made to stand to attention and being yelled at - that sort of thing. Fortunately, not many of them were like that, but it was just my luck to have the worst one as my direct superior.

For the first year, I worked in the HQ office, and the chief clerk was one Sergeant Molly Machin. She could be a real cow, and ruled us with a rod of iron, and it took me a long time to learn how to handle her, and not before I'd had a few spells of jankers, all for the same old thing - not being able to keep my mouth shut. Luckily, I was quite popular with the officers, and they were well aware of Molly's nature, so I always got off lightly. She eventually got pregnant by one of the other sergeants, who was married, much to the delight of all, and had to leave the Army. I feel a bit sorry for her now that I'm older and wiser, but she was nothing if not a very capable lady, and I expect she handled things quite well.

I came in for my fair share of strife at Burniston, inevitably, due to my nature, as did Jim and Arthur, mostly for insubordination.

"Not you again Brimson", our company commander would say wearily, then listen to the evidence -

"I heard him mutter an obscenity sir, after being told to.........".

"What did he say Corporal?".

"He called me a **** sir".

"Anything to say Brimson?".

"No sir", (always the wisest response).

"Do you accept my punishment?".

"Yessir". (again the wisest response).

"Three days Confinement to Barracks. March him out".

"ESCORT AND ACCUSED - RIGHT TAHN - QUICK MARCH - LEFRILEFRILEFRIRIGHTWHEELLEFRILEFRI!!".

I was always treated lightly, I think because I was for the most part good natured, and a bit of a comedian, and the officers knew all of us well, and as long as you did your work and kept yourself clean and smart, and was not an evil bastard, they'd treat trivial transgressions fairly tolerantly, and were able to tell the difference between spirit and malevolance. They were also well aware of which NCOs were charge happy, and those that would only charge someone as a last resort. For instance, a certain WRAC corporal made me double round the parade ground once, after a bit of good humoured cheek. Fair enough, but she then made mark double time. I said, all out of breath, still running on the spot, -

"Leave it out Sally for Christ's sake", whereupon she gives me a wicked smile and tells me to double round the parade ground again. I halted, smiled back at her and said -

"No, I don't think so - I've had enough of this", and walked away, with her yelling at me to come back, and me saying over my shoulder -

"No - You're just being horrid", and continuing on my way. The upshot of it was that she put me in for a charge for disobeying an order, and that meant going up before the Old Man, Lt/Colonel Sladen, and if found guilty, a month at least in Colchester glasshouse. The Orderly Officer quickly put the mockers on that thank God, as he wasn't daft, and knew that it was just a storm in a teacup, and made her alter it to an ordinary 252 - "Conduct to the Prejudice of Good Order and Military Discipline" - the blanket charge that covers all minor indiscretions. And I got away with that!. I just said that I thought she was joking, and was given an admonishment, which is bugger all, another word for a warning come telling off.

I had some astonishing luck as well. During my service, I went AWOL twice, and both times got away with it, scot free. The first occasion was during a detachment. It was when the Government called up the 'Z' reserve. It was a sort of massive exercise to see how quickly the country could mobilise a large Army of trained men, and that meant blokes who had been through the war, but were still of military age. These 'Zedmen', as they came to be called, had been demobilised and settled for the last seven years in domestic life, and it was the last thing that any of them had expected. They didn't call all of them up of course, but enough to see whether it could be done, and they just came back into the Army for two weeks. They were kitted out with all the gear, and did some drill and a few battle schemes, and then went home. I think it was something to do with the political situation of the time - the war in Korea, and those bloody' Russians getting all stroppy in Europe.

I was sent to a camp which was the temporary home for a battalion of Highland Light Infantry - hard bitten old bastards who had fought at Tobruk and in Italy, and all of them just treated it as a laugh and a good excuse to get away from the missus and have a monumental piss up with all their old mates. I can't remember what town we were camped near, just that they wrecked it. If they couldn't find anyone to fight, they'd fight each other.

Thank God they were on our side during the war, that's all I can say.

I was told that I would be working some of the time in the office, as well as taking the odd PT period, as I had recently done a PT course. Fat lot of chance of them doing PT, they would probably have eaten me, and there was very little office work to do, so myself and a few of the other National Servicemen staffing the camp were told to more or less stay out of the way till we were needed. We skived around in our huts most of the day, with a lookout, in case we saw someone coming who might be going to make us work, whereupon we would disappear out of the other side of the hut and make ourselves scarce. It was so chaotic there, that we got away with it most of the time. But come the weekend I was bored out of my skull, and buggered off home to see Jeanny. What with one thing and another, I missed the train back on the Sunday night, and thought 'Ah well, might as well be hung for a sheep as a lamb', and didn't go back till Wednesday afternoon. I was convinced that I'd be spending the next month in the nick, and I was resigned to it. When I walked into the hut, the lads were playing cards, and informed me that no-one had bothered them since the weekend. I sat down and joined in the game, and soon after, a sergeant walked in and said, "You - can you type?". "Yes sarge". "Come wi' me then", and he took me over to the HQ marquee and put me to work. Incredibly, I hadn't even been missed.

The other occasion was soon after Jeanny and I had become engaged.

I had finished my seven days leave, and knew that I wouldn't be seeing her again for at least six weeks. We were very much in love, and I just couldn't stand the thought of going back, so I didn't.

"Won't you get into trouble love?" says Jeanny.

"Nah, don't worry. I'll get a note from a doctor".

Much easier said than done. We spent two whole days traipsing round all the surgeries in Tottenham, and I'd walk in with a carefully rehearsed pack of lies about stomach aches and head aches and bollock aches, and they all listened very attentively until I said that I'd overstayed my leave, and that was when I was very firmly shown the door. They'd heard it all before. Bastards. I'd already phoned the regiment telling that I was sick, so I was in very big trouble. Colchester for sure.

We'd given up, and were walking very sadly along Lordship Lane, so depressed. I had to go back that very night, or I would be classed as a deserter, much more serious than AWOL. Then Jeanny said - "Look, here's another doctor". We were standing outside a house with a couple of brass plates on the door. 'DR LASKI. MD'. one of them read. Our legs were aching from roaming around all day, and we were very tired and it had started to rain.

"Might as well give it a try", I said wearily. I was shown into the surgery, and there sat Dr Laski, a small, chubby Jewish looking man, with a kind face.

"Yes young man - vot is de trouble?". I thought - 'sod it, I ain't telling any more lies.

"Truth is doctor, I'm in the Army see. I should have gone back last Sunday, but I've just got engaged and........"

He held up his hand, shut his eyes and said - "Shh". He got up, walked round the table, leaned down and said -

"Open your mouth pliss". I opened my mouth.

"Vider pliss". He peered into my open mouth then walked back round the table tut-tutting, sat down and opened a drawer, taking out a bottle of pills.

"Now den. I vant you to take two of these a day, and come and see me next Monday morning", then began to write me out a certificate.

Dear marvellous Dr Laski. Jeanny and I walked home through the rain, two feet off of the ground we were so happy, with me firmly grasping the bottle of asparins he had given me, occasionally patting my pocket which held the back dated certificate with 'Quinsy' scrawled on it. He kept me home for another week, bless him.

I know that this has nothing to do with my time in the Army, but I'd like to tell you a little more about Doctor Laski, gentleman and ardent Spurs supporter.

He became our doctor of course, after I left the Army, and I got to know him very well. He was a marvellous man, a German Jewish refugee, who had lost all his family in the holocaust, and two sons who had been killed fighting in the British Army. I told him once that I had just read a book called 'Das war mein Liebe', by a professor Saurbruch, who had been Hitler's personal physician, and was the inventor of the pressurised operating theatre. I remember his eyes opening wide with surprise, and he told me that he'd studied surgery under him when he was a student. "Oh, he vos a real tyrant - a martinet, but a very fine surgeon, even if he vos a Nazi". He himself had been a very prominent surgeon in Germany, but the law being what it was in those days, could only be a GP in Britain. When our Stephen was just a few months old, we had a bad time with him. He was always crying and covered in little spots, but the midwife at the clinic said not to worry, he was perfectly healthy, and just a naughty baby. Finally, in desperation we took him to Dr Laski. He held him up and lc ked at him, yelling his head off.

"Are you giving him full cream milk?". Jean told him that we were, on the express orders of the clinic.

"Wrong wrong wrong. He should be on half cream. Den no more spots". He examined Stephens little winkle, and looked up horrified.

"Vy has dis boy not been circumcised?". We told him that again, that bloody midwife had said that it wasn't necessary. He shook his head.

"Not necessary! Dear God, the boy will be dead within a week if he is not. Bring him back here this evening".

As I told Steve when he was old enough - "You had your nob end cut off by one of the worlds best surgeons. Not only that, but he was Jewish, so he was very well qualified".

But I digress......

The only serious trouble I was ever in, and for which I did spend time in the nick was, in my opinion, all a mistake. Occasionally, we would have small detatchments of Territorial WRAC posted into Burniston. All Territorials have to do two weeks camp every year, and these girls would spend them with us. I met, and had a brief romance with one of these, a Corporal Doreen Wilkinson, who was a teacher at Durham High School for Girls. She was twenty six, dark haired and pretty, very intelligent with a good sense of humour. This I hasten to add, was before I'd become engaged. What she saw in me I don't know, as I was much younger than her, and a bit farther down the social scale, but there you are. We really hit it off for the brief time we were together. When she returned to Durham, she was given a lift in a car, so she still had the return half of her ticket, which she sent to me with her first letter, the idea being for me to use it for a weekend visit. The visit never transpired however, for one reason and another, and the ticket had an expiry date on it, and I thought waste not want not. I was going home on leave, and as it was made out via York, I'd use it, saving myself ten bob, just paying the fair from York to Kings Cross. I pushed the ticket under the grill at the station, and this miserable looking Yorkshire sod of a clerk asked -

"Where did you get this ticket?".

"What do you mean - where did I get it. What's wrong with it".

"I said where did you get it?" he said nastily. I was in a hurry as I could hear the train puffing in the station, and I only had a couple of minutes in which to catch it.

"Give us it back then" I said, and put my hand under the grill to retrieve it, but the old bastard slid it out of my reach.

"Give me a return to Kings Cross" says I, shoving the money at him.

"I wanna know where you got this ticket" he said.

"Mind your own fuckin' business" I shouted - "Hurry up will you, I've got a train to catch".

"What's the trouble here?" says a voice behind me, and Christ Almighty, there's one of our officers standing there. Oh dear.

Unluckily for me, I hadn't noticed the little 'W' nicked out of the ticket, which said that it had been issued to a women. Also, on every Army warrant ticket there is written 'Non Transferable'. I had to give the snotty old sod my name and all the rest of it - no choice with the officer there.

I thought no more of it, but on my return from leave, I was put under close arrest, and charged. I didn't take it seriously, and neither did anyone else, it seemed such a trivial matter.

So, there's me standing in front of Lt/Col Tom Sladen,

"ESCORT AND ACCUSED TEN SHUN" and all the rest of it. I wasn't very worried. The charge was read out, and the Colonel says quite kindly

"Now then Brimson. What have you got to say for yourself?". I launch forth on a long, what I thought plausible explanation, that I was only trying to save myself ten bob, and it was a shame to let the ticket go to waste etc. The Colonel listened, smiled and nodded.

"Well then, how do you plead - guilty or not guilty".

"Well guilty I suppose sir, although technically I'm not. You see the charge says I was trying to get all the way home with it, but....".

"Be quiet. You plead guilty do you?".

"Yessir".

"And do you accept my punishment?".

"Yessir".

The Colonel smiled happily and said - "Fourteen days detention. March him out".

"PRISONERANESCORT - RIGHT TUHN. QUICK MARCH. LEFRILEFRI LEFRIRIGHTWHEELLEFRILEF..".

I couldn't believe it. I'd only expected three days CB. 'You rotten old sod' I thought.

Fourteen days detention very fortunately, meant that I would have to spend the time in our own little nick, behind the guardroom, and not go away to that hell hole in Colchester. You had to get at least a month to be sent there. I was the only one ever to serve time in the cells at Burniston while my regiment was there, and it was quite an occasion, as everyone had to read up on all the procedures, and I became a sort of celebrity. I'm fairly sure that was one of the reasons the Old Man did it, as a sort of exercise, as well as teaching me a lesson, knowing full well that I'd got away with murder on a few occasions. He also knew just as well, that there was quite a trade in that department - chaps hitch hiking home on leave and flogging the tickets to a mate at half price. No harm in it, and everyone was happy, but never-the-less, against regulations. I'm sure of this because the adjutant visited me in my cell during my first morning.

"Well matey - you've done it this time haven't you?".

"Yes sir, but Blimey it's a bit strong". He smiled and said -

"Quite. Tell me Brimson, have you ever heard of Admiral Byng?".

"Yes I have sir. 'Pour encoureger les autres'".

He was quite surprised at this, both eyebrows going in an upward direction.

"Well done", he said.

It wasn't too bad at all, as the RPs were all decent blokes who I knew well, and I spent a lot of that fortnight playing cards with them. It became a bit of a joke actually, although everything was done to the letter of the law, such as doing two hour long periods of drill every day by the orderly sergeant, all by myself on the parade ground, but I didn't mind, and anyway, the girls would be watching out of their block window sometimes saying, "Aah, poor Derek, leave him alone you big bully". I had to double everywhere, with an escort, every time I left the guardroom, and my kit was inspected very thoroughly every morning, but I had all the time in the world to get it right. My meals were all brought to the cells which I thought was nice, and every evening was spent on fatigues, but nothing to arduous. I was allowed the regulation two cigarettes a day, but that was even more of a joke, as every-one was keeping me well supplied, especially my WRAC mates who were always pushing them through the little window on their way to switchboard duty. I've never smoked so much in all my life. Once, for a laugh, I wrote - 'HELP - I'M BEING HELD PRISONER' on a piece of paper, and stuck it up on the window. The Orderly Officer of the day, a young subaltern saw it and came into the guardroom.

"Sergeant, tell the prisoner to cut that out".

"Whassat sir?".
"He's stuck a note in the window. See to it will you".
"SAH".
"Then you can beat him up".
"YESSIR - RIGHT AWAY SIR". All with perfectly straight faces.

There was a lot of humour in our regiment. We had one Lance Jack who used to pretend that we were all in the Wermacht. He was always shouting 'RAUS - SCHNELL!' instead of the usual 'MOVE YERSELVES'. and 'LINKSFAHREN' and 'RECHTSFAHREN' instead of left turn and right turn. A really comical character who we all liked. He had a small squad of us once, outside the stores, and when he dismissed us he shouted "ZEIG HEIL!" and flashed up a Nazi salute. We all went along with it, and as one, crashed to attention, shouted back "ZEIG HEIL" and returned the same salute. We're all standing there rigid, with our arms up, when the Colonel appeared from the stores to investigate. He glared at us with his big moustache bristling - gave the corporal a withering stare, then shook his head sadly, turned, and went back into the stores.

Not a bad old bugger.

We had another character, I forget his name, who was a quiet, sad sort of bloke - lugubrious is the word that fitted him. He never had much to say, but he did have one attribute that marked him out as very special. Quite simply, he could fart whenever he liked. He could also control the pitch and volume perfectly. We'd never heard of Petomain at that time, or that would have been his nick name, so we just called him 'The Farter'. Every barrack room in the British Army sounds like the Battle of the Somme every morning at reveille as a matter of course, but this bloke was a menace. He got me three days CB once. You see, there's nothing that can induce giggling so much as a fart at any solemn occasion. It can render you helpless, and our hero knew it. He'd always get in the front rank if he could, on the Saturday morning parade.

"OPEN ORDER - MARCH", and the front rank would step forward two paces, the rear rank back two paces.

"ORDER ARMS" - slap - slap - Crash.

"FRONT RANK - Ten -SHUN". Crash.

"PORT ARMS". And along would come the Colonel, the RSM, the troop sergeant, pace sticks and canes under their arms, examining every squaddy from top to toe, peering down the rifle barrels looking for any tiny speck of dirt, then along the back of the rank, checking haircuts and webbing. All very slowly and solemnly done.

"FRONT RANK - ORDER ARMS. Slap - slap - Crash.

"STAND AT EASE". Crash. That's them finished.

"CENTRE RANK - Teen-SHUN"....Now it's our turn.

And that's when the farter would strike. He's in front of us remember, and he'd wait till the Colonel was up the other end, out of earshot. Then he'd let one go. His expression would never change, he'd just look sad, but all of us poor sods would be standing there, rigidly at attention, gripping our rifles at the port, jaws clenched and eyes shut trying desperately not to giggle. But he had one more trick up his sleeve, or in his pants to be more exact. Just as we'd get it under control he'd always squeak out a tiny little one, which he himself called - 'The frightened mouse'. This always resulted in a few splutters and coughs and a 'SILENCE IN THE RANKS' from the sergeant.

So that was the situation that particular day just as the Old Man and his entourage came to me. Sladen inspected my cap badge, then stared straight into my face. I was biting my lip and holding my breath.

"What's the matter boy?" growled the Colonel.

"Nothing sir", I said between clenched teeth. He frowned, and then continued his inspection, his eyes travelling down - belt buckles, then boots, then someone else in the front rank dropped one, just for a laugh. There were suppressed splutters all round. "Oo done that?" said the sergeant whirling round, and I just couldn't help it - I laughed straight into the Old Man's face.

"Take this man's name sergeant", then two or three others exploded - "That man there - and that man" said the Colonel pointing with his cane. He was furious. Then a few more cracked up.

"SILENCE!", roars the RSM - "WHASSUP WIV YER? - YOU'RE LIKE A LOT OF BIG TARTS!".

We all spent that afternoon back on the square, drilling, and myself and the other two all got three days jankers. After that, we always made the Farter go into the rear rank, and warned him to keep his bum quiet, on pain of death.

. . . .

It was a happy regiment, by and large. The only chap to be sent away to Colchester, for all of my time there was a bloke called Wadsworth. He was a nice feller, with no harm in him at all, but the poor bugger had a very bad piece of luck.

Guard duty was a real chore, especially in the winter. Two hours on and four off, from six pm to six am. That meant at least one spell in the middle of the night, the worst one being the two am guard. We used to stand out there in the dark, freezing our arses off, marching up and down, and doing arms drill to try and keep our blood moving. That two hours used to seem like four. No time off the next day either, and it was a job trying to keep awake all day. So poor old Wadsworth was sheltering from the rain in the guard box, three o'clock in the morning and he nodded off. We've all done it. I was fast asleep myself once and was woken by a shove in the shoulder.

"You weren't asleep were you son?", snapped the orderly officer.

"No sir, I was just thinking about something".

"Really? - don't let it happen again, right?".

"SAH". and he stomped off to the guardroom. Laissez Faire as they say.

Wadsworth was gently snoring, standing hunched up in the box, just as I had been, (and many others), but unfortunately for him, the Orderly Officer for that particular night was a young WRAC subaltern, new to the regiment. She didn't wake him up, but went and got the guard commander as a witness, and charged him. Asleep on duty - a very serious charge, and a mandatory twenty-eight days up the Swannee. Everybody was very pissed off, and she was one very unpopular officer, but the damage had been done. OK, you shouldn't be asleep on guard, but this was North Yorkshire not the Russian border. A bollocking and an extra guard would have been enough. When Wadsworth came back from the nick, he looked terrible, and was very quiet and withdrawn for some time. He was a little, gentle chap - not really the type to be sent to that awful place. That silly bloody woman should have realised that.

. . . .

Chapter 13

THE LAST STRETCH

I realise that so far I've dwelt mostly on strife and punishment, but I wouldn't like you to get the idea that all of it was like that. Indeed, as the months wore on, the intervals between charges got longer and longer. We all learn in the long run, and I was no exception. Right to the end of my service, I would still have a job keeping my temper when an NCO shouted in my ear, but I gradually learned to avoid giving them any cause to. I like to think that I was a fairly good soldier, well thought of by most.

I was never promoted of course, because of my disciplinary record, but I didn't mind that in the least.

Despite the fact that I can only see out of one eye, or maybe because of it, I was a crack shot, in the top half dozen in my regiment. I didn't get my Marksman badge, because I couldn't get a decent score with the Bren gun. The reason for this was that the sights on a Bren are on the left side, and you have to sight along it with your right eye. No way you can do it with your left one, so that let me out. They don't make left-handed Brens. But with the 303 Lee Enfield I was mustard. I always used to get a small audience when firing five rounds rapid, because it must have looked quite funny. I had to fire from the left shoulder you see. No problem there, except that the bolt is on the right, and a normal man doesn't have to move anything but his right hand when he pulls the bolt back to reload. If you can imagine it, I had to roll my head to the right, cross my right hand over past my face, and slide the bolt backwards and forwards past my left ear. But I could do it, and get the five aimed shots off in ten seconds, all accurate.

Every regiment has an armoury of course, and twice a year, all the weapons have to be zeroed - which means having the sights set. All the 303s, Brens and Sten guns are loaded onto a lorry, and taken to a range, together with four of the best shots, an officer and an armourer. I was picked twice, and loved every minute of it. We had all day with unlimited ammunition, and did our very best to outshoot each other. We'd take it in turns, firing at a target that was only a hundred yards away, with the armourer sitting by us with his telescope on a tripod. Five rounds, carefully aimed from the lying position, with the weapon resting on sandbags. CRACK - five times, taking our time. Then the armourer would adjust the sights with his screwdriver, and we'd have another five with it. A look through the telescope. Another tinker, then two more rounds to make sure. One more accurate rifle. We had about two hundred rifles to do, so we needed the shoulder pads and earplugs. We only had a few Bren guns, and having plenty of ammo, and all the time in the world, I was able to experiment and learn to sight along the studs on the right of the weapon, firing from the left shoulder. After a few rounds, with the armourer telling me where my shots had hit, I was able to hit the bull every time. The Bren is a beautiful weapon, incredibly accurate with single shots, and hardly any kick. Unfortunately, the studs are not as reliable as sights, each gun being a tiny bit different, otherwise I'd have earned the crossed rifles on my sleeve.

The Sten is just a close combat weapon, and we fired at a twenty five yard cut-out, blasting away in bursts from the hip, just to make sure that they were working properly. Great fun though.

There is a very rigid and proper range drill employed in the Services. Very wise, and very necessary, especially when a whole company is firing. Accidents can so easily happen, which is why that drill is so rigidly adhered to. But when you're firing all day, you can easily get careless.

We were loading the weapons back on to the lorry, after finishing for the day, and the Stens were all in a pile at the butts. I was picking them up, carrying them across, four at a time. I went back for the last lot, picked up two of them, and put them under my arm, then leaned down and picked up the third one. BANG BANG! and two rounds missed my foot by inches. Bloody near broke my wrist. There was no way of knowing who was at fault, anyone of us could have left those two rounds in, with the weapon still cocked. Very stupid. The magazines should all have been taken out and checked before being replaced, but it taught all of us a lesson.

"Better keep this quiet chaps" said the officer, (it might even have been him).

And so we did.

Our biggest enemy was boredom. I was good at my job - I must have been, because I was selected for an advanced clerical and typing course, and spent a very pleasant two weeks at Welbeck Abbey, near Worksop. I was the only non NCO in the class, and I breezed through it with high marks - handy, as it meant a few more bob in my pocket. The trouble was that there wasn't enough work to go round, and we spent a lot of time doing crosswords in the office. We could easily have done our days work in a couple of hours, no bother. This applied to everybody. Arthur and Jim spent half their time washing their three ton Bedfords, and cleaning up the garage.

I had a few chats with the officers about it, putting forward the view that with the number of experts in every regiment, not just ours, and the amount of spare time that was actually available, all National Servicemen were in a very good position to benefit, for the good of the community in general.

Sport is very actively encouraged in the Army, and if you show any talent at all, they are right behind you. As well as boxing, I threw the javelin in the athletics team, and played hockey for the regiment, and was given plenty of time off to train and compete. All well and good, but supposing everyone was given a compulsory first aid course for instance. You'd have all those thousands of blokes leaving the Army with that knowledge, and the laws of average would mean that over the years, many lives would be saved. Our medics sat round scratching their arses most of the time, when they could just as easily been teaching us. We could have all been taught to drive, very handy in civilian life. Further Education was there if you wanted it, but only on a voluntary basis, whereas I think that all the semi-literate (20 per cent of all National Servicemen, believe it or not), should have been given a couple of periods instruction per week whether they liked it or not. Better than mooching around picking up paper, cutting grass and whitewashing stones. The Army hates to see men idle. Quite right, but far more often than not, it employs them in a very wasteful manner.

We'd do anything to get out of the camp for a couple of weeks. Jim Arthur and myself, and a couple of other blokes, volunteered as human guinea pigs once. We did it purely because there was seven days buckshee leave at the end of it. We were sent to Porton Down, on Salisbury plain - the Army Chemical Research Centre. We had a medical that lasted all day, Christ, they tested everything that was possible to test. Then we had to do exercises till we were exhausted, and I mean exhausted, close to fainting. Then another medical, the same as the first one. The next day, we had to walk through a long sort of tunnel made of transparent sheeting, breathing deeply. Then the exhaustion exercises again, then the same medical. That was all there was to it. None of us felt any ill effects at all, and I think that we must have been used in a placebo capacity. We had to sign the official secrets act, but I don't suppose it matters now, forty odd years later, but when we got back to Scarborough there were all our names up on Part 2 Orders. Mine read -'Awards of Gallantry. 22447932 Signalman Brimson D.H. did voluntarily expose himself to .... agent'. How about that then. Awards of Gallantry!. Load of cobblers really, we only did it to get a free weeks leave. Just to be sure, I'd better not put down what '........' was.

We were standing round the notice board that morning, well pleased with ourselves, and Arthur said to a passing officer -
"You seen this sir?. Can we 'ave a medal?".
"Piss off Nutt".
"Yessir".

I had some nice detachments. An Army Cadet camp at Whitburn, a PT course - I forget where, two weeks in Carlisle with the Coldstream Guards, another two weeks in Nottingham, and a week in London, and the Z men thing with those mad Jocks. All helped to pass the time. Nothing like new faces and a change of scenery. Also, our pay increased up to full regulars rate in our last six months, and that helped.

So the months slipped slowly by. When I look back two years now, say performing at a club, knowing it was that long since I'd been there, it seems such a short interval.

I sometimes think that life is like sliding down a chute, picking up speed all the way. Looking back on those long hot endless summers when I was a boy, and the all too brief summers of recent times. And that endless two years in the Mob. But why does Christmas come round every six months now?. My little Grandson Ben was only two last year. How come he's five already?. And my youngest son Eddy. They tell me he's thirty-one, but I know bloody well he's only twenty-six. I think it's all a conspiracy.

. . . .

"I'll write to you if you like", said Jeanny Smyth.
"Yes, that would be nice", I replied.

And so she did, and I got my first letter a couple of days after I was posted to Burniston Barracks. There was a cigarette in the envelope too. I replied of course, and so it all began. Pen pals for the first few months, then a sev-enty-two hour weekend pass after which we were sort of boyfriend - girlfriend. Nothing heavy, just 'chatting', to use the parlance of the time. I think perhaps that we were both a bit wary at first, me because I'd seen too many lovelorn blokes being very depressed, missing their girls so much, just living for their next leave, and Jeanny knowing full well that I was a bit of a flash sod, who'd let her down once already. She was a lovely girl though.

There was something about her. Shy and a bit quiet, yet always the centre of her circle of mates, sort of top of the pecking order without even trying - not actually being aware of it. We were very different, extrovert and introvert, and except for a shared sense of humour, had very little in common. Whatever she saw in me I don't know. But we liked being together.

Still do.

So the long distance courtship began, and over the next year, it gradually seeped into my thick skull just what a fabulous bird she was. I've already mentioned how lucky I have always been in the big things, how things have a habit of turning out right in the end. Being in the Army slowed down our relationship, making it solid, something that might not have happened of we'd been seeing each other every day.

I can't remember when we actually fell in love, but we did all right, hook line and sinker - no grey areas. I guess it would have been about half way through my service. We spent all my leaves together, and I wangled as many weekend passes I could, spending an awful lot of time on the old Great North Road with my thumb out, hitch-hiking south, most times with Arthur and Jim. In those days it was easy, as most people would give squaddy a lift, and we were usually in London before Friday midnight. Then the three of us would meet on Kings Cross station to catch the Sunday night train to York. From there, the milk train to Scarborough, which stopped at every station, getting in at about six-thirty in the morning.

So I became one of those lovelorn squaddies, and that of course, made the weeks drag even more slowly, but this was offset by the feeling that I had someone special, something to look forward too. Well worth it. We got engaged round about my twentieth birthday. I'd always fancied being married and settled down, not like some blokes, who just want to spend their lives getting pissed and bonking everything in sight. Nothing wrong with that I suppose, but in my case, I think that it was because I'd never had a happy home life, never really felt part of a family, with that protective wall of affection round me. I'd always loved children too, and looked forward to having some of my own one day. I wasn't ever in any hurry mind - wasn't looking for a partner, but I knew that Jeanny was the one for me. She was quiet and shy, but she also had a lot of spirit, and a fiery temper on occasions. That red hair was Irish, a legacy from from her Grandfather Donovan, who came from Dublin. Quite an attractive combination.

Yeah - my dream girl.

We intended getting married when I was twenty-one, with a steady job and a few bob saved up, but what with one thing and another, it didn't work out like that, and we tied the knot at Tottenham Registrar's Office on the sixth of December, 1952, just a few weeks before I left the Army. Super wedding it was too, and as you can see in our wedding photos, a thick smog was descending, and about a hundred assorted friends and relatives had to walk back to the reception in Jeanny's house, as the cars couldn't move in that peasouper. Great cockney knees-up of a party too, despite Jeanny's cousin George going out in the fog, drunk, to find a better piano player, and ending up in hospital after getting coshed. He was a tough little bugger though, an ex-paratrooper, so he was none the worse for it. Then the bell, which unknown to us, someone had tied under our bed going 'DONG', followed by a cheer of approval from those still merry-making downstairs. I only had a seventy-two hour pass, as I had used up all my leave, so we had to have a very tearful parting the next day, but I returned to Scarborough a very happy man.

As was the custom, I walked into the mess for breakfast the next morning to a cheer, and a rousing chorus of 'Here Comes the Bride'.

I was standing on Scarborough station, just a few weeks later, a free man. At last, all over. I was still in uniform, as I had to report to No.1 SAS Signals Regiment TA, in Worship Street before I went home. All National Servicemen had to spend three and a half years in the TA after demob, but that only meant an evenings drill once a month and a two week annual camp. No great hardship, and you were still a civilian.

I was the only one on the platform, sitting there smoking, feeling absolutely marvellous.

"Hello there". I looked up, and there was Lt Warrender, a young and very pretty WRAC officer. I didn't really know her very well, and had always thought she was a bit of a snob, very straight-laced. She was the Orderly Officer of the day. I stood up and saluted.

"Afternoon ma'am. Where are you off too?".

"No-where. I thought I'd come and see you off".

"That's very nice of you ma'am" I said, as I heard my train approaching. It was very nice of her too, and we chatted for the couple of minutes that were left. The train hissed to a stop, and I opened the door and put my case and kit bag in.

"I hear that you were married recently".

"Yes ma'am". She smiled and said -

"Well look, I hope everything goes well for you. I'm sure it will".

"Thank you very much ma'am". A whistle blew and then - 'ALL ABOARD'.

"Well cheerio ma'am, and thanks for seeing me off", and I grinned and held out my hand. She smiled back then suddenly leaned forward and gave me quick peck on the cheek, then laughed at my look of surprise.

"You look after yourself. We'll all miss you you know", then turned and strode off.

'Well I never', I thought.

POSTSCRIPT

So, that was me first twenty years. Nothing special, except for me of course, but for the most part, it's a fairly typical story, and perhaps it's given you some idea of what it was like to live in those times.

I'm still in touch with Alby, Kenny and Terry, but I lost touch with my other teenage mates many years ago. I did see Kenny Goldstein in Hemel Hempstead back in the sixties. He was selling ties out of a suitcase in the High Street, and we were talking so much, he didn't see the copper coming and got nicked. I lost his address I'm afraid, but knowing him, he's probably a rich man by now.

Arthur Nutt came to see me in Tottenham, soon after I left the Army, but apart from that, I never saw him or Jim Hanson again. I tried to find them when I started writing this book, but with no success.

Dad was eighty-one when he died, and Mum ninety-six. She was still a fierce old bugger even then. June died of stroke when she was sixty-three. Right out of the blue – never had a serious days illness till then. Heartbreaking.

I've seen Arthur twice in Australia, and three times when he came back to England for visits, once accompanied by Jesse. He and I had a nice little trip visiting the First World War battlefields in France. He's still the same little pepperpot, but likes a laugh for all that.

Ivy is a widow now, and lives in Falmouth. Still my lovely big sister.

Frank and Pip live in Northampton and we keep very much in touch.

And Me? Well, Jeanny and I had five sons and a daughter, and they're just about the best kids anyone could wish for. Ten grandchildren too, (so far).

To cut another long story short, I eventually, and incredibly fortunately, became a professional folk and blues singer, and for the last thirty odd years have enjoyed a successful career. Done a good bit of travelling too. At the very beginning of all this, someone spelt my name wrong in the 'Melody Maker'. From then on I became Derek Brimstone.

I'm in the book. give us a ring.